INSIDE STUDIO 54

The Real Story of Sex, Drugs, and Rock 'n' Roll
from Former Studio 54 Owner

INSIDE 54
STUDIO 54

MARK FLEISCHMAN
with Denise Chatman and Mimi Fleischman

A Vireo Book | Rare Bird Books
Los Angeles, Calif.

Publisher's Cataloging-in-Publication data
Names: Fleischman, Mark, author. | Chatman, Denise, author. | Fleischman, Mimi, author.
Title: Inside Studio 54 / Mark Fleischman ; with Denise Chatman and Mimi Fleischman.
Description: First Hardcover Edition | A Vireo Book | New York, NY; Los Angeles, CA:
Rare Bird Books, 2017.
Identifiers: ISBN 9781945572579
Subjects: LCSH Fleischman, Mark . | Studio 54 (Nightclub). | Nightclubs—New York (State)—New
York. | Nightlife—New York (State)—New York—History—20th century. | Popular culture—New
York (State)—New York. | BISAC BIOGRAPHY & AUTOBIOGRAPHY / Entertainment &
Performing Arts | BIOGRAPHY & AUTOBIOGRAPHY / Personal Memoirs | BIOGRAPHY &
AUTOBIOGRAPHY / Rich & Famous
Classification: LCC F128.52 F55 2017 | DDC 792.7/09747/1—dc23

Contents

Introduction:
The Studio 54 Effect

I'VE HAD A THING for clubs since childhood. Social clubs, officers' clubs, nightclubs, and supper clubs—I love them all. It started the night my parents took me to The Copacabana for the first time. I was ten years old and it colored my world forever. Looking back, everything that has happened in my life from that point onward propelled me on a trajectory toward Studio 54.

I became the owner of Studio 54 in 1980 and from the very first night we opened, in 1981, I was swept up in a world of celebrities, drugs, power, and sex. I was the ringleader for nearly four years and I became intoxicated with the scene—bodies gyrating on the dance floor, sex in the balcony, and anything goes in the Ladies' Lounge and Rubber Room. Every night, celebrities and stunning women made their way through the crowd, up the stairs to my office to sip champagne and share lines of cocaine using my golden straw or rolled up one-hundred-dollar bills. Nighttime can make you feel somehow protected, operating under a cloak of darkness. It alters your perception of right and wrong, sane and insane, in an arena far more cutthroat than the corporate world I had known before.

I was the guy in control, the owner—the host of the party. It was my duty, my job, to make sure everyone had a good time. It was a responsibility, a heady feeling, one that I gave myself over to wholeheartedly. The legendary New York City nightclub was at the "center of a strange bit of American history that touched a powerful nerve in our culture."[1] It was an exclusive world where anything could happen. New Yorkers and visitors alike were desperate to get inside and be a part of it. Studio 54 was part of a journey that I was meant to take and one that nearly killed me.

---

1   By columnist Liz Smith

After a long battle with the State Liquor Authority, I reopened Studio 54 in September of 1981. That night, ten thousand people stormed the main entrance in a near riot and the police were forced to close the block to traffic. Celebrities like Mary Tyler Moore and others were unintentionally turned away while Ryan O'Neal, John Belushi, and Jack Nicholson managed to slip in through the back door.

Did I think about how this might impact my life or how it could change me and nearly destroy me? If I did, I don't remember. Nothing would have stopped me. I fell under the influence of Studio 54, along with many others, from owners, managers, competitors, bartenders, and DJs to lawyers, patrons, and friends.

My involvement with Studio 54 began years earlier, on the night I walked into its main room for the very first time. The heavy bass and the collective energy of so many bodies dancing as one drew me in. The crowd was hot and beautiful. Next to the dance floor, on a long silver banquette, several stars relaxed together passing around a joint as if at their own private party. I envied the original owners, Steve Rubell and Ian Schrager, for creating this pleasure palace. When I heard about them getting in trouble and then losing their liquor license, I made my move. My visits with Steve and Ian, at two different federal prisons, were orchestrated by their pit bull of an attorney, Roy Cohn, who was famous in his own right.

Articles have been written about Studio 54, but the "behind the scenes" story has never been told—the 1998 film, 54, didn't come close. Mike Myers did an incredible job of playing Steve Rubell, but Ian Schrager was never mentioned. The film revolved around the life of a fictional bartender from New Jersey and had little to do with the story behind the club itself. I was invited to the premiere of 54, and at the after-party, I asked Miramax Films' Harvey Weinstein why the film hadn't told a more accurate story. He answered, "I just couldn't do it to my friend Ian." In 2012, Ian gave an interview on Sirius 54 radio claiming, "The drug thing got blown way out of proportion and it's kind of unfair. There were no more drugs going on at Studio 54 than there were going on at Yankee Stadium." The truth is, drugs were celebrated at Studio 54 from the very first night Steve and Ian opened the doors. A ten-foot-high neon prop known as the "Man in the Moon" dropped down from the ceiling, dominating the dance floor, scooping spoonfuls of cocaine up his nose throughout the evening. The beautiful Christmas gifts of cocaine in Ian's possession during the raid at Studio 54 and the stories of basement parties all belie Ian's assertion.

Nicholas Pileggi's article "Panic Hits Studio 54" (*The Village Voice,* June 12, 1978) documented the widespread use of drugs at Studio 54.

Before opening Studio 54, Steve was unknown and his partner Ian was just another guy practicing real estate law. After the Studio 54 effect took hold of Steve, he changed. Columnist Liz Smith summed it up: "Steve went crazy." Maybe it was all the Quaaludes and cocaine or some of the other stuff he was doing, but something caused a major lapse in judgment when he bragged to *New York* magazine, in the article written by Dan Dorfman, that he and Ian were "making more money than the Mafia."

The *New York* magazine article put Studio 54 on the radar screen of the Internal Revenue Service's Criminal Division. They took one look at Studio 54's tax return for 1977 and discovered they had paid a paltry $7,000. Game over. The Feds raided Studio 54 and it became clear that Steve and Ian were going down.

The effect of the raid on Studio 54 plagued Ian for years, but he was able to move on and create a stellar career as an hotelier. Steve wasn't as fortunate. The Studio 54 effect destroyed him, leading to his untimely death at age forty-five. It almost destroyed me as well. I didn't want the party to ever end. I could have headed home at four or five each morning when we closed the doors to the club, but I didn't. Night after night I'd jump in my limo and hit the after-hours clubs, or I'd remain at Studio 54 and hang out with a crowd of VIP regulars, actors, and an assortment of hangers-on looking for cocaine. With complimentary drinks flowing and an exotic assortment of drugs to please my guests, we'd sit around my office sharing our personal stories. Then, around 9:00 a.m. or so, rubbing our eyes, we'd walk out of the dark, cavernous space into the bright morning light. And while other people rushed up and down Broadway on their way to work at the start of a brand new day, we headed home from the night before.

I didn't realize it at first, but by the beginning of my third year at Studio 54 my body had become addicted to the drugs that supported a lifestyle of very little sleep and working day and night. I was swallowing Quaaludes and Valium each morning so I could calm down from all the cocaine I had snorted the night before and fall asleep. When I woke up each afternoon, I was so slow and groggy from all the Valium that my body demanded more and more coke to wake up. I enjoyed doing lines of coke with all the new and exciting people I was meeting, but while most of them did coke occasionally, I was doing it every single night. After three years my body was no longer cooperating; it was demanding much more to get high. I justified some of the fucked up things I did by telling myself that it was up to me to lead the party—be a good host, show everyone how to have a good time at Studio 54. It was my job—or so I told myself.

There are many stories of how Studio 54 changed people, and I will get to many of them in an effort to explain how people can be driven to altered states, often self-destructively, by the beat of infectious music, pulsating lights, and a generous assortment of sex, drugs, and alcohol. For eons, people have found release in music and dance. There is a rich tradition in African tribes and aboriginal cultures of getting swept up in the mind-numbing religious fervor of music and tribal dance, sometimes enhanced by hallucinogens. I have witnessed the different aspects of tribal dancing and its effect on people in my travels to Brazil and Haiti and how it influenced people at Studio 54.

It's not difficult to imagine how the primal feeling of so many bodies moving in unison and dancing as one became a part of people's lives—it became a ritual. Studio 54 sucked people in, luring them back night after night, affecting their personalities and emboldening them to do things they might not otherwise have done. It became a way of life to some: that was the power of Studio 54. This is my story of the incredible highs, the debilitating lows, the consequences I suffered, and the many people I got to know and care about over those years.

Let the party begin.

Chapter One:
Behind the Velvet Rope

THE FIRST AND ONLY time I went to Studio 54 without being on the guest list was in 1977. I had met Steve Rubell once and I figured, "How difficult could it be to get in?" The truth is, most people who stood waiting outside never got in. The door host Marc Benecke already knew the crowd Steve was going for on any given night—and if you had it, he knew it the minute he laid eyes on you.

When my chauffeured black Cadillac stopped at Fifty-Fourth Street and Eighth Avenue, Fred, my driver, asked if we wanted to walk the rest of the way. We stopped talking, looked out the window, and there it was—a long line of taxis ahead of us interspersed with a few town cars, some limos, and a mass of people crowding the sidewalk shoulder to shoulder in front of the famous Studio 54 marquee. Daunted by the size of the crowd, we almost turned and left, but we didn't. I wanted to dance and so did my date, Michelle, a willowy blonde with long hair and a couple of inches on me with her heels on. We walked down the long block between Broadway and Eighth, pushing ourselves forward as the mob of hopeful partiers got thicker. Some people stood patiently, while others shouted and waved, "Marc, over here" or, "Marc, Marc, it's me."

I'd never seen anything like it before. I couldn't take my eyes off of this Marc guy. Wearing a jacket and a crisp white Brooks Brothers–type shirt, he was good-looking in a preppy kind of way. His face remained neutral—a smile here, a nod there. I was fascinated by how he scanned the crowd but avoided eye contact. He was completely in control of the front door. He was surrounded by a tough-looking group of guys—with sideburns and baseball jackets—that I reasoned were there to protect him.

The crowd was a mixture of the absurd and the sublime. Two people off to my right were dressed like beachcombers, putting lotion on each other and carrying metal detectors, even though it was cold and close to midnight. Another costumed group could have been waiting for the curtain to go up at a Puccini opera back in the 1800s. Limos dispatched people I assumed to be A-listers. I noticed that some of them were immediately granted entry, while others joined the mob. It was a throng of the beautiful and the not-so-beautiful, gay, straight, young, not-so-young, blue-jeaned, and spandexed souls throbbing with a mutual desire—admission. Two heavyset guys in matching gold lamé suits, black shoes, Ray Bans, and black hats, carrying black briefcases—very Blues Brothers—shimmied and moved nonstop to a beat. I could tell by the way they moved that they were really good dancers. It was a wild mash-up of characters, like a scene out of Central Casting at a Hollywood film studio. All-American beauties and their beaus passed joints to stunning models speaking Italian, French, and German. Sequins, satin, feathers, leather, Levis, long legs, hot legs, tweeds, cashmeres, mink, emeralds, diamonds, gold, and silver. Perfume, cigarettes, cologne, and marijuana permeated the late-night air. The anticipation was making me crazy.

Marc would point to a couple, then signal the tall security guys to help bring them forward through the crowd to the velvet rope. Each time this happened the crowd would immediately look in the direction of the action and try to figure out who the people were and why they had been chosen. Were they famous? How were they dressed? Why them? It was a character study just watching it all.

After thirty minutes it was no longer entertaining and I was ready to leave, but Michelle pleaded with me to wait just a few minutes more, so I focused on a guy wearing only chicken feathers and a jock-strap selling Quaaludes. A crowd had formed behind us but we hadn't moved any closer to the red velvet rope. Behind me, several drag queens were shouting, "Marc, it's me, darling! It's me, Marc!" I was bending down to tie my shoelace when Michelle said, "Oh my God, he's pointing at us. Stand up, stand up, let's go." I stood up and all eyes were focused on us. The security guys went into action. Another security man nodded and shouted, "Move aside please—move aside and let them through." Suddenly we were important. The crowd turned to see who was gaining entrance. People were staring and glaring. Checking us out from head to toe. Who were we, and why did Marc pick us? I felt like a much-in-demand celebrity. It was magic and there it was—the red velvet rope. "Let them through please, stand back, people—please, stand back." All these people

were in my face and then I saw Marc and heard, "Good evening." He smiled—
it was wild and exhilarating. The big burly security guard opened the door and
I again heard, "Enjoy your evening." I turned to acknowledge him but he was
gone and the door closed behind us.

We were in. I could hear Gloria Gaynor singing "Never Can Say Goodbye."
We were bathed in a warm golden glow from the low-lit crystal chandeliers
above. There were mirrors everywhere, teasing me with a floor-to-ceiling
reflection of me and the woman I was hoping to make crazy love to later that
night. I felt wild and ready for anything. We walked the wide carpeted hallway,
the music getting louder and louder. I gladly paid the forty-dollar-entrance
fee for the two of us. Everyone we passed, happy and good-looking, wished us
a good evening. It was a different world from outside on Fifty-Fourth Street.
The girls in the coat check were smiling and relaxed. Pretty faces, long hair,
short hair, dancing, and twirling, "Enjoy your evening." We turned around and
WOW—there it was—the main room.

"Let's dance."

Chapter Two:
The Raid on Studio 54

STUDIO 54 FIRST OPENED in April 1977 and became the most famous nightclub of all time. Its quick ascent was confounding because creators Steve Rubell and Ian Schrager were just two guys from Brooklyn in their early thirties. But they had talent. Steve's contribution was simple: people loved him and always had. He was the most popular kid in grammar school, high school, and at Syracuse University, where he met Ian. He was short—about five foot five—and slight, weighing probably no more than 125 pounds. Stevie, as he was often called, spoke with a thick Brooklyn accent and frequently wore a goofy grin. He exuded charm and charisma. You simply felt good when you hung out with him. He had unstoppable confidence. He knew you were going to like him.

Ian was taller and much more powerfully built. Also from Brooklyn, his accent was somewhat more mainstream, with a slight speech impediment and a gruffer voice. He didn't talk that much. Quiet and reserved, he listened. The girls loved him and along the way he had a series of attractive and talented girlfriends, including American fashion designer Norma Kamali. Ian was a lawyer with a precise and creative mind—he was the driving force behind the concept and design of the original Studio 54 and the renovation when I took over.

Regardless of the project at hand, Ian was the producer and Steve the director. Ian would always be the one working behind the scenes, watching everything, always mindful of the smallest details. Steve was the people person. Nobody enjoyed the party more than Steve the Schmoozer.

It was a winning combination.

It took Steve and Ian six weeks and less than $500,000 to transform the space into a nightclub. Richard Long and Alex Rosner designed the outrageous, bass-heavy, full-spectrum sound system. The extraordinary lighting effects were designed by Broadway-gurus Jules Fisher and Paul Marantz. The sound and lights worked together with unusual and ever-changing visual effects, such as the club's famous moving backdrop depicting an illuminated Man in the Moon snorting cocaine from a silver spoon. It also had numerous theatrical drops and sets, each creating a revolving vibe to further stimulate the scene on the dance floor. But what really made Studio, as it was called by regulars, unlike any club in New York, or for that matter the world, was that on any given night, some of the most famous celebrities from film, theatre, music, art, fashion, politics, and sports could be found partying with abandon. Dancing alongside the world's most recognizable people were an assortment of wildly dressed characters from all walks of life. It was the place to be at the height of the disco craze, capturing the attention of every major media outlet on the planet.

Then, suddenly, after only two and a half years, the party came to a crashing halt. The State of New York closed Studio 54 in February 1980 on the heels of the federal raid that led to Steve and Ian's incarceration.

The beginning of the end of Steve and Ian's Studio 54 era came about in November 1978. An article in *New York* magazine by financial writer Dan Dorfman quoted Steve as saying that profits at Studio 54 "were [so] astronomical, only the Mafia does better," and that the club "is a cash business, and you have to worry about the IRS. I don't want them to know about everything." Unfortunately for Steve and Ian, these remarks got the attention of the head of Criminal Investigations for the IRS in New York City, who made a few phone calls that prompted an investigation led by United States Attorney Peter Sudler.

On December 14, 1978, Sudler got a federal judge to sign a search warrant and Studio 54 was raided. Upon arrival, his task force proceeded straight down to the basement and emptied out the metal safe where Steve and Ian hid their real books. They also found garbage bags full of cash inside holes and cracks in the walls and ceiling that amounted to more than a million dollars. Sudler knew exactly where to look because Steve, who everyone knew liked to brag, was known to have shown it to people.

According to newspaper reports, Ian walked in through the back door during the raid carrying a package of envelopes filled with baggies of cocaine, which were to be given as Christmas presents to key celebrity clients. Each one had a ribbon on it, along with cards addressed to such famous names as

Calvin Klein, Bianca Jagger, Andy Warhol, Halston, and so on. Not realizing what was going on, Ian put the bundle on the floor so he could shake hands with Sudler. Once Ian no longer had personal possession of the cocaine, it was subject to search and seizure; Sudler called Drug Enforcement Agency agents and Ian was arrested on narcotics charges. These charges were in addition to the tax evasion charges levied by IRS agents, assisted by members of the NYPD. The authorities later found Steve in his Mercedes and he was taken into custody after the officers confiscated another $500,000 in cash from his trunk and apartment.

The federal case against Steve and Ian went to trial nearly a year later, in November of 1979. Their partner, Jack Dushey, retained his own attorney, and the three of them pled guilty to tax evasion. In exchange for a lighter sentence, Steve and Ian agreed to provide incriminating information against other nightclub owners who were known to be skimming profits. On January 18, 1980, they were sentenced to three years in federal prison, a harsher sentence because the judge believed they skimmed an inordinate amount of money. However, Steve and Ian's attorney, Roy Cohn, well-known for brokering deals for high-profile mobsters, was able to get the drug charges dropped. He put forth the ingenious argument that there was so much "cut" in the cocaine that the actual quantity of cocaine was insufficient to break the law at that time.

I saw the *New York Post* story in the fall of 1979 reporting that Steve and Ian had plea-bargained and were going to jail. I remember immediately realizing the opportunity that lay before me. Having owned a number of hotels and restaurants in New York, I had had extensive dealings with the State Liquor Authority (SLA). I knew that it would be unlikely to renew Studio 54's liquor license for Steve and Ian now that they were convicted felons. I also believed I had the experience, the right lawyers, and the spotless record to overcome the SLA's objections to the liquor license being granted in my name.

I was right. After Steve and Ian went to jail, the license was not renewed when it expired on February 28, 1980, and the club shut down. Steve and Ian thought that they could keep it alive by appointing a celebrity board of directors to oversee operations, but that was completely unrealistic. There were some talks with Dick Clark and interest from Neil Bogart, the owner of Casablanca Records—but the liquor authorities quickly put the kibosh on those plans.

By that time, I was a known commodity to Steve and Ian. I had had several successful restaurants in the city as well as the Executive Hotel, and I had talked with them on and off about a Studio 54 franchise at the Virgin Isle Hotel, which I had acquired in 1978. My high school buddy Eric Rosenfeld's law partner, Bobby Tannenhauser, had gone to Syracuse University with Steve and Ian, and I figured he was the perfect person to represent me and get the ball rolling.

The first negotiation to buy Studio 54 occurred on a visitor Sunday at the Metropolitan Correctional Center near Chinatown, where convicted felons in New York were held before being shipped off to federal prisons around the country to serve their time. It was a modern twelve-story building but was also a scary, dark place with slits in the concrete for windows and a long line of unhappy visitors waiting to see loved ones in jail. After several hours, Bobby and I were finally allowed past reception and up a secure elevator to meet with "The Boys" (as they were often referred to) and directed to a large visitor cell. Steve turned on his charisma and gregarious personality. Ian was removed and sullen. He had recently been disbarred of his license to practice law due to his conviction and, understandably, seemed none too happy about it.

Both Steve and Ian were eager to get things moving. Their major concern was making sure the club would reopen. Most of the discussion focused on my past ventures and the impact they would have on licensing. Once they felt comfortable with the fact that I had been licensed in the past with no infractions, we got down to negotiating how it would all work.

Toward the end of the hour-long visit, Bobby asked Ian if the Mafia might in some way "interfere" with our operation. It had been reported that Ian's father, Louis Schrager, was an associate of Meyer Lansky, well-known to be the financial wizard for the Mob. In any case, Ian, who had a *Goodfellas* look, said, "Don't worry. I'll take care of it."

A few days later I got a call from Roy Cohn's secretary, asking me to meet him regarding Studio 54. Cohn was the infamous attorney who rose to stardom helping to convict Ethel and Julius Rosenberg of spying in 1951 and then aiding Senator Joseph McCarthy in his crusade against "suspected Communists" who were treated as "guilty until proven innocent" during the Red Scare of the 1950s. Reputations were ruined and lives were destroyed as a result of their campaign, better known as the "Blacklist." By the time I met Roy Cohn, he had represented Donald Trump, publishing mogul Si Newhouse, Cardinal Francis Spellman, Andy Warhol, Calvin Klein, Mafia boss Carmine Galante, Barbara Walters, and countless others.

Like Steve, Cohn was short, slight, and had a prominent scar on his nose, which was reportedly from a botched nose job from his youth. He graduated from Columbia University Law School at nineteen and was shaking up the world from his office in Washington, DC by the time he was twenty-six. He was about fifty when I met him and, by then, dozens of nefarious deeds had been attributed to him. One was that he had arranged to make public Vice Presidential Candidate Thomas Eagleton's medical records. When everyone found out that Senator Eagleton had been treated with electroshock therapy for depression, he was forced to drop out of the race. This scandal was a serious blow to George McGovern, who I had campaigned long and hard for in '72, to the extent that I had earned a place on Richard Nixon's "Enemies List." Nevertheless, I liked Roy and was charmed by his friendliness. I wasn't alone. Robert Sherrill wrote in the left-leaning magazine *The Nation* on August 9, 2009: "Large slices of the upper crust of New York and Washington snuggled up to him, laughed and entertained one another with stories about his crimes as though they were choice insiders' jokes, and wrestled for the privilege of partying with Cohn and his crooked and perverse friends." Ronald Reagan was one of Roy's biggest fans in the end, endorsing Roy during his eventual disbarment proceedings while Reagan was president.

To the best of my knowledge, Roy arranged the final plea bargain for Steve and Ian, wherein they were forced to inform on other club operators. However, before that, he made a last-ditch attempt to get them off entirely by having them rat out Hamilton Jordan (Chief of Staff for Jimmy Carter) for allegedly snorting cocaine in the basement of Studio 54. Roy was deeply involved in Ronald Reagan's presidential campaign in 1980 and was probably the source of this accusation becoming so well publicized and a very public embarrassment for Carter.

In any case, the attempt to discredit Hamilton Jordan didn't help Steve and Ian. However, as a result of it, they were put into bulletproof glass cells for their own protection because their next attorney, Howard Squadron, was afraid of CIA retaliation against them in federal prison. Nevertheless, Roy was successful in damaging Carter's administration, which was probably his aim to start with.

My meeting with Cohn took place in his impressive townhouse in the 1980s off Madison Avenue that served as both his home and workplace. Roy lounged at his desk wearing a bathrobe. Behind him a photograph of his old boss, Senator Joe McCarthy, was hanging on the wall. He called for his assistant to bring coffee for both of us. A very handsome young man wearing loose-fitting athletic shorts and a tight T-shirt revealing a muscular physique appeared. The young man put the coffee down and ran his hand across Roy's back tenderly. Roy patted his butt affectionately and gave him a warm smile. As Le Jardin was one of my favorite clubs back in the mid-1970s, I had become familiar with and appreciated the gay community, especially in fashion and the world of dance and music. I felt flattered that Roy felt so comfortable in my presence.

Roy calmly and politely informed me, "If you pay a certain amount every month, there will be no problem." I was being shaken down by the Mob through Ian and Steve's attorney before any real business had taken place! I knew as well as everyone else that Roy had represented the Mafia in a number of cases, and this was one of the many instances where Roy was playing all sides of the table. It's a rare person who can be associated with the Mob, Studio 54, and the Reagan administration all at the same time. Ultimately, we made a few payments to the designated person, but decided to stop a few months after opening, and fortunately nothing happened.

While all this was going on, I got a call from Studio 54's former publicists, Michael and Ed Gifford, asking me to meet them one Sunday at their elegant townhouse. A married couple, they had a top PR firm and extensive contacts in the theater and entertainment industries. Ed had also been a television director for CBS and had actually worked in the Studio 54 space when it was a CBS Television studio named Studio 52. When Steve and Ian first met Michael and Ed and retained their services, they were struggling to figure out a name for this huge emporium they'd just taken on. Ed told me before he died that Michael suggested, "Why not call it Studio 54?" reasoning that the main entrance was on Fifty-Fourth Street.

The Giffords represented a number of my enterprises at that time including the Virgin Isle Hotel. We had become close friends and they had sent their daughter Muffin down to the island to work at my hotel. They begged me not to do business with Steve and Ian because they were "sinister criminals" who were outrageous in the way they defrauded the government. When I didn't heed their advice, the Giffords resigned from all my establishments, just as they had resigned from Studio 54 after reading about what they considered the owners' greed in the original indictment.

One of the people that Steve and Ian informed on, and who was subsequently indicted, was Maurice Brahms, the owner of the nightclubs Infinity, New York, and The Underground. It turned out that Maurice Brahms and his cousin John Addison had taught Steve and Ian the nightclub business when they were partners in a Boston club, 15 Lansdowne, several years earlier. Older than Steve and Ian, but also from Brooklyn, Maurice wore business suits and didn't quite seem to fit in the club world. I remember meeting him for the first time in 1980 at a pre-opening night construction party of Bonds, his cavernous Times Square disco that proved unsuccessful soon after it opened. Brahms had heard I was negotiating to purchase Studio 54 and sought me out in a crowd of five thousand people wearing construction hard hats to ask if I was going through with the deal.

I responded, "Yes, provided I get the liquor license in my name."

Brahms put his face close to mine in the midst of the crowd and, with burning eyes, he said quietly but menacingly, "If you go through with the deal, I will curse you, and my children and my children's children will curse you, for the rest of your life."

That was quite a scene—and though I tried to make light of it, I would be lying if I did not tell you that Brahms sent a chill up my spine. Though it would be several months before I finalized the purchase, I realized immediately that I was about to have a mortal enemy in the disco world, particularly once I heard that Brahms was incarcerated a few months later because of Steve and Ian's information.

One day, Roy Cohn invited me to lunch upstairs at the 21 Club in New York to discuss strategy. In the middle of the entrée, Roy's driver ran up to our table hysterically shouting that Charlie Brown, Roy's Cavalier King Charles Spaniel, had jumped out of his red Eldorado convertible, which was parked outside, run down the street toward Sixth Avenue. Roy calmly asked the waiter to bring a phone to the table and then called the mayor's office. By the time we exited the restaurant and quickly walked to Sixth Avenue, we found that five or six NYPD cars with sirens blaring had closed down the block. A few minutes later, a couple of beaming cops came walking up to us with Charlie Brown clutched in one of their arms saying, "Here's your dog, Mr. Cohn." It was an impressive demonstration of Roy's power. Robert Sherrill's exposé in *The Nation,* quoted earlier, ends by saying, "the one true love in Roy Cohn's life was his spaniel, Charlie Brown." A short time after our lunch, Charlie Brown sired a litter and I was fortunate enough to be given one of the puppies, which I named Oliver. Over the years, every time I met Roy, he would ask "How is Oliver?"

Roy arranged for me to meet with Steve and Ian a second time at the same federal prison in Manhattan, where they were still being held while the authorities got all the information they needed from them. By that point, we only had a short window of time to conclude the deal before the boys would be moved to a facility in Alabama to finish out their sentences. Roy's secretary called and instructed me to meet him on a Tuesday morning in front of the prison.

Roy pulled up in his red convertible with his driver dressed in black. This time it was a nonvisiting day, and I knew from my first visit that only lawyers were admitted. I asked Roy, "What's going on?"

Roy handed me a business card that read "Mark Fleischman, Attorney at Law" and told me to show it to the administrative guard on my way in. This gambit seemed over the top as far as I was concerned. I looked at Roy as if to say, "Are you sure about this?"

In his glib fashion, Roy said, "If you want to own Studio 54, this is what you have to do."

Like most everyone who dealt with Roy, I did what he told me to do. Steve and Ian's protective custody meant they were in a glass cell. A series of glass doors, all opened and shut electronically by the guards, led into a large room with several transparent "cages." I'm not normally claustrophobic, but this scene with multiple layers of bulletproof glass shutting behind me did a number on my psyche. As I walked down the aisle to their cell, I couldn't believe my eyes when I saw Michele Sindona, a banker I had met ten years earlier, in the cell next door. I had read he was there for ordering the murder of the lawyer charged with liquidating banks when Sindona was laundering the Mafia's heroin money. Suddenly, this jail seemed even more sinister. Several years later, Sindona was extradited to Italy and poisoned in his prison cell.

Seeing Steve and Ian sitting in jail was bizarre. Up until now, it seemed that the two of them had always gotten what they wanted. A lot of this power came from their partnership. They were very different people. Steve was outgoing, gregarious, the life of the party, the guy who drew all sorts of different people together. His energy and enthusiasm were infectious and you couldn't help but get swept up by it. Ian, on the other hand, was straight, introverted, calculating, controlling, and plotting—in many ways, a typical lawyer. But something happened when Steve and Ian teamed up that was quite extraordinary. It was as though one was the yin to the other's yang. It was almost as if they became one person. No matter the issue at hand, the two held the same position and attacked it together with such strength that whatever or whomever stood in their way didn't stand a chance.

At least, until they took on the Feds, that is. I wondered how they had let it get so far out of control. But later, after running Studio 54 for a while, I would understand.

With Roy presiding over the meeting, it was to the point and all business. "We'll help you from here," exclaimed Steve.

"Don't worry about the liquor license," said Roy.

Ian wasn't as enthusiastic, due to his own situation, but he chimed in to agree with Roy and Steve. "My contacts are your contacts," he assured me.

They were convinced that Studio would reopen and be successful because they could continue to advise me via a pay phone from jail. (I had agreed to bring them rolls of dimes for the telephone whenever I visited.) And it was true, and to their credit most of their closest celebrity friends remained loyal to them. Diana Ross, Bianca, Andy, Calvin, Halston, and Liza—the whole crew supported them. Their unfortunate circumstances seemed inconsequential to their crowd. Steve and Ian were Teflon-coated.

Several weeks later, this time on an official visiting day, we signed the papers prepared by Bobby Tannenhauser in their prison cell. Since there were rules against doing business in prison, we had to stuff the signed papers in our jackets on the way out. That was the easy part. Getting the liquor license was another story, and it turned out that Roy was no help whatsoever.

In retrospect, I don't believe I made the best deal I could have. Whenever I visited them in jail, I was met with yellow legal notepads that had pages of deal points scribbled out by two guys with nothing but time on their hands and the benefit of knowing the intricacies of exactly how the money was made and the expenses it took to make it. The truth is I wanted to own Studio 54 so badly that I overlooked Steve and Ian's influence on my attorney, a buddy from their days at Syracuse, and the effect that Steve's thousand-watt charm, the driving force behind all of their joint successes, was having on me. I succumbed to it. I liked him and felt sorry for the both of them sitting in jail. Bobby seemed to hold them in awe, accepting without question most of the representations about potential cash flow (there were no financial statements presented) when drafting the agreement.

The reality is that I was thoroughly seduced by the idea of controlling the world's most important nightclub, and I proceeded headlong and recklessly toward that end.

Chapter Three:
Hooked on Clubs

W HAT DROVE ME TO such lengths that I was willing to impersonate a criminal attorney in order to bypass a security guard to enter a federal prison? Studio 54! I would have done almost anything to cut the deal that would lock me in as the new owner. At the time, it seemed like an adventure, a mythological journey wherein I would claim my rightful throne by executing a series of daring deeds. But at a deeper level, from the time I was a child growing up first in the Fort Tryon Park area of Manhattan and then in Great Neck, Long Island, the Golden Fleece of my dreams had been owning grand nightclubs.

When I was young, my parents would go dancing at some of the major clubs of the day, like The Latin Quarter and The Stork Club. One night, they took my younger brother, Alan, and me to their favorite club, The Copacabana, in Manhattan. I was mesmerized. I took it all in, relishing every moment. It was the 1950s and Harry Belafonte, whom my parents had met a few years earlier when he was appearing at a friend's resort hotel in New Hampshire, performed that night. It was a glamorous scene featuring a crowd of well-dressed people, delicious food, and a big orchestra featuring The Copa Girls, who wore tiny panties, sparkly sequins, and fluffy feathers. To me, a ten-year-old, the girls were practically *naked*, and the scene made an indelible impression on me. In the 1940s, the era before television became popular, nightclub owners were considered to be celebrities because of the big-name acts that performed in their clubs like Frank Sinatra, Ella Fitzgerald, Patti Page, Diahann Carroll, and Milton Berle. Barbara Walters talks about her friends being envious when she was growing up because her father was Lou Walters, who owned the famous Latin Quarter nightclubs in New York, Miami, and Boston.

I was a child hooked on nightclubs and the men who ruled over them. And then I saw two films that forever sealed my fate. The first was *Casablanca*. I became enthralled with the character of Rick, the owner of Rick's Café, an upscale club and gambling spot in exotic Morocco. He was irresistible to women and had a thing for white dinner jackets. The other film, *New Orleans*, starring Arturo de Córdova, was about a dapper nightclub owner named Nick who was a magnet for beautiful women and a promoter of a new musical sound called the blues. I was blown away by Nick's charisma, love of music, and the talent of Louis Armstrong and Billie Holiday.

We moved to Great Neck, Long Island, when I was eight or nine, by which time my father, Martin Fleischman, a wiry, good-looking man with startling blue eyes, had become fairly wealthy running modestly priced hotels in the New York area. He had a European accent and a dictatorial manner and I rejected his authority, and perhaps all authority in general, through much of my youth. He insisted I go to Hebrew school at age twelve to prepare for my bar mitzvah, for which he staged a major dinner at New York's Essex House, but afterward I stubbornly refused to go to synagogue. On the other hand, my mother, Sylvia Zausner Fleischman, could do no wrong. She was beautiful, smart, and loving. She graduated from Hunter College, spoke five languages, and I adored her.

When I turned sixteen, my father insisted I get a job if I wanted my own car. When he was only fifteen, he was sailing to America alone about to invent his own destiny. While many of my teenage friends in Great Neck were given Corvettes, I had to work to buy a souped-up 1951 used Ford convertible. I got a job as a soda jerk and was soon promoted to short-order cook. Earning that promotion felt good and I enjoyed short-order cooking, but I never told my father that.

By the time I was seventeen, I'd venture into Harlem along with some friends to dance at the hot spot Smalls Paradise on Seventh Avenue near 135th Street. It was a risk because I was driving illegally, having only a junior driver's license, and Harlem was considered dangerous for white boys, but I got away with it. While most kids my age were still dancing to swing, I was moving around the raised platform at Smalls, dancing with my date to the music of Muddy Waters, Etta James, B. B. King, and Big Joe Turner. It was my first taste of what I later realized was tribal-style dancing. I was so turned on by the sensuality of the R&B music and the all-out seductiveness of the beautiful black women on the dance floor. It was hot—the music, the sweat, the gyrating bodies. Everyone around me on the dance floor was feeling it. Early on I fell in love with the blues and R&B, listening to my favorite radio shows *Symphony Sid in the City* and Alan Freed on what was then called WJZ. My every experience at Smalls was unforgettable, and I would go on to spend my life believing in the joy and power of music and dance.

Over the years, people have asked me how I had the balls to hang out in Harlem as a teenager. That's when I tell them about Cornelia and how lucky I was to have had her in my life. In the mid-1940s when we lived in Washington Heights, my brother Alan and I had only one babysitter. Her name was Cornelia and we were crazy about her. She was a heavyset black woman who looked like Mammy in the film *Gone with the Wind*. Cornelia would occasionally take Alan and me to her home in Harlem when my parents were gone for the day. Back then, Harlem had a completely different vibe. I remember the streets being clean with nice brownstones and polished stoops. I got to know and like Cornelia's boyfriend, a big, friendly, dapper black man named Mr. Smith, who wore zoot suits and spats and had a big black car with white sidewalls. I thought he was very cool and the two of them felt like family to me. To me, everyone in Harlem seemed happy.

After Great Neck High School, my education toward becoming a club owner continued at Cornell University where I attended the School of Hotel Administration and joined a fraternity, Phi Sigma Delta. It turned out to be a great place for me because it was a party house. In my sophomore year I was elected social chairman; that was the beginning of my appreciation for being a party host and getting high on booze. I was finally able to overcome my social immaturity, which had persisted throughout high school and into my early college social scene. I was born in February and so my mother had the choice of starting me in kindergarten a year early as a four-and-a-half-year-old, or a year later as a five-and-a-half-year-old. She chose to start me earlier and as the youngest and smallest I was always trying to keep up.

At the fraternity parties, I hired popular Dixieland bands to play on the main floor for dancing, while in the basement I played Sinatra records with the lights dimmed low for making out. I made the punch, which I spiked with plenty of alcohol, handled the décor, and all the other little details. I had an affinity for the role, which I enjoyed immensely. The next year, our fraternity parties became really hot when word spread across campus in 1958 that we had great rock-and-roll music that I introduced, reminiscent of Small's Paradise in Harlem. I found the band Bobby and the Counts, and we were dancing to Chuck Berry, Buddy Holly, Jerry Lee Lewis, and Elvis cover songs. It was infectious and the dance floor was packed. I was elected social chairman for my junior and senior years as well. Although it required real effort, it had social benefits and honed my hosting skills.

To avoid being drafted into the Army after college, I went to US Navy Officer Candidate School, which was both jarring and enlightening. There I learned navigation, seamanship, gunnery, and how to make a quarter bounce on my tightly made bed during daily morning inspections. I was one of three Jews in a class of several hundred officer candidates. My new circle of comrades was far different from my life in Great Neck and my predominately Jewish fraternity at Cornell. Although, even at Cornell, I had a brush with anti-Semitism as a freshman in the form of a group of guys who called themselves "The White Citizens' Council." I was an easy target because I wasn't very serious about my studies and goofed around a lot, so they chose to blame me for the flood caused by someone flushing all the urinals simultaneously in the freshman dorm. They dragged me out of my room and seemed ready to beat the shit out of me but I somehow used humor to defuse the situation. I got the message: I was the right color, but the wrong religion. I'm not sure what lessons I may have learned from that experience but I got along well and was considered a good naval officer in a totally Gentile environment.

In 1962 as a Lieutenant JG (junior grade) in the US Navy, my first assignment was to run the officers' club and Bachelor Officers' Quarters (BOQ) at Naval Air Engineering Station Lakehurst in New Jersey, the site where the Hindenburg burned. My participation was part of a special program for Cornell Hotel School graduates; and I was really happy about this because by that time the Army was already building up forces in Southeast Asia. I immediately set out to do the best job with it as possible, changing the club into a popular watering hole for the officers and their ladies. I threw great parties, hired fun bands, produced interesting menus featuring my version of comfort food, organized happy hours with great hors d'oeuvres, and presented personally chiseled ice carvings of navy eagles as buffet centerpieces. These innovations increased the receipts, which, together with implementing the inventory controls that I had learned at Cornell, lowered the food and beverage costs, making the club profitable within a few months. I also developed a sense of how to become a leader of a diverse group of people including black and Filipino stewards' mates, wave receptionists, and local "redneck" civilians who bartended.

As the Club Officer, I found myself drinking more and earlier in the day. Five days a week the club opened at noon, and like clockwork there would be a line of navy pilots lined up by 11:45 a.m. waiting for the bar to open. Lakehurst had become a testing facility for new jet fighters as well as an anti-Russian submarine airbase, and no one blamed the pilots for having a few stiff ones. I was drinking with commanders, captains, and occasionally admirals. If I was standing at the bar talking to someone, my glass would be refilled without question by one of the bartenders, and I rarely declined when a fellow officer said, "Mark, have a drink with me." The bartenders wanted to keep me happy. When they poured my shots, they were bigger; when they poured my drinks, they were stronger; and my glass was never empty. This practice would continue throughout my career as a hotel, restaurant, and club owner.

Besides my duties running the officers' club, I was assigned "Officer of the Day" (OD) duties one weekend per month. I was in charge of the entire base while the rest of the officers were on weekend leave. One of my duties as OD was to oversee the Shore Patrol, who served as military police. I was required to carry a pistol while in uniform when I was off the base. If we received a phone call from a local bar in town reporting a fight involving navy personnel, I would head over there with the Shore Patrol, who would break it up, and then haul the navy servicemen back to the base. We didn't want our people arrested and put into the local jails; we'd rather bring them to our own brig to sober up so they could be reprimanded by their own company officers and be able to report for duty on Monday. One time, during my watch, we had to break up a fight involving a man who, unbeknownst to us, was mentally unstable, and we put him in the brig. Later that evening the petty officer in charge of the brig called me on the phone at the BOQ and in a frightened voice said, "Lieutenant Fleischman, you've got to come down here right away." When I arrived at the brig, I was led to the prisoner. He had hanged himself with his belt. That is an image I will never forget. These experiences as the OD helped to train me to oversee the security guards every nightclub depends on. It's a skill to use their brawn intelligently to keep a drinking scene under control.

Just before my scheduled release after four years of active duty, I signed a deal to take over the three-hundred-room Forest Hills Inn with financial help from my father, who had always planned on going into business with me. The

Inn was a venerable hotel that looked like an English country manor, with a formal dining room and a wood-paneled bar. It was located in an upscale neighborhood in Queens, and it was in foreclosure. It stood adjacent to the Forest Hills Tennis Stadium, which hosted the Nationals (now known as the US Open). I had grand plans for reviving the Inn, but there was a small complication: though I was scheduled to be discharged from the Navy in early 1965, with tensions mounting in Vietnam, President Johnson surprised us all and extended everyone's tour of duty indefinitely. However, the deal was done, so along with my father and several investors, we took over the hotel.

I raced back and forth between the Naval Air Engineering Station Lakehurst in South Jersey and the Forest Hills Inn in New York, hoping there would be no consequences. I worked hard doing both jobs, managing to literally wear two hats for four or five months, until I finally received my honorable discharge from active duty later that year. It was on one of those trips to New York in 1963 that I heard on the radio that President Kennedy had been assassinated. He was my commander in chief and had offered such hope for the future. I was devastated. I pulled over to the side of the Garden State Parkway and broke down crying.

Renovating the Inn was a daunting task in and of itself, made harder by the fact that my father and I had very different ideas on how to go about it. My ideas were designed to create excitement, get us noticed, draw crowds, and keep them coming back for more, night after night. I believed that to make money you had to spend money, while my father thought that the only way to make money was to save money. His motto was, "The eyes of the boss keep the fat on the horse," which is a fancy way of saying, "Squeeze every last dime out of every dollar." He thought that my generation "had it too easy and that's why we squandered money." He used to say about himself, "Instead of Cornell, I learned the business at the school of hard knocks."

Looking back, I realize we were both right and I should have compromised more, as our goals were essentially the same. Instead, I competed with him. He was tough, but he was kind and I loved him. I discovered later that my father helped my uncle Hy out financially without my mother knowing about it when her brother went through a bitter divorce from his second wife, who wanted to take as much money from him as she could. My father was a generous man and I wish I had appreciated him more during his lifetime.

Reviving the Inn involved more than just upgrading the food in the formal restaurant, the Windsor Room, and bringing in a new maître d'. I had to change the stuffy attitude of the staff as well. I went head-to-head with the Hotel Employees and Restaurant Emplyees Union. Running a union operation was an education in and of itself after my experience in the navy, where everyone followed my every word. I hired some new personnel and transformed the outdated Tournament Grill into the Three Swans, an authentic English pub that became a successful neighborhood hangout. In addition to updating the food, I modernized the music for both listening and dancing.

At the Forest Hills Inn's Grand Opening, we invited local VIPs and politicians—including Mayor John Lindsay—as well as members of the press. This was the first time I was savvy enough to work effectively with the media to generate publicity, thanks to my first publicist, Richard Auletta. The Grand Opening also marked the first time I would get some serious personal press of my own, including a story in the *New York Daily News* by Tom McMorrow with the clever headline "Inn-Presario Gives a Hypo to Famed Spot." The telephone awoke me before 8:00 a.m. the day after the opening, and I groggily heard my mother's cheerful voice as she proudly read me the entire article that began:

> Mark Fleischman, the new twenty-six-year-old executive director of the old Queens landmark–the Forest Hills Inn– wasn't born when Big Bill Tilden, General Pershing, Sinclair Lewis, and Peaches Browning were making the name of the famed inn familiar around the world. The youthful Fleischman is a Cornell alumnus, class of '62, who still looks like an undergraduate, spends a good deal of his time listening to suggestions from those who remember the era when Daddy and Peaches might be seen at the bar with Mayor Jimmy Walker.

It was a long, complimentary story and gave me the sense I could go on to greater things. I remember feeling very proud—a Jewish Naval Officer taking a sprawling, broken-down, formerly anti-Semitic hotel and relaunching it in the modern era.

I loved coming up with press-generating ideas, including the creation of a Celebrity Walk in front of the hotel's sidewalk café. It was a real coup when we got Frank Sinatra to put his handprints into a block of wet cement when he headlined the Forest Hills Music Festival at the nearby tennis stadium. As soon as other celebrities heard about Sinatra's handprints and signature, they agreed to be included in our Celebrity Walk when they performed. Eventually Barbra Streisand, Trini Lopez, Woody Allen, Buddy Hackett, and a number of others participated. I was also able to get tennis stars playing for the US Championship to participate in our Celebrity Walk, including Rod Laver, Arthur Ashe, John Newcombe, and my hero from Spain where I attended summer courses at the University of Madrid, Manuel "Manolo" Santana.

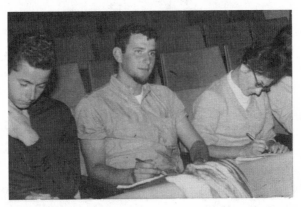

I tried to concentrate on my studies at the University of Madrid.
My classes were in Spanish, a language I was still learning.

From the 1930s through the 1960s, gossip columnists were extremely popular and very powerful in New York. The legendary Walter Winchell led the charge with a few well-placed mentions of the Forest Hills Inn in his column. His items resulted in getting people to drive from Manhattan and all over Long Island to enjoy dinner and dancing in the Windsor Room and drinks at the piano bar in the Three Swans. I continued to cultivate my relationship with the press, staging events and stunts to garner their interest, including the annual "Live Turkey Derby" on Thanksgiving, which made the local New York TV news.

As the press reported on the goings-on at the Inn, both bars and restaurants became popular with people from all over Long Island and a favorite neighborhood hangout where once a year the local Irish drunks came to festively break chairs over each other's heads on St. Patrick's Day. We were also booking three or four weddings and banquets every weekend, although that didn't always go smoothly. On one occasion, the maître d', a black man, Bill Nance, a former waiter and valued employee, who had worked at the Inn for thirty years, walked a white bride into the wrong wedding in the old English courtyard garden, shocking everyone. However, a few glitches notwithstanding, the Forest Hills Inn was a hit. It felt good when I overheard my father bragging to his friends about my accomplishments.

Chapter Four:
The Candy Store

A BOLD TEXAN NAMED Marion Roberts, who was a frequent guest at the Inn, often invited me to join him on his jaunts into Manhattan. His generosity in including me was probably related to his appreciation for my extending thousands of dollars' worth of credit to him (which drove my father nuts). As the manager of the comic Pat Henry, who often opened for Frank Sinatra, Marion had currency everywhere we went. Sinatra and his Rat Pack owned the era, and any connection to them was gold. Marion had a gruff voice and a brash personality. Although stocky and not a looker, he wore top-of-the-line silk suits with cowboy boots and cut a figure that you could not miss. Moving through Manhattan with Marion in his chauffeured Cadillac was an exhilarating experience.

After a little club-hopping, we usually ended up at The Copacabana, which for me was still as exciting as ever. Nothing much had changed since my visits with my parents; it was still *the* place to be in the mid-1960s. It was located on Sixtieth Street between Fifth and Madison and known for serving great food. It was decorated with tall fake palm trees, wild Brazilian décor, and a kick-ass Latin-themed orchestra. Going to The Copa was still like stepping into another world. The guests were dressed to the nines—men in sharp suits and women in cleavage-baring cocktail dresses. The downstairs main room was filled with movers and shakers, celebrities, and, of course, gorgeous women, mainly in their twenties, dripping with jewelry. People usually had a cigarette or cigar in one hand and a cocktail in the other. No one talked about alcoholism or cancer. The air had an ethereal quality from all the smoke drifting under the spotlights.

Big names played there—Frank Sinatra, Nat King Cole, Dean Martin and Jerry Lewis, Ella Fitzgerald, Sammy Davis Jr., Sam Cooke, and Harry Belafonte.

The Supremes made their debut at the club in 1965, paving the way for The Temptations and Marvin Gaye. We've all heard Barry Manilow's famous song "Copacabana" about Lola, The Copa showgirl. The Copa Girls performed each night and were not only beautiful, they exuded sexuality. They still wore skimpy mink panties, sequined brassieres, exotic-looking plastic fruit-laced turbans, and sky-high heels. Both Joan Collins and Raquel Welch started off as Copa Girls. There was also a crowded, smoke-filled street-level bar upstairs populated by characters that seemed like they were straight out of *Guys and Dolls* and *Goodfellas*. The place was owned by Jules Podell, widely known to be connected to the Mafia.

It had been fifteen years since my first visit to The Copa with my parents. It was just as magical at age twenty-five as it had been at ten and I still felt that pull to own a major nightclub.

If a single word could define nightlife in Manhattan during that era, it was "swanky," and I was in the middle of it all. I remember feeling that this was the pinnacle of nightlife, as good as it could ever get. Eventually I became somewhat of a regular at The Copa, as well as at Jilly's across town, which was owned by Sinatra's best friend and bodyguard, Jilly Rizzo. I also frequented Jackie Kannon's Rat Fink Room above the Round Table, owned by Morris Levy, a man with a lot of connections.

One night at The Copa bar I met a tall, heavyset but dapper man in a shiny silk suit named Larry Mathews. He was a businessman who owned a nightclub on West Fifty-Fifth Street named Disc-Au-Go-Go. Larry was another one of the Sinatra hangers-on and his particular claim to fame was his very successful "Larry Mathews' 24-Hour Beauty Salon" chain. If a woman wanted a shampoo and set at 5:00 a.m. before an early-morning flight, or a touch-up to her color and manicure before heading out to the clubs at midnight, then Larry Mathews was the go-to guy. His salons were the first twenty-four-hour beauty parlors in the city and they catered to insomniacs, talk show guests, showgirls from The Copacabana and Latin Quarter, and luminaries including former first lady Eleanor Roosevelt, author Jacqueline Susann, Marilyn Monroe, and everyday women with special circumstances. He eventually had dozens of salons in New York City, and in the early 1970s expanded his after-hours beauty enterprise nationally with over 125 salons from Miami to Las Vegas to Hollywood.

Larry and I got to talking one night, and he mentioned that his nightclub had a fully licensed upstairs room that was not being used. He asked me if

I had any ideas for it. This was the question I'd been waiting for all of my young life. Ideas? I had them in spades. I was finally going to do a nightclub in Manhattan!

The space Larry was offering me wasn't big and luxurious, but I immediately thought of a little hole-in-the-wall club on West Forty-Fifth Street in Manhattan called The Peppermint Lounge that had closed a year or so earlier. Some friends and I had caught the action at The Peppermint Lounge and we had a blast. I was captivated by the waitresses who periodically put down their trays and jumped up on the railings to dance for the crowd: the first ever Go-Go Dancers.

That nightspot helped to catapult a new dance called The Twist when the house band Joey Dee and The Starliters cut a smash-hit record "The Peppermint Twist" and a photographer captured Russian Prince Serge Obolensky twisting the night away at the club. The next morning the photo was plastered on the front pages of newspapers around the world. That picture caused an explosion of interest and the following night, it took barricades and police on horseback to keep the crowds in line. The Peppermint Lounge became a hit and the hip hangout club of the International Jet Set for several years, attracting such regulars as Ava Gardner, Norman Mailer, Marilyn Monroe, Frank Sinatra, Judy Garland, Truman Capote, and Jackie Kennedy. It was reported in the news that Jackie O. had a "Peppermint Lounge" temporarily installed at The White House for President Kennedy, as the twist was his favorite dance.

But what could I add to the Peppermint Lounge-concept to make it new and fresh? In an instant I thought of Candy Johnson, featured in all of the Annette Funicello and Frankie Avalon *Beach Party* movies as the "Shimmy Girl." I would call the club The Candy Store, bring in Candy, surround her with hot Go-Go Girls, and make it the wildest live show in Manhattan. Candy, dubbed Miss Perpetual Motion, and her very good-looking and outrageously well-dressed band of seven guys, Mickey, Larry and The Exciters—one of the best bands I have ever heard—had just set attendance records at the 1964 World's Fair as the Candy Johnson Review. The World's Fair had recently closed, and Candy and her manager Red Gilson had been staying at The Forest Hills Inn. When I pitched my idea to them, they loved it.

I opened The Candy Store to a line of people waiting to get in that stretched down West Fifty-Sixth Street for half a block. It was a wild and decadent scene for that time period. I personally auditioned the dancers/

Go-Go Girls/waitresses—hand-picking an assortment of beautiful, cute, tall, and short, redheads, blondes, and brunettes—all wearing bikinis, black fishnet stockings, and white leather go-go boots. The Candy Store Girls didn't have the headdresses of The Copa Girls but they could dance, and dance they did. The guys went wild! The two lead singers, Mickey and Larry, did splits and flips and swung their microphones around like yo-yos. They were a huge draw to the ladies. They rocked out to the hit songs of the day, popularized by Mitch Ryder & The Detroit Wheels, The Temptations, Tom Jones, James Brown, Sam & Dave, The Rascals, The Righteous Brothers, Otis Redding, Ray Charles, Jackie Wilson, Chuck Berry, and Little Richard, to name a few. It was the best live music in the city and the band featured some outrageous choreography including some members of the kick-ass horn section playing upside-down as they hung from their knees on trapezes suspended from the ceiling. Candy sang and shimmied nonstop to wild applause from patrons like Tom Jones, Little Richard, Sam and Dave, and Paul Anka.

As I took in the scene around me on opening night—the wild colors, sights, and sounds, the sexy girls dancing, the musicians swinging upside down through the air, Candy shaking it for all she was worth, and the room filled with smoke as guests drank cocktail after cocktail—I realized my first foray into the nightclub business was a success. Columnists Earl Wilson and Walter Winchell faithfully reported on it the next day, securing a spot for The Candy Store on "the list" of the Manhattan Night Set at the time.

However, something else happened on opening night. Larry Mathews called me into a back office to introduce me to his "partners," nicknamed Joe the Wop, who was the real boss, and Sal, who told me his hobby was raising white doves in his Westchester mansion. Dressed in silk suits and wearing gold chains, they were friendly and congratulated me, toasting my success. However, something about them made me extremely uncomfortable, because Larry, usually the bon vivant, acted so nervous around them. During that period of time the Mafia was at their peak of power and, from what I understand, these two guys controlled the West Side. Larry and his partners were hoping my success would spill over to their downstairs club, but it didn't. A month or so later, Tony, their squat, tough manager who reminded me of the Joe Pesci character in *Casino*, sat me down one night and, in his thick Bronx accent, said, "We gotta change da deal." He informed me that we needed to modify our arrangement and become "real partnas."

There was no way I wanted to get any further into bed with the Mob, so I sent my buddy from Great Neck High School, Eric Rosenfeld, who had only recently started practicing law, to Larry's office to meet the "partnas." His goal was to remind them about our signed agreement but the meeting didn't go as planned. Eric got so scared he dropped The Candy Store as a client, explaining, "Mark, they could break our knees!" This was obviously not part of his curriculum at Harvard Law. Although I was nervous, I figured if I showed the Mob respect and never borrowed money from them, they probably wouldn't hurt me.

As time went by, I continued to talk to Joe and Sal on my own, making small concessions, and they seemed to take an almost paternal interest in me, even offering me the presidency of a small Las Vegas casino. However, when they continued to pressure me and told me that they wanted to comanage Candy and make her a big star, I had to take a step back, and I decided it just wasn't worth the risk. I definitely didn't want to end up like Larry Mathews, owned by the Mob, so I slowly stopped promoting The Candy Store. Business dropped and I told them I couldn't continue paying Candy and the band. I found Candy and the band a gig in Mallorca, where I knew people from my many trips to Spain, and, after I got her safely out of town and away from the boys, I moved on.

Chapter Five:
I'll Take Manhattan

THERE WAS NOTHING MORE stylish and hip than New York City in the 1960s. It was the center of the universe and after The Candy Store, I knew that I belonged in Manhattan, not in Queens. It was a heady time to be young, single, and successful in Manhattan, so I moved to an outrageous bachelor pad right in the middle of it all on Thirty-Eighth Street between Madison and Park Avenues. It was a one-bedroom with high ceilings, carved moldings, columns, a working marble fireplace in the living room, and an elevated mirrored dining area off to the side—a real knockout. It had previously been the formal grand room of a Delano-designed mansion. It was a great spot for entertaining.

At night, the city had a special quality to it. Trader Vic's at the Plaza Hotel was often one of my first stops in the evening. It felt like a spot off the beach somewhere in exotic Bali with the thatched roof over the bar, spears, carved masks, and an enormous dugout canoe from Marlon Brando's film *Mutiny on the Bounty*. My dates loved the deadly rum-laden Scorpions, a guaranteed aphrodisiac, served with a fresh gardenia floating on top. It was one of Johnny Carson's favorite places to hang out after hosting *The Tonight Show*. I always left by the Central Park South door, loving the sight of the twinkling lights in the windows of residences surrounding Central Park. If I was in an uptown mood, I'd take my date by the hand and we'd walk one block east to the lively-celebrity-laden Playboy Club on Fifty-Ninth Street, have a few drinks by the fire, and hear some good jazz. It was five floors of Manhattan-chic.

Or, if after leaving Trader Vic's I felt like something more Bohemian, I'd hail a cab and we'd head downtown, taking in the blaring overhead neon of Times Square as it cast its unflattering light on the sleazy street below where prostitutes, panhandlers, and tourists mingled. Down in Greenwich Village there were so many small clubs filled with cigarette and pot smoke and the amazing live music anywhere. One night my date and I went to see Howlin' Wolf at Cafe au Go Go; we were having a drink and smoking a joint when out of nowhere, The Chambers Brothers got up and jammed with The Wolf. Sometimes we'd head to Little Italy to stuff our faces at Umberto's Clam House where "Crazy Joe" Gallo would be gunned down years later. If we felt like dancing we'd head over to Trude Heller's nightclub. Francis Grasso, mentor to many DJs of the early 1970s, worked there not as a DJ, but as a dancer. He danced twenty minutes on, twenty minutes off—all night long. "It was the hardest twenty dollars I ever made in my life," he later said about the experience.

And then the pill coupled with Helen Gurley Brown's 1962 book *Sex and the Single Girl* created the perfect storm for what lay ahead—the sexual revolution. The book sold two million copies its first three weeks on the shelves of America's bookstores. It challenged the very core of the American family. The author encouraged women to become financially independent, experience fun with sex before settling down to marriage and children, and perhaps even opt out of marriage altogether. The pill gave women a choice. It was liberating, radical, and many will argue that it was the beginning of the end of the family as we had always known it. But until that mindset took hold, I was stuck with the reality that most "nice" girls still wouldn't go all the way. They were saving "it" for Mr. Right and marriage. The girls I could have sex with somehow didn't really interest me for more than one or two evenings. And then I met Susan.

She was twenty-five to my twenty-seven, Jewish, and already a law school graduate with an impressive job. She dressed in tight miniskirts, which were all the rage in 1967, and fitted tops that accentuated her small waist. She was just as smart as I was, maybe smarter. We made a great couple. I could immediately see the possibilities of a serious relationship with Susan.

We kissed on the first date, and she encouraged me to run my hands all over her hot little body and get a good feel on the second date, but the events following date number three proved to be a problem. Susan was far more experienced sexually than I was and I liked that, but at the same time I felt intimidated, thinking I might not please her. It was the beginning of the sexual revolution, and Susan seemed to be really enjoying her sexual freedom. I knew that she'd made it with other guys.

At the end of our third date we ended up at her apartment. We'd been fooling around and took our clothes off. At one point she reached into this little yellow box full of poppers (amyl nitrate), broke open the capsule, and held it under my nose, and all of a sudden I went limp. It was clear I wasn't going to be getting it on that night. The poppers freaked me out. She freaked me out. I was clueless—I didn't know what they were for or how I was expected to react to them. The experience left my confidence so shaken that the next time we went out, I didn't even try to get her in bed. I was frightened by her intellectual brilliance, assertiveness, and sexual superiority, and so we drifted apart.

I had dated a lot, but, sexually speaking, I was a novice compared to Susan, and that one experience of failing to perform worried me and led me into therapy for the first time in my life. For four or five months I saw a Freudian shrink who, as you may or may not know, said almost nothing. You could sit or lie there in silence for fifty minutes if you, the patient, chose to say nothing. But you paid for it. I chose to open up and share some of my innermost thoughts and fears about growing up and my relationship with my father and mother. Then the good doctor explained he was leaving on vacation for the entire month of August. I was not ready to put my therapy on hold. I was intrigued by an experimental psychologist I had heard about who believed in using psychedelic drugs as part of his therapeutic process. We talked for hours about life and how LSD affects awareness, consciousness, and the mysterious workings of the subconscious. He explained that LSD turns off the regions of the brain that constrain consciousness, allowing for an increase in the flow of free thought. Your imagination shifts into high gear and takes you to places that can be terrifying or exhilarating. LSD can give you a feeling of enlightenment about yourself and the world you live in.

After about three months of LSD therapy with him, he referred me to a spiritual psychologist, a practicing Buddhist. He taught me a style of meditation with breathing techniques that helped to diminish mental anguish and tension. This would prove to be a useful tool in my life. All of this took place over the course of almost a year, giving me a greater understanding of and insight into myself. The experience cracked open a window on a newfound curiosity for truth and enlightenment.

Then, one evening, as luck would have it, I bumped into Susan at a party and the spark was immediately reignited within me. She was the kind of girl I wanted at my side and in my life. In our excitement we planned a long getaway weekend together in the Caribbean. Part of me was looking forward to going away with her; the other part was terrified. The idea of what might happen once the two of us were alone in a bedroom for days scared me, even after my months of therapy. But, as scheduled, we traveled to the Dutch island of Bonaire. We stayed in a small, two-story hotel, which offered nothing but dark, damp rooms, and it felt like anything but a sexy island getaway. That didn't deter Susan—she would've been hot to trot in a mortuary. I thought if I drank enough rum I'd get over my fears and rise to the occasion. But each night that I didn't, Susan became more and more fixated on me, using every trick in her repertoire. And the more fixated she became, the more frightened I became. By our last day in Bonaire, she was hysterical.

"I can't stand it!" she cried. "I can't stand being with someone who can't make love with me! What's the matter with you?"

I wondered the same thing.

I was beside myself. Here I was with this beautiful, successful, smart woman—whom I was really attracted to—and I couldn't make love to her. She was right—there must be something wrong with me. I didn't know what to say; it made no sense to me either. What the hell was it that was preventing me from getting aroused? In those days we didn't discuss erectile dysfunction. TV commercials depicting an amorous couple in a seaside bathtub enjoying four hours of erection thanks to the wonder pill, Viagra, were unheard of. In 1968, I was convinced it was just me.

Finally, Susan and I left Bonaire and flew through Aruba on our way back to the US, though this time we went out of our way to book a night at a really nice hotel, giving us one last shot at paradise before heading back home. Our hotel could not have been more different than the one in Bonaire. It was a beautiful white modern high-rise hotel with bright, cheerful rooms opening onto beautiful terraces with comfortable chaise lounges, all of which overlooked the glistening blue ocean, dotted with little white sailboats. It was uplifting, to say the least, and it shifted my mood immediately. I started to relax.

Lounging around, sipping an Island rum drink, I watched Susan prance around our room in nothing but a pair of panties. Life felt good again. We decided to sit outside on the terrace, and after a while she leaned over and gently kissed me. Her hysteria was gone. She was calm, loving; it was wonderful. And then it happened. I started to feel the rush of sexual excitement.

We slowly and gently touched each other in a loving way and suddenly I was fully aroused. I immediately started to worry and I could feel my body tensing, and then something new happened and I snapped to it, just as I had practiced in exercises with my Eastern shrink. I changed my breathing. I could feel my heart rate slow and I began to relax. Just like that, I was back in business.

Susan didn't pressure me. We just let it go to wherever it was going to go, and before I could think of anything that might stop it from happening, we both climaxed. We smiled with satisfaction and I kissed her passionately. I woke up the next morning happy to be cuddled up behind her and very aroused. I kissed her tenderly and after much foreplay we made love to each other like never before. I broke through my mental barrier and from that moment on I couldn't get enough of Susan.

Susan became my first long-term girlfriend. We enjoyed evenings together down in The Village, eating steaks at Nick's while listening to live Dixieland music. Other evenings we went to Little Italy to eat at my favorite restaurant there: Paolucci's. Some nights we'd go to Bianchi and Margherita where the waiters sang opera and the chef would burst out of the kitchen to join in the "Anvil Chorus" from *Il Trovatore*. I've always loved opera, so I'd sing along in Italian, which always impressed Susan. There was always great dance music at Shepheard's in The Drake Hotel on Fifty-Sixth Street and Park Avenue, one of the early discotheques in New York City. You never knew who might be hanging around in the wee hours since the hotel was home to Hendrix, The Stones, and others when they were on tour in America. I drank Dewar's on the rocks. She drank white wine. We were drunk on each other.

We sort of lived together, going back and forth between her apartment and mine; we traveled to Spain and France and skied in Aspen and Europe. I was crazy about her, the sex was amazing, and we were well-suited for each other in so many ways. Eventually, though, I was forced to face reality and the fact that Susan wanted to marry, settle down, and have children sooner rather than later. I wasn't ready for that. I was thinking only about how much fun we were having. It was painful, but finally, Susan and I mutually decided to call it quits.

I was in the middle of it all: New York City in the 1960s, a time of cultural, political, and social upheaval that changed America's mindset. America had been through tumultuous times before, but nothing like the 1960s when, for the first time ever, an entire generation of America's young people rejected their parents' values and beliefs, "the establishment," and formed a generation gap the likes of which the country had never experienced before. We questioned the political system, the economy, social standards, and sexual mores. It started on the college campuses but became a cause for many Americans. We supported the civil rights movement, opposed the Vietnam War, and then fell head over heels in love with sex, drugs, and rock and roll. Marijuana and LSD were the most popular drugs of the day, and we dismissed anyone who doubted that pot was as harmless as beer or that psychedelics were mind expanding. The 1960s were a time to make love not war, and I reflected my generation's views. I worked diligently to raise money for presidential candidate Eugene McCarthy and later for George McGovern. I preferred sleeping around to marrying and starting a family, and I used both marijuana and LSD to better my life. The mindset of the day was "if you can't be with the one you love, love the one you're with"—a smash hit by Stephen Stills.

The sexual revolution took hold and suddenly, everywhere I went, there were long-legged, miniskirted girls who wanted to have sex with me. I soon discovered that as a successful entrepreneur I never came across a shortage of women, especially after being named *Cosmopolitan*'s Bachelor of the Month. I was twenty-eight years old and excited about the unknown. As I ventured out into the social world of the late 1960s with a newfound confidence in my sexuality, I chose to pay attention and continue to learn from women, wanting to enhance their pleasure and my experiences with them. Some men were too busy enjoying themselves to have a clue as to what women wanted or needed sexually, but that was not entirely their fault. A lot of girls never said anything, either because they didn't know and were afraid to ask, or they were trying to come off as innocent. The problem with that scenario is that quite often the guy hits his climax, rolls over, and falls asleep, and the girl is left lying there wondering, "Is that all there is?" She never experiences that "fire down below" passion. I was determined to be a considerate lover, mainly because I derived so much more pleasure from the experience of knowing whoever I was with was satisfied. Now that my impotency issue had been resolved once I discovered that some women just didn't turn me on, I no longer questioned my masculinity but understood it was just the chemistry of the moment. I was fearless and ready for the 1970s.

In the 1960s and '70s, I dated a lot, frequenting some of the hottest, most elegant discotheques of the time. If it was a Sunday night I'd head over to Doubles in The Sherry Netherland Hotel, a chic members-only hangout for Jackie Kennedy. Sandy Stack, a pretty little blonde DJ from London, always blew me away with her selection of The Stones and R&B tracks. Sandy's son,

DJ Patrick Oliver, travels the world playing some of the best Electronic Dance Music I have ever heard

Arthur opened in 1965, created by Richard Burton's first wife Sybil, after he dumped her for Elizabeth Taylor. It was the precursor to Studio 54—a hangout for Andy Warhol, Truman Capote, Rudolf Nureyev, Roger Daltrey, and Wilt Chamberlain. It was obvious how important Sybil thought it was to jam-pack the club with young and beautiful girls. She turned Manhattan upside down with her admission policy—it was no longer about who you were but how hot you looked. Terry Noel was the DJ and the music he played was seamless and brilliant. The band ended each set with a cover song and Terry would take over—blending in the original on vinyl.

L'Interdit in the Gotham Hotel was another spot that I really enjoyed. It was decorated in red velvet, intimately lit, and the DJ played a great selection of sexy French dance music. The chicest of all was Le Club, a Kennedy family hangout. Le Club was my favorite, the first European-style discotheque in New York City. The DJ, Slim Hyatt, dictated the mood, set the pace, got the people up and dancing, and was a master at picking the right music to please the sophisticated, worldy crowd. I started spending time there once my former Forest Hills partner Philippe, known as Philippe of the Waldorf, sponsored me for membership. The crowd was beautiful, wealthy, and international with members such as Gianni Agnelli, Aristotle Onassis, and Hollywood's Ray Stark, dancing the night away with some of the wealthiest, most beautiful, and most intriguing women in the world.

These new discotheques in New York City were fashioned after the famous Parisian nightclub Castel, where I loved to dance when I was studying abroad in 1960, and again as a naval officer when I managed to get free flights to France. Discotheques in Europe were all the rage, and I spent a lot of time in them. In lieu of bands, they played records, whereas American nightclubs mostly featured live music. Throughout the night, the bands would play a forty-five-minute set, then take a thirty-minute break, leaving the club with dead air. In the European discotheques, DJs used two turntables making the music seamless and their selections were amazing—a mix of American rock and roll, and moody, atmospheric, European music. The juxtaposition was intoxicating in and of itself. When discotheques finally started to open in New York City in the mid-1960s and DJs followed the same format as Europe, young Manhattanites were enthralled, and I took note of how the DJ controlled the crowd.

In 1968, I acquired an interest in the Executive Hotel on Thirty-Seventh Street and Madison Avenue in Manhattan for $10,000. It was in receivership and I figured I could turn it around with a vision for an unusual restaurant/club to market the property. I developed my plans for the hotel's basement bar and restaurant. It was once known as "The Den at the Duane," where up-and-coming singers like Barbra Streisand had performed many years earlier. My concept was an intimate lounge with a piano bar, designed for couples where every table was enclosed with glittering strings of beads for privacy. I called it "A Quiet Little Table in the Corner." We advertised using headlines such as "Corner Her Tonight," and "After Our 4 Romantic Corner Tables Are Taken We Have 19 More." Something told me "word of mouth" marketing and promotion would build business quickly, so we invited all the residents from the neighborhood to come in for a free cocktail and hors d'oeuvres. "A Quiet Little Table in the Corner" became an overnight success.

Ultimately, the unusual name drew crowds, although not everyone agreed in the beginning. When I first floated the name by my publicist Dick Auletta, he said, "My God, that name is a press agent's nightmare!"

I shook my head incredulously and asked him what he was talking about.

"There are too many words in that name," he explained. "Gossip columnists always have to worry about how many words they have space for in their columns. I guarantee you, Mark, they'll be hesitant to say, 'Richard Burton and Liz Taylor were spotted at A Quiet Little Table in the Corner.' You should call it something else."

"I don't think so, Dick," I objected. "The name itself will attract people's attention. Besides, I don't see this as a celebrity hangout for Elizabeth Taylor and Richard Burton."

I saw A Quiet Little Table in the Corner as a place that would cater exclusively to the New York dating scene. It was the Swingin' 1960s—the era of the sexual revolution. *The Dating Game* and *Love, American Style* were among the most popular shows on television. What better time to develop a restaurant especially for couples out on dates? We served tapas that would be cooked over a Hibachi with tasty dips. If a couple out on their first date didn't have a lot to say to one another, this gave them something to do, thus avoiding that awkward and embarrassing silence that could occur. There was also live music from the piano bar, setting the tone for romance.

A Quiet Little Table in the Corner wasn't just a hit—it remained a New York dating hot spot for the next fifteen years. The success spilled over into the hotel itself. At the end of the night, it wasn't unusual for busboys to find panties under the tables as they were cleaning up the booths. One would imagine that, on more than one occasion, a couple who began their evening at the Quiet Table, as it was referred to, continued it upstairs in one of the rooms of the Executive Hotel.

The pill was made available in the early 1960s, but it wasn't until the mid—to late 1960s that large numbers of women started to use it. When that happened, things really got loose. Once girls knew they could screw around with little consequence, it was game on. Women were ready and eager to experiment with this newfound freedom and they often became the aggressors. It was great timing for Quiet Table and for me. I was up for almost anything.

Soon after we opened, my publicist set up an interview with Carol, a reporter for a major restaurant industry magazine. As the owner of a Manhattan supper club, I had gained some currency with the opposite sex, and I could tell right away upon meeting Carol that she was attracted to me. Though we had our interview during the day, it didn't make sense for Carol to write a piece about A Quiet Little Table in the Corner and not experience it at night. Plus, I had high hopes that our flirtation might continue into the nighttime hours, so we made an appointment to meet that evening. When Carol showed up, I was confused to see she had brought along her friend Bonnie.

"We're here to do an interview about A Quiet Little Table, so why don't we go experience one?" I suggested. The girls agreed. All of the booths were surrounded by beads, so you could see the outlines of people sitting at the tables but not what they were doing—and if someone wanted service, there was a gold tassel to pull, which turned on a small red light signaling to the slender, slinky waitresses in black tights to take a drink order. But otherwise the tables were very private, which was what A Quiet Little Table in the Corner was all about.

The three of us slid into a booth—with me in the middle—and continued our evening. Our bartender Buster always gave me and my guests doubles of whatever we ordered. He and I had concocted a Trader Vic's–like drink with vodka and fruit juices—the kind of cocktail where you couldn't taste the alcohol, but you knew you were drinking something strong. Bonnie and Carol were drinking the specials, while I was drinking Dewar's on the rocks, and we were getting drunker and drunker as the night wore on. Carol started rubbing my leg, letting her hand drift to the inside of my thigh, a real turn on. Perhaps, if I played the evening right, the three of us could end up together. A ménage à trois was something I had imagined but had certainly never experienced myself, but within seconds of telling the girls I kept a room for myself in the Executive Hotel just above the restaurant, the three of us were in the elevator heading upstairs.

Within a few moments it became a frenzied tangle of limbs. We were all hands and mouths on skin in a scene so unimaginable to me only a few hours earlier. I'd have thought it fictional had I not lived it. Looking back, I'm guessing that Carol really wanted to have sex with Bonnie but it took me to set the scene and make it happen. This was my first ménage à trois, and once I had opened this Pandora's Box, I was hooked. That night was the first of a series of increasingly common sexual forays that, with the addition of the recreational drugs of the day, made settling down with one woman a less and less likely scenario.

As wild and exciting as my nights were at A Quiet Little Table in the Corner, my daytime activities upstairs in the Executive Hotel offices were about to become a different kind of "wild." The Executive Hotel was controlled by attorney Harold Peller, who did a great job selling me on joining him as a working investor. However, as time went on, I realized he was not nearly as charming as I had originally thought. He was nuts and devious. Thinking back, I recall how he used to say, with intense eyes: "I'm not Jewish, I'm a Hebrew warrior." I was still young and learning my way in both business and the world and I was somewhat stunned to realize that truly crazy people weren't all wearing straitjackets and locked away in institutions—many of them operated in the normal world as businessmen. As I put pressure on Peller to pay me the percentage of gross I'd negotiated for opening A Quiet Little Table in the Corner, which had become a financial success, certain problems came to light. When we originally invested, Peller had separately persuaded each of the hotel's investors (including me and well-established stockbrokers Joe Cserhat and Fred Mates) to give him a proxy to vote each of our shares, giving Peller control of the corporation and its funds even though he owned only 20 percent of the stock. We ultimately realized that Peller was a thief and a scoundrel, and we needed to prove it. I convinced my other partners to take action.

We hired Jonathan Lubell, a mild-mannered Harvard-educated criminal-defense attorney who in 1970 had fought for the prisoners involved in the much-televised riots at the Attica Correctional Facility in upstate New York. A genius and a renegade, Jonathan was one of those lawyers who always had a different take on things. After hearing our story, he let me in on a little secret called the Doctrine of Self-Help, a vestige from English common law that has been around for centuries. It reads as follows: "When one's property has been seized unlawfully by another party, and it is impossible to seek recourse under the law because the courts are unavailable or closed, people have the right, under certain conditions, to retrieve the property." Knowledge of this would serve me well on a number of occasions throughout my career.

Our plan was to break into Peller's office at the hotel and take his files, providing us with the evidence needed to prove our case. We would first transfer the hotel funds into a new account under the same corporate name as the old one, giving us, the 80 percent majority shareholders, the control we were entitled to. We hired an off-duty NYPD cop I knew from The Forest Hills Inn to provide security if needed. Unbeknownst to Peller, Frank Pallone, the hotel's trusted comptroller, and a signatory on the bank account, had switched his allegiance to us and agreed to help. So at three o'clock on a Friday afternoon in 1968, Frank sent his assistant Sal to meet me at the Franklin National Bank in Manhattan. Sal looked and acted like a tough guy, but when my cab pulled up at Fortieth Street and Park Avenue, he was vomiting in the gutter, he was so scared.

Our goal was to move $40,000 of the hotel's working capital to a new corporate bank account controlled by us. Frank was sitting in Peller's office at the hotel waiting for the call from the bank to authorize the transaction. Around 3:30 p.m. the call came in and Frank, pretending to be Peller, gave his consent to the transaction. And just like that the working capital was deposited into the new corporate account. With all of Peller's records at our fingertips, our attorneys and CPAs spent the weekend preparing our case proving that Peller had misappropriated funds, spending over $25,000 for carpeting and appliances for his home in Brooklyn, as well as jewelry for his wife.

As expected, early Saturday morning, a desk clerk notified Peller that we were in his office. Then he called the local police precinct, telling them there had been a break-in. A squad car was sent over, but our cop told them it was a civil matter and they left. First thing Monday morning, we took our case before a judge, proving significant theft, and we got a court order signed that kept Peller off the premises for a year. He never set foot in the hotel again. The judge had nullified the voting trust, shocked to see the blatantly unethical and illegal behavior of an attorney. Within the year, we bought him out.

A Quiet Little Table in the Corner continued to thrive until 1984, when the Executive Hotel was sold.

Chapter Six:
Reefer Madness

THE STONEWALL RIOTS OF <u>1969</u> in Greenwich Village changed the dating game even more by advancing the cause for lesbians and gays. A radical feminist wrote the SCUM Manifesto and then shot Andy Warhol, declaring a war on men and our male-dominated society. Meanwhile, straight women everywhere were celebrating the pill and a newfound joy in sex, emphasizing that it was just as important for a woman to have an orgasm as it was for a man. I agreed wholeheartedly. <u>Unwanted pregnancies were a thing of the past thanks to the pill</u> and Roe v. Wade, which <u>made abortions legal.</u> Timothy Leary's now famous quote of the decade, "Tune In, Turn On, Drop Out," encouraged us to find our inner nature by getting high on LSD and dropping out of the rat race. Most of us opted not to drop out and instead remained within to enjoy the benefits of a new attitude—free love. People were free to love whomever, whenever, and wherever they pleased without attachment or commitment or risk of unwanted pregnancy.

We were all still recovering and trying to come to terms with the assassinations of President John F. Kennedy and Dr. Martin Luther King Jr. and the war in Vietnam. Clips of American soldiers returning home in body bags could be seen nightly on the 6:00 p.m. news. It was the only war America ever lost, and, worse yet, many pundits proclaimed that it had all been in vain and that it was a war that should never have been fought. "Have a drink," "drop a tab," and "smoke a joint" were the popular solutions of the day.

I will never forget how pop culture stood up and took notice of the pornographic flick *Deep Throat*. The plot revolved around a young woman, played by Linda Lovelace who, after much frustration, discovers that her clitoris is in the back of her throat, and the only way she can be sexually satisfied is to give a man oral sex. This was a fantasy come true for every man whose "dream girl" is as hot to give a blow job as he is to get one. The film provided endless fodder for late night television hosts like Johnny Carson—his guest celebrities, Jack Nicholson, Norman Mailer, and Truman Capote touted the charm and talents of Linda Lovelace. The film grossed $600 million and elevated porn from sleaze to the Avant Garde. The demographics for pornography and sex toys were forever changed, paving the way for the billion-dollar porn industry as we know it today.

Life was good. I was doing well as I neared my thirtieth birthday and took over the bankrupt, publicly traded company Davos Inc. I settled the bankruptcy by issuing stock, and within two years I used the public company's shares to make acquisitions of food-processing companies, which resulted in gross annual sales of $100 million. I also acquired the ski resort Mt. Snow, with miles and miles of slopes and dozens of ski lifts, three hotels, five restaurants, an airstrip, and a golf course—much of it not quite finished. I was on a roll.

I was using LSD again, but this time around therapy had absolutely nothing to do with it. It was all about fun. I spent my weekends dropping mescaline and acid with one of my best friends, Robert Giller, a medical doctor and acupuncturist. I'd begin the day with a glass of orange juice and a big fat joint of some high-quality marijuana. Those were the days when you could light up a cigarette or a joint practically anywhere—restaurants, movie theaters, and clubs, just walking down the street—it made no difference. Technically, marijuana wasn't legal, but tobacco was, and by the early 1970s, nobody in New York City seemed to care what it was you were smoking.

At the time, a good friend of mine was my former fraternity brother Bob Millman, a psychiatrist specializing in drug addiction at Cornell Medical School. He was hired part-time to supervise young interns at a makeshift drug overdose Emergency Center—located in Bill Graham's famous theater, The Fillmore East in New York's East Village, where kids on a bad trip were monitored and helped. Along with Bob, I was lucky enough to hang out backstage in a crazy drugged-filled scene with The Rolling Stones, Jefferson Airplane, Moody Blues, Grateful Dead, and then-unknown Elton John opening Leon Russell's show. That's where I heard Elton's beautiful "Your Song" for the first time. The Fillmore East looked deceptively small from the outside but inside there were 2,500 seats. It felt intimate and had a mind-blowing energy, courtesy of all the people inside the building being high on pot or tripping their brains out on acid and enjoying some of the greatest rock and roll music ever played.

That same year, I bought and renovated a farmhouse on eighty acres next to a large reservoir near Mt. Snow. Bob Giller moved in with me when he returned from studying acupuncture in China. During the warmer months, we'd usually arrive on Friday night with our weekend dates, often dropping acid when we were half an hour away, so that just as we pulled into the long dirt driveway we'd be tripping our brains out. Then we'd wander through the woods barefoot in the dark, hallucinating that we were Indians like the characters in Carlos Castaneda's *Don Juan Trilogy,* which we were all reading at the time. I felt myself to be living in the image of a Native American and some nights took to the lake in my wooden canoe, cutting silently through the water, surrounded by tall trees under a full moon and starry sky. It was otherworldly.

A year earlier, I had purchased a Mercedes sports car that I bought after the success of A Quiet Little Table in the Corner. One night, I was speeding up Interstate 91 on my way to Mt. Snow, completely stoned and rockin' out to The Stones' new album *Sticky Fingers,* when suddenly, I saw a flashing light in my rearview mirror. I quickly turned the music off, put out the joint in the ashtray, and opened the window in an effort to air out the car. I pulled over to the side and hopped out of the car thinking that if I could get to the cop before he got to me and smelled the pot, I'd be a whole lot better off.

Suddenly, he was standing right in front of me and said, "Don't you know you were doing ninety? Get back in the car!" I did so and then he stuck his head in the car and said, "I smell marijuana."

"I don't know what you're talking about," I said nervously.

"Gimme that ash tray," he said. I removed the tray and handed it to him. He fished around and found the roach I'd just put out. He held it up to my face and said, "That's marijuana!" He shot me an "are you kidding me" look and said, "Follow me," then got back in his car. I did as I was told and trailed him along Interstate 91 to a police station in Greenfield, Massachusetts. Once we got inside, I was instructed to sit and wait. He called to someone in another room, and in walks this narc—he wasn't introduced as a narc, but I knew he was. He was a redhead with long, curly, unkempt hair that blended with the beard that covered his whole face. Dressed in torn jeans, he didn't look like a cop; he looked like he was homeless. But that's how narcs disguise themselves.

He said to me, "Mr. Fleischman, I understand you've been smoking marijuana while driving at ninety miles per hour on I-ninety-one."

I calmly replied, "No sir, I wasn't smoking marijuana, just speeding."

Thus began a back and forth—them telling me I was lying, me insisting I wasn't. Finally, the narc said, "We have the roach as evidence. However, if you tell the truth, we're going to let you go."

I debated this as quickly as possible. I remember thinking, *Oh my God, I'm gonna admit this? Then what?* I had to decide if he was really going to let me go. Then I thought, *If the cops wanted to bust me, they'd have searched the car, where they would've found my drug stash—which included Dexedrine, black beauties, magic mushrooms, mescaline, acid, and a shitload of marijuana.* I decided they weren't going to prosecute on a roach. I gulped hard and I said, "Yes, okay, I did it. I smoked marijuana in the car." I continued, "Sir, please, don't arrest me. It will ruin my life."

I held my breath, waiting for him to respond. The narc watched me closely. The trooper said nothing. Then, after what seemed like an eternity, he said, "Well, now you're being honest. I'm going to let you go this time. Don't let there be a next time."

I'd never been so relieved in my life. I pumped his hand like he'd saved me from eternal damnation, which he did, and I walked out the door, shaken to my core. Had I been busted, I never would've been able to borrow another dollar in my life. Bankers don't look favorably upon people who do drugs and get arrested and my liquor licenses would have been in jeopardy. As it was, banks were already taking a chance loaning so much money to me—an arrest like that would have abruptly ended my career.

In the early 1970s, my most serious girlfriend was Suzy Chaffee, a downhill racer who had been captain of the Women's US Olympic Ski Team in the '68 Winter Games in Grenoble, France. She literally took the country by storm as "Suzy Chapstick" the fresh-faced, gorgeous blonde skier in all the Chapstick commercials. I met her in Vermont, but since we both had apartments in Manhattan, that's where we started dating. One evening after dinner we went to my apartment and I turned her onto marijuana. That was the first time we made love. After that, I started skiing all over the west with her.

As a result of my relationship with Suzy, I underwent a real metamorphosis. I went from being a mediocre skier, never having achieved much in competitive sports, to an amateur Giant Slalom racer, skiing and hanging out with

Olympians in Pro-Am races. This accomplishment fueled my inner strength, bolstering my self-esteem, giving me greater confidence and driving me to take on bigger and bigger challenges. In February 1972, *Signature Magazine* ran a complimentary story about me. I was pictured on the cover with Suzy seated next to me on a chair lift at Mt. Snow against a perfect blue sky heading up the mountain. It was a flattering article and cover photo that went straight to my head. I thought I could do no wrong.

Then came the 1973 energy crisis, making it a nightmare to get gas. If the last digit of your license plate was odd, you could buy gas only on odd-numbered days, and others had to buy on even-numbered days. To make matters worse, gas stations were now closed on Sundays, the day people had always filled up their tanks before returning home from a ski weekend. Between the gas shortage and two rainy winters in a row, business took a nosedive and I was forced to close down Davos, selling Mt. Snow to the Killington Ski Corporation. I sold my plane, as well as my beloved Chinese junk, and went from being on top of the world to having to start all over again. I was only thirty-three years old. It was time to move on, this time without the pot and acid for breakfast.

I signed the deal in Japan to borrow millions of dollars for Mt. Snow

Since one of my main lenders for Davos had been a Japanese bank, I had spent quite a bit of time in that country. One of many ideas resulting from my adventures was the Robata restaurant in New York City, a remake of a popular spot I frequented in Tokyo. I opened it in 1974 at Sixty-First Street and Madison Avenue, where the once famed Colony restaurant hosted the who's who of Café Society. Robata was way ahead of its time and became an immediate hit in Manhattan. People loved the Japanese country décor showcasing two chefs kneeling behind the open fire with an abundant and colorful display of fresh vegetables, fish, and meat to choose from. It was also one of the first restaurants in Manhattan to feature small plates. The reviews were terrific (including a rave review in *The New York Times*), and we became one of the most popular Japanese restaurants in the city until years later when the building was demolished to make way for a high-rise.

In 1974, I started spending more time at New Line Cinema, a company in which I had been one of the founding shareholders. I moved into New Line's offices on Broadway and Fourteenth, which I worked out of for the next five years. It was during this period that I met Laurie Lister. I was in my mid-thirties, and she was a recent Mount Holyoke graduate working as *Penthouse* magazine's interview editor. Although Laurie was only twenty-three, she was taken seriously in the publishing world and was on her way up. One day, I got a phone call from Laurie in her role of *Penthouse*'s Interview Editor. I found out later that she had read a piece about me in a book called *Young Millionaires*, taken from the *Signature Magazine* article with me and Suzy Chaffee on the cover. She had decided she wanted to meet me. Laurie had a beautiful voice, slightly breathy but with an elegant accent. She sounded young and sexy and I was always looking to promote my projects in the media.

Robata was inspired by the open-fire cooking method and presentation that I enjoyed so much during my time spent in Japan. Robata was the first of its kind in Manhattan.

We set up a dinner meeting at Robata. Laurie was stunning. She was slim and beautifully dressed in a high fashion outfit you might see in *Vogue*. She had long, straight, light brown hair with bangs and big green eyes. But, more than for the way she looked, I was attracted to Laurie for how bright, funny, and incredibly well-read she was. That night, we had the kind of conversations that I usually had with my guy friends. Laurie was political and, like me, a dyed-in-the-wool Democrat, but we still had spirited debates about some of the twists and turns of current happenings. After dinner, we strolled toward Park Avenue, and as we were waiting on the corner for a taxi, I leaned down and kissed her under the street lamp, her hair blowing in the wind. It was magical.

When we first started dating, she had another boyfriend—a successful, well-known publisher—someone who appeared to be above me in the social strata of the day. Although I still was co-owner of a small hotel and a couple of restaurants and was involved in a small film distribution company, I had just lost my status as the CEO of a $100-million company, which had motivated her to call me for the "interview" in the first place. I was afraid I didn't have enough to offer Laurie who, like others of the early women's rights movement, considered herself free to play the field. Laurie designated one night a week to go out with me, which I would look forward to all week. Laurie and I would laugh and talk through dinner, and I was on top of the world. Beyond just good times and conversation, Laurie had the ability to look into my soul with those big green eyes. She appeared to sympathize with my insecurities and understand my dreams. She was a good listener and I told her everything about myself. And then, after dinner, we would go to my apartment, and make love for hours. Ultimately, Laurie broke up with the publishing guy and we became more or less a couple, although we both continued to see other people.

New Line Cinema had some early success distributing films like *Reefer Madness,* which hit college campuses in the late 1960s and was enormously popular, and then again with John Waters' cult classics, *Pink Flamingos* and *Female Trouble,* starring the one and only Divine. The first film we produced was *Stunts*, a mystery thriller about a stuntman who dies while involved in the making of a film. I was instrumental in raising the funds for the film once NBC bought it as a future Movie of the Week.

In May of 1978, we took *Stunts* to the Cannes Film Festival to sell the foreign rights, cash out, and pay off our loans. We didn't have the money to throw parties or line the Croisette with giant posters to attract foreign buyers, but with so many reporters and photographers looking for a story, a scene from the movie—in which Robert Forster's character runs out of a burning house just before it explodes—triggered an idea. I found a local stuntman whose handler referred to him as a "torchman." We got the word out to all the foreign buyers and press to meet us on the beach in front of the Carlton Hotel to see a major happening. The torchman's handler poured gasoline on him then lit him up as dozens of cameras were flashing while the human ball of fire ran toward the sea for dear life. When the local police realized I had orchestrated the stunt, they threatened to throw me in jail not for almost killing a man but for setting a fire on the beach without a permit. Go figure. The following day, there was a huge color picture of this fiery scene on the front page of the major newspaper, *Nice Matin*, garnering us all the attention we needed. Mission accomplished.

New Line Cinema hosted a preview of *Stunts* in New York, and when the credits rolled at the beginning of the film and my name was not included, I was extremely disappointed. As a contributing partner, I should have received a screen credit, and with Laurie sitting next to me I was embarrassed by the slight. But that experience reinforced to me the fact that although Bob Shaye referred to me as a partner, New Line was Bob's company and I was the second banana—a position I wasn't accustomed to playing. I explored other opportunities and decided to pursue the Virgin Isle Hotel in St. Thomas.

Chapter Seven:
Adventures in Paradise

ACQUIRING THE FORMER VIRGIN Isle Hilton in 1978 turned out to be a significant step on my path to becoming the owner of Studio 54. I went down to the Islands to look at what the broker at Helmsley Spear Realty touted as the deal of a lifetime. The hotel had been closed for four years after two local, well-publicized tragedies. The first was the Fountain Valley Massacre in which locals machine-gunned to death a number of white residents at the Rockefeller's Golf Course. The second was the crash of an American Airlines jet into the side of a mountain at the St. Thomas airport due to a too-short runway. Tourism and hotel occupancy rates had plummeted.

I flew to the island and a reclusive caretaker with a talkative pet macaw on his shoulder showed me around the hotel and grounds. Even after the bird tried to take a bite out of my hand, I saw the property's potential—it was impossible not to. The beauty of the turquoise waters surrounding the island, with its quaint, formerly Danish town and lush tropical atmosphere, called to me. The hotel property—an impressive 230-room structure set in lush gardens atop a ridge overlooking the harbor of St. Thomas, designed by Morris Lapidus, architect of the Fontainebleau in Miami—could be bought for half of what it cost to build twenty years earlier.

My buddy, Harvard Law graduate Eric Rosenfeld (the one who didn't want his knees broken by my Candy Store partners), was specializing in tax shelters at the time. His law firm jumped at the opportunity to raise the $2.5 million needed and, by the fall of 1978, my brother Alan and I became the principal owner operators of the new Virgin Isle Hotel. With the hotel closed for so many years, there were many maintenance issues to overcome and only ninety days until the winter season began. We remodeled and upgraded the guest rooms, kitchen, plumbing, air conditioning, electric, water, and waste lines as best we could in such a short time. Within three months we were able to reopen the guest rooms, The Terrace Bar, the hotel's beautiful art deco dining room overlooking Charlotte Amalie harbor, and Lindy's, a deli-style coffee shop serving pastrami sandwiches and cheesecake. We worked the phones incessantly, drummed up some publicity and invited friends and a few VIPs for that first Christmas week.

Unfortunately, just as the guests were arriving for Christmas week, the shit hit the fan—literally. Before purchasing the property, we hired a well-regarded engineer from Florida who certified all the operating systems. However, the engineer did not anticipate hotel guests flushing toilets at the same time, causing many of the old pipes to give way, resulting in sewage draining all over the front desk and other parts of the lobby. We sued the engineer but it took years to settle the case with his insurance company.

In the meantime, we needed a beach club and restaurant to augment the hotel's hillside location. As part of the original deal when we purchased the property, we leased with an option to buy five acres on beautiful Brewers Bay Beach, just ten minutes from the hotel. To keep the area safe, we cleared out all the Rastafarians living in the brush. Then I remembered how taken I was with L'Age d'Or ("the Age of Gold"), a restaurant in France specializing in wood-fire cooking, which New Line Cinema's Bob Shaye had introduced me to during the Cannes Film Festival. It was the perfect concept for our beachfront restaurant. It would be designed by a creative local architect, Peter Brill, who had recently completed the Bitter End, a marvelous indoor/outdoor restaurant and hotel on the nearby island of Virgin Gorda. Alan and I took a day trip to Virgin Gorda on our sailboat *Gypsy Star* and we fell in love with the design of the Bitter End, particularly after a bowl of mushroom soup made with "magic" mushrooms picked along the way from the island of Tortola.

We hired Peter and he designed a functional and attractive beach restaurant and bar featuring the wood-fire oven. We then found Culinary Institute graduate Steve Melina, a talented young chef from New York who had been working as a sous chef for noted restaurateur Alan Stillman at the Manhattan Ocean Club. We gave him the opportunity to be the head chef at our new restaurant, La Grillade, on Brewers Bay Beach, which we opened in early 1979 as the hotel's second eatery. Every day we'd get fresh fish and lobster, as well as steaks and vegetables, and cook them over the wood fire. La Grillade was not only frequented for lunch on the beach by our hotel guests but also quickly became one of the most popular dinner restaurants on the island. It was one of the earliest restaurants in the US to use wood-fire cooking instead of Texas barbecue; although it was already popular in Europe, I expected the concept to develop further on the mainland.

Before long, we started to do well and made a real impact on the island. Alan became president of the Virgin Islands Hotel Association while I was having liaisons with an array of fabulous women. Cocaine was another island libation, since it was often transported through St. Thomas on the way from Colombia to the US. The island coke was clean and pure. Snorting coke was almost like having an orgasm, at least in the beginning. There was a quick burn and then an ecstatic rush to the brain, which could make you feel alert, powerful, and sexy.

With everything in place, we turned the hotel into a nightly party with Caribbean barbecues on the torch lit terrace that featured Calypso bands, steel drums, and Moko Jumbi stilt dancer Ali Paul, who became a good friend. He was also a local senator whose theme song was "have a paaarty, smoke a wattie." One of my favorite groups who performed there was Otis and The Elevators: they always put everybody in a good mood playing R&B classics. There was fun entertainment at the Terrace Bar, emceed by a beautiful local girl and former Miss Virgin Islands, Lorraine Baa, who, to my dismay, always refused my advances.

When we first took over the hotel, I put an ad in *The Village Voice* looking for bartenders and waitresses to replace many of the locals on our staff, as they were not providing good, courteous service. Since this was a hotel in the Caribbean, offering a job including room and board during the frigid winter of 1978, I received an overwhelming number of responses from smart and attractive young ladies who wanted to replace some of the surly locals. I flew to New York and personally conducted most of the interviews. Once we chose the staff, they flew down to St. Thomas to start their new work life. One of my hires for the waitstaff position was Shelley Tupper, a hot brunette with a razor-sharp wit and a dynamite personality, but after three weeks it was obvious that the heavy dining room trays were proving to be too much for Shelley. So I took her out of food service, and she joined my Social Hostess Staff arranging beach and hotel activities for our guests. Then, I met three beautiful blonde Swedish girls who were visiting the island, Birgitta, Anika, and Inga, and hired all three as hotel concierges. From that point onward, one of my partners, Fred Kassner, co-owner of Liberty Travel, dubbed the hotel "Mark's Country Club."

Chapter Eight:
Studio 54 Hits the Virgin Isle Hotel

B Y EARLY 1979, THE Virgin Isle Hotel was strapped for cash because of the unanticipated repair costs and the loss of revenue from the damaged guest rooms that sat empty as a result of the plumbing disaster. Recognizing the popularity of disco music and dancing, I knew the hotel could generate more profit with a dance club, and I had just the building available. It stood across from the hotel's front entrance porte-cochere and had a peaked roof that could house the needed sound, lights, and special effects. I contacted Steve Rubell and Ian Schrager about a potential franchise of Studio 54 in St. Thomas. A dance club would be a great amenity, and having a Studio 54 there would be a surefire way to promote the hotel.

Steve and Ian procrastinated for months deciding whether or not to give the Virgin Isle Hotel the Studio 54 franchise. Eventually, Ian visited St. Thomas, but they both continued to drag their feet. With no answer from Rubell and Schrager, I turned to Xenon. Like Studio 54, Xenon had once been a theater. Originally the prestigious Henry Miller Theater in the Broadway district on Forty-Third Street between Fifth and Sixth Avenues, it had been operating as a porn house called Avon-at-the-Hudson when Howard Stein and Peppo Vanini bought it in 1978 and went head-to-head with Studio 54, which had opened a year earlier. I signed a contract with Howard and Peppo to open a Xenon in the Virgin Isle Hotel.

While I actively handled the day-to-day running of the Virgin Isle Hotel, I spent long weekends in the Islands and conducted the rest of my business during shortened work weeks in New York, using my office at New Line Cinema. During the summer of 1979, I spent a lot of mid-week evenings in

Howard and Peppo's offices at Xenon doing coke with their celebrity pals. Peppo was a tall, handsome nightclub impresario from Gstaad, Switzerland. Howard was a former rock promoter who had brought rockers David Bowie, The Who, and The Rolling Stones to the Westchester Theater right outside of the city. He was a handsome guy with dark, slicked-back hair, blue eyes, and a New York accent. He was always friendly, but you could see he had a tough side. His background was similar to Ian's in that his father was known to be associated with the Mob. (However, unlike Ian's father, who died of natural causes, word had it that Howard's father's headless body had been found floating in Jamaica Bay.) Howard and I finally signed an agreement providing for the opening of Xenon at the Virgin Isle Hotel, and as part of that arrangement Howard agreed to bring his club's celebrities down to the hotel for publicity. Late that fall, we started the renovation of the unused building on what was to be the island's new nightclub, Xenon.

Steve and Ian were serving time by then. It was that fall when I began negotiations with them to acquire their Studio 54 in New York. During one of these talks at Metropolitan Correctional Center, Steve suggested that it would make more sense to open the club in the Virgin Isle Hotel as Studio 54 since I was going to own the New York Studio 54, but I told him I had already signed a contract to open as Xenon. Unbeknownst to me, there was a fierce personal and professional rivalry between Howard Stein and Steve and Ian. It started when Steve torpedoed Xenon's grand opening a few years earlier by hosting Andy Warhol's birthday party at Studio 54 on the same evening, thereby forcing Xenon to compete for a smaller list of available celebrities as well as for ink in the nightclub pages the next day. Word leaked about my visit with Steve and Ian at the prison, and the next day Howard called and asked to meet me regarding an important matter.

Howard picked me up in his dark blue limousine and got right to the point: "Mark, I hear you're talking to Steve and Ian about buying Studio 54 in New York." Howard frowned. "I want to preface what I'm about to say by telling you that those two guys are evil and it would not be in your best interest to go through with any deal."

I knew that Howard had the Virgin Isle Hotel deal in his mind, and I calmly said, "This is only a preliminary discussion and what I do with them in New York will in no way violate our contract in St. Thomas."

All of a sudden, the glad-handing Howard got tough and said in a menacing tone, "No way are you going to own Studio 54 when you have a contract with me for a Xenon."

I repeated myself: "Anything I do with Steve and Ian will have no effect on our business dealings in St. Thomas. We were merely engaged in exploratory conversations about Studio 54 in New York. I fully intend to open the club in the islands as Xenon."

I was hoping to calm him down, but Howard became even more agitated, and finally I just got out of the car when it stopped at a light and told him, "Nothing more is going to happen until you and I speak about this again."

When Howard read an item in *New York* magazine, "Intelligencer," the following Monday about my jailhouse negotiations with Steve and Ian (which may have been planted by their attorney Roy Cohn to produce these exact results), he exploded at me over the phone: "I am going to sue your ass, Fleischman!" Howard's corporation was called "Sosueme": the threat didn't seem all that idle.

Again, I assured him, "Nothing is final in regards to Studio 54 New York."

My reassurances did nothing to dissuade him from serving me with a lawsuit a few days later, hiring Weil, Gotshal & Manges, a major New York law firm, to represent him. He sought a Temporary Restraining Order (TRO) not just for opening the Virgin Isle Hotel Studio 54, but any involvement in New York as well. Fortunately, the judge saw through such obvious vindictiveness, and the TRO for the New York club was rejected.

With such bad vibes between us, it was going to be difficult for me to open Xenon in St. Thomas while negotiating to buy Studio 54 in New York. Howard and I ended up settling. I agreed to pay him $50,000 over a period of time, and my brother Alan and I were free to open Studio 54 in St. Thomas. Now, Howard hated me as much as he hated Steve and Ian. Though it would be eighteen months before I reopened the doors to Studio 54 in New York, I had already made another enemy in the disco world in addition to Maurice Brahms of The Underground.

Out of work and with nothing else to do, key members of the Studio 54 staff in New York flew down to St. Thomas and worked for Alan and me. They were eager to escape the depressing scene in New York after Studio closed, and I was offering employment. This talented group, which had run Studio 54 for the past two and a half years, helped me open Studio 54 in the Virgin Isle Hotel, which became the hottest nightspot in the Caribbean.

Marc Benecke, Studio 54's doorman in New York, was among the staff members who initially joined us in St. Thomas. Marc's aloof style may have worked fine in New York, but it wasn't long before we realized we would need a different type of doorman. Marc was white, while half of the population on St. Thomas was mixed and black, and it would prove impossible for him to play any "selection game" on that island without causing trouble. We hired a cool, local, light-skinned island cop to be our new doorman, and he worked for us during his off-duty hours. He knew the area, as well as all the popular people, and did a great job keeping the troublemakers out. We also hired Studio 54 New York's night manager, Chris Williamson, to be the general manager. Together, with Studio 54 GM Michael Overington, we replicated the excitement of the New York club in the Tropics, complete with Robert DaSilva's light show, DJs Gary Holtzman, Richie Kaczor, and Leroy Washington playing on a booming sound system, and long lines of people waiting to get in.

In addition to opening Studio 54, the Virgin Isle Hotel staged other promotions as well. At one event, we invited disco icon Grace Jones to join us for Carnival. Tall and strikingly beautiful, Grace was not only a superstar, but was also from nearby Jamaica, and everyone was excited to have her on the island. At Carnival, there is always a big parade with floats created by churches, merchants, and other local entities moving down the main street of town. We entered a float, calling it "Disco at the Carnival." We set up a great moving sound system on the hotel's truck and played all the disco hits that were popular at the time. The theme songs for our float were Sister Sledge's hit song "We Are Family" and the music of Grace Jones, including "Private Life" and "A Rolling Stone." We had a generator on the truck to power the sound system, and we built a large wooden platform on the cab for Grace to dance on. the Virgin Isle Hotel float was decorated with green fabric and glitter. The incredible sound from the five-hundred-watt speakers could be heard for miles.

My friend Senator Mike Gravel from Alaska brought Senator Bennett Johnston from Louisiana, and a number of other high-profile friends joined us as our guests for that year's Carnival. Everyone, including the staff, was dressed in white with green ribbons and powdered with green glitter to match Grace's green satin outfit. Whether we were on the truck, or in the street dancing around it, we snorted uncut coke (except for the Senators) and drank

151-proof rum straight from the bottle, while tall, sinewy Grace Jones gyrated as our "star" on top of the cab. It was almost one hundred degrees that day, but nobody complained. As we slowly made our way down the crowded main street, people were singing and chanting, "Grace...Grace..." dancing alongside and looking up to catch a glimpse of Grace Jones.

Carnival '79—a very adult parade indeed. A gyrating Grace Jones was the star of our float and everyone around us was snorting cocaine and drinking 151-proof rum.

Each float took one lap around the field and then one pass in front of the judges' stand. By the time our float got to the judges, Grace Jones had gone completely crazy. She tore apart the entire wooden structure of our float with her bare hands, one plank at a time. Then she started hurling the pieces of wood like javelins in the direction of the judges. Thankfully, none of the judges were hit. Before long, our float was in total shambles, but clearly we made an impression on the judges: we won one of the top prizes.

Jimmy Cliff was a huge star in the islands. His music was played constantly on the radio and his film *The Harder They Come* had developed a cult following all over the world. I became friendly with Michael Butler, the producer of *Hair,* who was friends with Jimmy and suggested coproducing a show with Jimmy in the islands, which we did the following summer. We booked the amphitheaters on St. Thomas and St. Croix and did some publicity and staged concerts on consecutive nights. It was a great idea, except we made the mistake of charging more than we should have. As a result, we had too many empty seats at both concerts and, not surprisingly, lost money.

But a funny thing happened at the stadium in St. Thomas. A huge crowd of locals stood outside the fence listening to Jimmy. They couldn't see him, but at least they could hear him. After the concert, I drove Jimmy and his entourage back to the hotel—I was the only white guy with Jimmy riding shotgun, while his retinue of five Jamaicans were hanging off the side of my Jeep, all smoking spliffs (cigar-sized joints). Jimmy's fans were lined up along the streets. As we were driving through town, people would yell out, "Hey, Jimmy! Hey, Jimmy! Why you charge so much, mon? Why not make it so all of us can see you?"

Back at the hotel, I talked it over with Jimmy, who was a really nice guy, and he said he'd perform gratis if we paid for the sound and staging. And so, while getting high on his ganga, we decided to put on a free concert in St. Thomas.

People came from all over the island. We set up the stage and sound in the town square and it was packed. They sat on every available tree limb and covered the rooftops. It was a wild scene. Jimmy played his entire repertoire of songs and took several encores. The audience loved every minute of it.

Another event that we brought to the island was Miss World America, a British beauty pageant. The first pageant was held in Huntsville, Alabama, in 1978, but in 1979 Griff O'Neil, president of Miss World America at the time, was looking for a more exotic location. St. Thomas was an obvious solution. We got together and made a deal to host and televise the second pageant at the Virgin Isle Hotel on September 15, 1979.

September 1979 proved to be the summer of Hurricane David, a Category 5 hurricane that was among the deadliest ever to hit the area. Most of the people involved with the pageant flew to St. Thomas on the same plane, experiencing severe pre-storm turbulence, and I could see how shaken they were upon arrival at the hotel. Large commercial jets were not permitted to land in St. Thomas, as the airport's runways had not yet been extended. Passengers were forced to land in San Juan, Puerto Rico, and make their way in a puddle jumper to St. Thomas. Making matters worse, much of the luggage, including clothing and makeup, didn't arrive at the hotel for three days.

Though I had been told it was against the rules to fool around with the girls, that didn't stop me from getting acquainted with them. Naturally, I tried to be very discreet, but it was difficult to play it cool around so many gorgeous women. So I smiled and flirted with them, walking that fine line between playing cute and being inappropriate, knowing that their island chaperones were watching me the whole time and doing their best to make sure that I didn't defile any of their precious flowers. When one of the contestants kept returning my smiles and flirtation, I knew it was only a matter of time.

The girls were on a strict schedule, with every minute of their day planned for them with things like show prep rehearsals, meal times, and an early curfew to ensure they got their beauty sleep. Even so, this contestant and I made plans to meet up that night. When I heard her knock and opened the door, neither of us hesitated—I pulled her into the room and we grabbed each other and kissed. She matched me in heat and passion, undoing my pants, tearing at my shirt, and before I knew it we were rolling around on my king-sized bed like a couple of horny teenagers trying to get it on before Mom and Dad got home.

Knowing that our time was limited at best, we got down to business quickly, and that's when it started: frantic, hysterical knocking at the door. I froze, deliciously trapped inside her, wanting desperately to fuck her senseless but sensing the jig was up.

"Mr. Fleischman," came the panicked but angry voice of one of her chaperones, calling out from the other side of the door. "Mr. Fleischman, we know she's in there! Stop what you're doing, right now!" The lovely little contestant was moaning as I called out, "She's not here!"

They wouldn't let up. *BANG! BANG! BANG!* "We know she's in there! We know you've got her!"

With great reluctance, the two of us got dressed. I unlocked the door to face two local, upstanding, heavyset, black Christian women who took their chaperoning job very seriously. With a sheepish look on her face, the contestant allowed one of the women to lead her out of the room, while the other one fixed me with a stern gaze, daring me to say something. There was really nothing to say. Next thing I knew, I received a phone call from Griff O'Neil threatening to cancel the pageant unless I agreed to stay away from the girls. Griff was stern, impossibly uptight, and very protective of the contestants; it didn't take long for me to realize he was serious. I agreed to back off.

Miss Virginia, Carter Wilson, was crowned the winner. Several fashion industry celebrities stayed at the hotel while serving as judges, including designer Scott Barrie and makeup artist Way Bandy, helping us garner even more press. Ultimately, the show was so successful that it was syndicated on TV throughout the United States, publicizing the hotel and the island of St.

Thomas. I invited then Governor Juan Luis of the Virgin Islands, along with his Lieutenant Governor, the Head of Tourism, and other local VIPs to the hotel for a private screening of the edited TV show. It was a glorious night as they enjoyed watching the pageant on a gigantic video screen set up poolside while feasting on an island buffet.

These and other well-publicized events—like the *Charlie's Angels* shoot with Cheryl Ladd, Jaclyn Smith, and Shelley Hack who were all knockouts and fun to spend time with—helped rebuild tourism on the island.

Back in New York one weekday morning, I got a phone call from Alan in St. Thomas: "Mark, something horrible has happened. La Grillade has been burned down and the security guard's head was cut off with a machete. Everyone is terrified. The two Dobermans are dead—they've been poisoned." We believed that the attack was perpetrated by the Rastafarians who wanted to get even with us for moving them off the land where we built our beach club two years earlier.

Everyone was scared out of their wits, including me. I even took the precaution of purchasing a gun, which I luckily never had the occasion to use. The chef of La Grillade flew off the island the following day, never to return.

Alan and I were in a state of shock and too scared to rebuild the beach club restaurant. In the meantime, I was concerned that the tabloids would have a field day if word of the tragedy were to get out. I instructed our staff not to discuss the beach club incident with anyone in New York. After several weeks, I thought the entire gruesome matter was behind us until I took what started as a pleasant phone call from Cyndi Stivers, who was writing for the gossip column Page Six at the *New York Post*. Cindy calmly asked me how everything was going with Studio 54 at the hotel in St. Thomas. I warily said, "Fine."

Then she said, "I heard there was a problem at the beach club..." and at that moment, I knew it was over. The next day there was a major piece on Page Six describing my dispute with Howard Stein and the island murder. The article almost suggested, in Page Six's circuitous manner of presenting gossip, that Howard was responsible, citing his filing of the lawsuit regarding Studio 54 replacing Xenon in St. Thomas and my negotiations to buy Studio 54 in New York. I heard he was furious. That was just one more nail in the coffin in the rivalry of the two most important clubs in New York.

Chapter Nine:
Battle for the Liquor License

I N SPITE OF THE raid on Studio 54 in December 1978, the club remained open and hotter than ever for more than a year. Time passed, and for twelve months, Steve and Ian continued to plea-bargain with the Feds, and then finally in January of 1980, they reached an agreement and reported to prison on February 4. The night before his incarceration, Steve sang "My Way" at their going-away party, which was attended by Diana Ross, David Geffen, and many of the Studio regulars. Studio 54 remained open, with Steve and Ian issuing directives to General Manager Michael Overington from the prison public phone until February 29, when the liquor license expired. On the following night, L. J. Kirby, Sal DeFalco, and the other bartenders offered platters of fruit to guests—the theory being, soft drinks and fruit, plus whatever drugs one might personally bring to Studio 54 to enhance the experience, could work for a few months—until another solution could be found. But without alcohol, the numbers dwindled, and after five or so days the club closed. I was already deep in negotiations with Steve and Ian to buy Studio 54 and had already filed the paperwork for a new liquor license with the New York City Alcoholic Beverage Control (ABC). This was the first step in a process that under normal circumstances would take about three months.

Once I filed, Steve wanted me to meet with Carmen D'Alessio, the Peruvian bombshell, who had booked many of Studio 54's major social events. Carmen had done some parties for Steve and Ian at Enchanted Gardens, their nightclub out in Queens, and then found them the space that would become Studio 54. She provided the list for Studio's opening night party in April 1977, bringing the fashion and glitterati crowd with her to launch Steve and Ian's first business in Manhattan. Carmen continued organizing events for them over the next few years and was promised a percentage of ownership, but the boys never delivered. In hindsight, this was probably fortunate for Carmen, because if they had given her a piece of the action, she might have been included in their trouble with the authorities.

I met with Carmen for the first time on a prison visiting day in Steve and Ian's Manhattan jail cell to discuss her working for me in the same capacity as she had worked for them. Fast-talking and flamboyant, with her distinctive Latin accent, Carmen and I became instant friends. She and I had a lot in common, including a love of parties as well as our mutual connection to Peru: my father's younger brothers and sisters had emigrated from Romania to Peru shortly after President Warren Harding significantly reduced immigration to the US in the 1920s, making it impossible for my dad to bring his siblings there. I visited with my aunts and uncles in Peru a few times as a child, and years later chose to go to school in Spain to learn Spanish, partly as a nod to my Peruvian relatives.

Carmen, Steve, Ian, and I began plans for a lavish Studio 54 reopening, thinking that it would take place within a few months. That was well before we realized that my application for the liquor license would be stonewalled for over a year by both the State Liquor Authority and the New York Alcoholic Beverage Control. There were still some issues to be ironed out with the sale, but Steve and Ian had been transferred to the federal prison at Maxwell Air Force Base in Alabama.

So in spring 1980, I flew to Montgomery, Alabama, to make sure the deal was on track. The Federal Bureau of Prisons permitted visitors to see only one prisoner per visit so I brought Steve and Ian's longtime secretary Honey Aldrich with me, thereby avoiding having to make two separate visits. It was a minimum-security prison with small buildings surrounded by well-manicured lawns and trees, and didn't seem all that unpleasant. But Steve and Ian hated it, particularly the food. I brought them corned beef sandwiches from the Carnegie Deli in Manhattan, which they gobbled up, but I doubted that was the only reason they seemed happy to see me. I had begun to think of them as close friends.

During that visit, Steve seemed anxious and talked about prison life, "It was very uncomfortable in the beginning, but I'm getting used to it now." He also bragged, "I talk to Calvin, Halston, and Claudia all the time." As editor of the *New York Post*'s Page Six, Claudia Cohen helped to put Studio 54 on the map. I guess this was Steve's way of assuring me that everyone was still his friend, and I could count on them all returning to Studio when I got my liquor license. Ian was also encouraging and more upbeat than he had been in the Manhattan prison. From what I remember, many of the other prisoners were nothing more than crooked Southern politicians who got caught with their hands in the cookie jar. Steve and Ian had each other for moral support and they managed to get decent work detail, mostly gardening jobs. I recall Ian saying that Steve was like the mayor of the prison—everyone loved him and they received great treatment because of him.

Originally, the purpose of my trip was not intended to be about fun, but I made the most of it with some extracurricular activities. After sending Honey back to New York, I decided to spend a few days in New Orleans, which was and is one of the most charming and happening cities in the world with food and music to delight the soul. On my first night, I began the evening in the Garden District at the award-winning Commander's Palace, a New Orleans landmark dating back to the 1880s, and then later that evening I crossed the river and headed over to Aaron Neville's hot club where I was introduced as the new owner of Studio 54. The brothers rolled out the red carpet for me and the party lasted into the wee hours of the morning.

The weekend's major highlight turned out to be Camille, a young lady who wanted to meet the new owner of the world-famous Studio 54. She had heard about me from a friend of hers, a Louisiana girl I was having sex with in New York. Camille was most definitely my type. Although she wore outdated, matronly glasses, she was attractive, voluptuous, and incredibly sexy. And she was not alone; she brought a friend with her, Tara, who was slender and much more reserved. I sensed that Tara had come along for the ride—wherever that ride took us.

Speaking of hot rides, my driver for that trip was a very foxy lady with a white classic Cadillac limo for hire. So, there I was in sensuous New Orleans with two hot dates and a hot driver for the night—which sounds like a lead-in to a porn flick. It was a harbinger of things to come as the owner of Studio 54.

I met up with Camille and Tara that evening which was to be my last night in New Orleans. I chose Antoine's for dinner, as it was the oldest and most elegant and prestigious restaurant in New Orleans dating back to 1840. It has entertained several US Presidents and Pope John Paul II. I was determined to impress these new friends with my choice in fine dining, but from the moment the three of us sat down, Camille's hands were all over me, teasing me under the table. By that time, I was ready to forego dinner and head back to the hotel.

We returned to my room and I ordered two bottles of French champagne. We shared a few lines of coke, and as I was passing around a joint, Camille undressed and then talked Tara out of her clothes and before long it was a happy threesome.

That was day one.

The next morning, I rolled over in bed—Camille on one side of me, Tara on the other—and then I looked at the clock. No way in hell was I leaving the scene that was happening in my bed. I made a game-day decision. I called the airline and switched my flight to the following day.

Camille was teasing Tara, telling her, "You know we've never made it together." And before Tara could say anything, Camille slid over and kissed her. As the girls caressed and touched each other passionately, I was mesmerized. Almost immediately they were panting and moaning, embracing each other as if I wasn't even there, but I was there so I joined in. It was a long time ago but I vividly remember, two girls crying out: "I'm coming, I'm coming" and so did I. It was so erotic. What a way to begin the day.

We decided that our last day together should be a true New Orleans experience and so the three of us set out—assisted by my foxy female chauffeur—to check out the town. We hit all the tourist spots, ate oysters and gumbo on Bourbon Street, walked the charming French Quarter, then hopped from bar to bar, drinking Hurricanes. Camille spotted a sex shop, so we went in. She insisted that I buy a few toys for us to play with back at the hotel that night.

The next morning, I was exhausted but happy, and my sexy driver took me for one last ride and dropped me off at the airport, where I caught my plane and returned home to take up where I had left off in my battle for the Studio 54 liquor license.

Back in New York, I went through a string of attorneys who failed to expedite the application process with the ABC. The authorities were considering the legal proscription of the premises as a "den of iniquity" that should never be operated again. A year went by while I continued my efforts to secure the license. I was so thoroughly invested in becoming the new owner of Studio 54 that I rarely set foot in my corner office at New Line Cinema, but I did attend the Cannes Film Festival in May 1980, and brought Laurie along with me. We had a nice lunch with Claudia Cohen at a popular beach restaurant where we discussed the future of Studio 54. On our way back to the

US, Laurie and I spent a few days in Paris with Carmen D'Alessio, checking out all the hottest Parisian clubs.

By early 1981, friends and acquaintances insisted that the disco era had ended, and that I should give up my relentless pursuit of Studio 54. I remained optimistic, even though I was seeing more and more "DISCO SUCKS" bumper stickers around town, I still believed that I could successfully reopen the club. My friends thought I was insane. Roy Cohn and I continued to have discussions about securing the licenses. He assured me he would work behind the scenes to make it happen. We both knew the ABC wanted Studio 54 closed forever.

I then retained Jerry Kremer, the New York state assemblyman who was chairman of the Ways and Means Committee that funded the New York State Liquor Authority. He was mild-mannered, yet very aggressive when it counted. When the ABC and SLA gave him the runaround, Jerry informed Warren Pesetsky, the tough-minded attorney for the State Liquor Authority, that he was prepared to file a lawsuit against the state in Federal Court to enforce my constitutional rights to be considered for a liquor license at Studio 54. That was when their position changed, and the ABC finally processed the application and ultimately approved it.

Then, *Billboard* magazine reported in the December 13, 1980 issue that the New York ABC had approved a liquor license for me that paved the way for the reopening of the long-shuttered Studio 54. Lawrence Gedda, the CEO of the State Liquor Authority (SLA), was pretty adamant that nothing could be further from the truth about Studio 54 soon reopening, because the SLA's litigation against Steve and Ian had to be cleared up first, and the pair was still serving time in federal prison. He predicted that litigation in the SLA's case against Steve and Ian could drag on for some time.

Anything related to discos, especially Studio 54 and its possible reopening, fascinated the press. New York loved Studio 54 and its prolonged closure was considered a major loss. The *New York Daily News* ran a piece on their People page titled "Behind Bars, He Gets Liquor Nod." The article went on to say:

> *Maurice Brahms, once one of the disco kings, is sitting in jail, but the liquor licenses were renewed yesterday for the three spots he owns: Underground, Bond's International, and New York, New York. It's the latest maneuvering in the disco scene in which the State Liquor Authority OK'd the renewals pending outcome of charges filed against Brahms by the agency.*

Brahms was convicted of skimming profits and dodging taxes, based on information given to the feds by Studio 54 owners Steve Rubell and Ian Schrager. In return, Steve and Ian had their own profit skimming and tax-evading sentences of 3 ½ years reduced.

But Rubell and Schrager aren't off the hook. As they serve time in a halfway house, the SLA lawyers are asking a US magistrate to release grand jury evidence of alleged drug sales at 54. And, the state has violations against 54 that block a new liquor license for the disco. The two are prepared to plead "no contest" to all the SLA charges, we learned, so they can clear the last hurdle for the sale of the disco.

By early 1981, Steve and Ian were released from prison and back in New York, living in a halfway house. They settled up with the SLA and I was granted the liquor license. It was finally over. After a year-and-a-half-long battle with government agencies, I had finally won the right to reopen Studio 54, and people all over town were treating me like I was some kind of conquering hero. I hadn't even opened the doors yet.

As per one of the conditions for granting me the liquor license, I was required to sign a document promising that I would not run a basement operation as part of Studio 54. This, of course, was a direct reference to the famous VIP parties that Steve hosted most nights in the basement, featuring a bowl of cocaine for special guests.

I had no problem signing the agreement—and just for the record, during the years I owned Studio 54, I can honestly say that to my knowledge nothing like that ever took place in the basement. (Well, there was that one time with The Rolling Stones and the Four Tops, but I'll go into that later.)

Additionally, while writing this memoir I had occasion to reconnect with Henry Eshelman, who is now a publicist in Hollywood, but back in early 1982, he was a director of the Studio 54 mailroom. Recently, over lunch in Beverly Hills, Henry confided in me that every Friday night, a dealer would come by Studio with an ounce of cocaine ordered by the mailroom staff working in the basement. They bought an ounce, instead of individual grams, to get a better price. It was then divided up and distributed, keeping everyone happy while working late into the night and early morning. I was clueless to all of it until that moment, nearly thirty years later. I was so damn lucky not to have been shut down for violating the signed agreement with the ABC.

That said, while I may have promised the ABC that I would not (knowingly) run any sort of basement operation, that agreement did not preclude me from moving the action upstairs into my office. I had no choice. Making cocaine available to our nightly influx of A-list celebrities was simply business as usual. It kept Studio's name in the papers which guaranteed a line of people waiting to pay to get in. In those days, providing cocaine was expected at all VIP-oriented nightclubs, and my office provided the prerequisite privacy.

Once I obtained the liquor license, the next step was dealing with the State of New York taxing authority and the IRS. They both had tax liens on the Studio 54 premises, and I needed their agreement to reopen the club. As I recall, it was determined somewhat arbitrarily that Steve and Ian owed in excess of $3.5 million in unpaid taxes to the State and Feds, including penalties and interest. A dispute then erupted over which government agency would get paid first and who would get the $500,000 that my investor and I would put up for Studio. The State, always in desperate need of funds, eventually won priority over the IRS.

These negotiations were tense because no one wanted to be accused of cutting any slack to such high-profile convicted felons. At one of these meetings I attempted to break the tension with a note of levity. I arrived at the conference room a little early, laid out six lines of Sweet'N Low made to look like lines of coke, and placed a newspaper over it. Once everyone was sitting around the large conference table and the negotiations began, I lifted the newspaper and Steve and Ian immediately freaked out and ran out of the room. They were both so scared, but the guys from the State and Treasury Departments cracked up.

From the very beginning of my negotiations to buy Studio 54, I knew that I would need a respectable and financially sound partner in this business venture. I approached Stanley Tate, a successful Miami-based businessman and Republican bigwig. He was a frequent fixture at the White House, having once been the national budget director for the Republican Party.

Initially, Stanley may have been enticed by the prospect of being in the middle of all that Studio 54 was famous for, but he ended up working very hard. He commuted to and from Miami and was always on top of the finances. He was a good partner, but we had our differences—actually, we drove each other crazy at times. But in 1981, Stanley jumped at the opportunity to be my partner in Studio 54 and arranged for the necessary $500,000. With his help, I assumed the governmental debt as our purchase price and was able to generate enough revenue during the three years we operated the club to pay off the $3.5 million to the State and Feds, as I'd promised Steve and Ian I would.

More than fifteen months had now passed since Studio 54 lost its liquor license. A guy named Mike Stone had been packing the club one night a week without a liquor license, catering to a young black and gay crowd that went crazy over DJ Kenny Carpenter, but the building had seen better days. By this time, Steve and Ian were out on probation and working as my consultants. Ian, who at some point in his life had aspired to be an architect, was in charge of the redecoration and restoration of the facility. We spent a considerable amount of money to restore the magnificence of Studio 54.

The original building at 254 West Fifty-Fourth Street, The Gallo Opera house, was designed by well-known Italian-American architect Eugene De Rosa, built for opera lover Fortune Gallo in 1927. CBS bought the building in 1943 and named it Studio 52, because it was the fifty-second stage set owned by the broadcast network. Over the next thirty years, some of America's most popular shows, ones that many of us grew up watching with our parents—*The $64,000 Question, What's My Line, Password*, and *To Tell the Truth*—were all shot there. CBS moved out of Studio 52 in 1976.

In 1977, the theater found its calling as Studio 54. Eugene De Rosa left us with endless beautiful details to explore. The grandness of the stately entry hall once again dazzled all who entered, with the unforgettable crystal chandelier updated with a touch of lasers. The stage, previously used for TV productions, became Studio 54's dance floor. The balcony, where the live audience once sat for the TV shows, remained untouched, providing an escape from the center of attention below and a darkened place for illicit activities of all kinds.

Chapter Ten:
The Lights Go On at Studio 54

ONE AFTERNOON, A FEW days before opening, Steve, Ian, and I were running around the club finalizing all the last minute details when James Brady, the legendary gossip columnist and founder of *The New York Post*'s Page Six column, strolled in, naturally quite curious about the renovations—as all of New York was. The ABC had insisted that Steve and Ian could have no involvement in the club at all, so had they been spotted in the club, an item would've surely landed in the press. When Steve and Ian spotted Brady, Steve quickly hid behind some props and Ian ran out the back door.

Steve was quoted in an article by Marie Brenner, "I can't give interviews. Interviews and publicity are not important to me right now. You have to believe me. I don't want to do anything that's not by the book. I still consider myself incarcerated. I don't want to look arrogant; I'm just trying not to make waves."

In the beginning, however, Steve did advise me on how to handle the PR, having done so from 1977 to 1979. He knew all the right people, how to hire the best publicists and when to use promotional gimmicks. At first, I almost always agreed with Steve, because he was usually correct. The one time we disagreed was when he learned that Marie Brenner, whom I was friends with before Studio 54, asked me if she could write a cover story about opening night for *New York* magazine. Steve was emphatically against any piece involving Marie, saying, "Did you see what she wrote about us after we got out of prison? Forget it."

I discussed Steve's concerns with Marie, and she promised a fair and honest story. Steve didn't buy it, and, despite his haranguing, I let her hang out with me for one week prior to the opening, as well as in my office on opening night itself. The story made the cover of the magazine and was helpful in reestablishing us as the place to be and be seen. Marie even quoted my father in the article, referring to him in a sweet way after she witnessed him asking me why we were spending so much money on giant fans. "What do you need wind for?" he said, thinking I was "spending recklessly as usual"—not understanding that a storm of fake snow created by the wind from the giant fans was another visual, in addition to the extraordinary light show and other special effects used to entertain the crowd.

Carmen D'Alessio had persuaded me to host a private VIP party a few hours prior to the Studio 54 opening night party at my newly built penthouse apartment at the Executive Hotel. I heard that my penthouse was so crowded that, according to Carmen, at one point Robert De Niro and his friend locked themselves in my candlelit master bathroom to chill next to the large Jacuzzi filled with ice and champagne. I say "I heard" because I was at Studio, so taken up with the last-minute chaos at hand prior to the actual opening night party that I never made it back home to greet my guests. My father and brother were there, and by the end of the evening, after observing all that took place, they were both convinced that I was completely out of my mind to want to get involved with such craziness.

The theme for the opening was "incandescence." More than five thousand invitations had gone out in the form of a small light bulb in a box imprinted with "You are invited to the relighting of Studio 54." On September 15, 1981 New Yorkers were so psyched for the opening of their beloved Studio 54 that more than ten thousand people showed up, plus reporters from just about every major news outlet. Inside, the crowd was masterfully controlled by Chuck Garelick and his security force. At one point in the crush of the evening, Chuck was blindsided and pushed up against a wall to the beat of "Devil's Gun," but Chuck, in a split second, instinctively determined the action was inadvertent. Allowing ego to rule could have turned the party into an all-out brawl. He was the consummate man in the skills of security, keeping it all safe and fun for everyone. Outside was a different story—it felt like a riot. The fire department had to close down the entire block on Fifty-Fourth Street, which prevented me from leaving to host the party at my penthouse. Many celebrities snuck in the back door—some couldn't get in at all, including Mary

Tyler Moore. The scene surrounding the club was best described in *Women's Wear Daily* as:

> *Outside, sheer pandemonium reigned all night as entrepreneur Mark Fleischman reopened Studio 54 with an all-out bash...*

...declaring Studio once again the center of Manhattan nightlife.

Before the night was over, I greeted many of the regulars, including Andy Warhol, Calvin Klein—accompanied by sixteen-year-old Brooke Shields, Cher, Liza Minnelli, Halston, Barry Diller and his future wife, Diane von Fürstenberg, David Geffen, and just about everyone else who made the night scene in New York, as well as Cary Grant, Lauren Hutton, Jack Nicholson, Ryan O'Neal and Farrah Fawcett, Gloria Vanderbilt, Paul Simon, John Belushi, and Gina Lollobrigida.

The scene inside Studio 54 on opening night was best described by Marie Brenner's *New York* magazine cover story, "Can Studio 54 Be Born Again?" It said:

> *The first one in was a Greek named Eustaithiou, and for some reason, he had chosen to wait hours in the rain, as had hundreds of others, to keep his place along with the granite-faced men in tuxedos and the almost nude man spray-painted bronze, the garment center models and the mime waving the Punch and Judy mask. They were all frantic to be a part of the event, pushing and shoving rather cheerfully at first, as if they actually expected to have a good time. But these were the early ones, the ones who were socially insecure. The camera crews kept coming out to tape them, as if they, too were somehow news: Desperation Returns. Studio 54 Open Again.*
>
> *The mobs, the desperation, the potential danger. That was what they had missed. That was the fun. Marc the doorman was back, too. Marc is a powerful man at Studio 54; it is Marc who determines who is in, who is out. And so, as Good Morning America covered him, he positively glowed.*
>
> *It takes a certain mentality to covet this type of position. You have to understand about power and guarding the bunker, of course, but you also have to be egalitarian enough to let in*

a mix. You have to know that the crowd that comes early is merely the filler, the boys who will strip off their shirts and keep dancing; you don't exclude the kids who have taken the train in from Queens. Not when they're paying $25 a head on opening night. You just let in any bald transvestite who happens to have on a skirt. The back door is something else. The back door is for the special friends, the comp list and the celebrities. That group never pays a thing.

But for an hour or two on opening night, the back door was closed. Nobody could get in and nobody could get out. A bus full of the owner's friends had to circle the block. The limousines were backed up, and the rich people on West Fifty-Third Street were screaming too. "Marc, Marc, Marc"—they all knew to call him Marc—"let us in!" The sublime irony is that now, at Studio 54, there are two Marks with power. The other one, Mark Fleischman, owns the joint.

He was inside, walking around in the crush, looking somewhat numb, but still in control, just not sure of how he was going to cram anybody else in. And there was a problem: although thousands were there, sweating and dancing, crushed together having a wonderful time, nobody was there yet. Not Halston or Andy, not the promised Lauren Bacall or Christopher Reeve. Just minor celebs like Uzie and Julie Budd. It was too early for the truly famous, and the Fire Department was telling the manager "Nobody else comes in."

And so many wanted in. They could feel that floor pulsing, even on the street, and they wanted it, wanted to be a part of the decibel level, so deafeningly high that all feelings would be annihilated. All you had to do was move past the bar up to the balcony, to check out the gold-and-scarlet light poles from the Steve and Ian days pumping over the dancers as if nothing had ever changed.

The idea was to make the transition between the old and the new somewhat fuzzy.

> *Days before the opening, 40 people work all night long. They*
> *are cheerful. A Busby Berkeley show comes to mind. The floor is*
> *waxed at 3:00 a.m. The sprinklers are installed. The new neon*
> *around the Steve and Ian chandelier "to make the link between*
> *the old and the new" is in place, Steve and Ian are being helpful.*
> *If they want to see their payment—some $4 million in notes—*
> *they had better be very helpful. Mark is ordering caviar for the*
> *members of the press. He's calm enough to turn his attention to*
> *his own party for 200 winged Portuguese—the mainstays of a*
> *Studio 54—who are flying in for the evening.*

Marie spent part of opening night sitting in my office watching the lunacy at the front door on the closet-circuit monitors.

> *…his TV sets are on, and one sees so clearly in miniature black*
> *and white everything that is going on outside, every awful*
> *detail. It seems so safe somehow, up here in the quiet. The fists*
> *fly, but there is no noise; the police are on the way, but the*
> *sirens are like sound effects in a dream. Marc the doorman has*
> *taken to the sidewalk now, his hair askew, his bellhop's jacket*
> *torn. The Studio 54 staff is shrieking piteously at him, "Come*
> *back, Marc, come back." They know it isn't safe for him either*
> *and their wails reverberate on West Fifty-Third. But Marc*
> *knows his duties. He turns around and bellows—as if it were*
> *his last sound on earth—"I can't come back in. Steve Rubell is*
> *arriving. I have to be out here to let him in.*

Though everyone assured me that Studio 54 "was a success again," I was still nervous. Hoping to overcome that, I drank a little more than I should have, and gladly obliged when people offered me cocaine, which was every time I turned around to meet someone new. Cocaine was definitely the star of the show—a valuable commodity. Finally, at 2:00 a.m., I started to calm down, relax, and enjoy myself after I swallowed the Quaalude that Steve gave me. Up until that night, alcohol, pot, acid (occasionally), and coke were my drugs of choice; Quaaludes were Steve's. I soon discovered that women loved them too—making them feel all warm and fuzzy inside, breaking down their inhibitions. The same held true for guys.

Studio was electrifying on opening night. DJs Preston Powell and Viviano were invited to hit the turntables after Steve had heard them spin in the Hamptons earlier that summer, and the one and only Robert DaSilva worked the lights. The excitement of several thousand beautiful and outrageously dressed people, dancing and moving in unison to the rhythm of the beat, made Studio 54 once again the only "place to be." At one point, at the center of it all, Liza and Cher were photographed dancing together, and the picture went global the next morning. The party, with all the visual and special effects masterfully controlled by Studio 54's tech crew headed by Neil and Harold Wilson, included insane amounts of confetti, fake snow, and glitter shot from cannons into the crowd repeatedly throughout the evening until our 5:00 a.m. closing. At the end, I was spent. When the house lights came on, I waded through a thick layer of confetti and made my way out the back door to my waiting limousine. I arrived home and collapsed, satisfied that I had pulled it off in spite of all the naysayers who said that disco was dead.

Chapter Eleven:
Cocaine and Quaaludes

MY GOOD FRIEND RICK James often referred to cocaine as a woman because, and I quote:

"Only a wild and crazy bitch could have wreaked such havoc on the American Psyche."

Cocaine has been working her magic as far back as 3000 BC when the Incas of Peru, living at high altitude in the thin mountain air of the Andes, chewed on coca leaves to escalate their heart rate and stimulate their breathing. People in Peru today still share the coca leaves with tourists arriving in Machu Pichu when they're hit with altitude sickness. When cocaine was extracted and processed from the leaf into a powder in the mid-1800s, Sigmund Freud got his nose into some of it and published an article touting its magical powers in treating depression and impotence. In 1886, John Pemberton introduced a new soft drink called Coca Cola that actually contained cocaine. Proprietors of drug stores and soda fountains all over America believed it to be, and I quote: "a valuable beverage containing the nerve stimulant properties of the coca leaf and cola (Kola) nut. It is not only delicious but exhilarating, refreshing, and invigorating—a Brain Tonic and cure for all nervous afflictions, neuralgia, hysteria, and melancholy." Cocaine remained an active ingredient in the Coca Cola formula for the next seventeen years. From 1910 to 1920, the silent movies produced in Hollywood portrayed cocaine in a positive light to millions of movie goers. By 1905, cocaine use had become popular, but more and more incidents of nasal damage as a result of snorting were reported. In 1914, the Harrison Narcotics Tax Act outlawed cocaine in the US.

In 1974, *The New York Times Magazine* ran an article with the headline, "Cocaine: The Champagne of Drugs," making the culture of cocaine sound glamorous, an essential part of the fast-track to success. The article went on to say that cocaine was "a good high achieved without the forbiddingly dangerous needle and addiction of heroin." Coke's euphoric effects, as well as its association with wealth and status, were also lauded in magazines such as *Newsweek* and *Rolling Stone*. Cocaine started out as a wealthy man's drug for elite members of Wall Street and the film, music, and fashion industries. But that would soon change when college students who could afford it would blow some coke and hit the books.

Cocaine and the era of sexual freedom could be felt everywhere I went. Doing some lines of coke at a party was nothing out of the ordinary now. Woody Allen's 1977 film *Annie Hall* took the humor of the cocaine culture to Middle America when Woody's character sneezes all over some lines of coke worth about $2,000, blowing it into nothingness. I remember going to a party at a movie producer's apartment and partaking from a silver platter heaped with what must have been $10,000 worth of cocaine sitting on a coffee table for all to enjoy and Robin Williams remarking, "Cocaine is God's way of telling you that you're making too much money."

At most parties, people would carry their own stash in a tiny oblong glass vial, available at almost any newspaper stand. It was about two inches long and a quarter of an inch in diameter, with a little black lid from which a tiny metal spoon hung down. It was a brilliant design. There was always a line to get into the bathroom at parties and clubs; most people couldn't afford to share so, rather than doing it out in the open, people would go it alone or take their date to the bathroom and do their hits together. The culture of cocaine was the opposite of the drug culture of the 1960s, when we would willingly pass a joint around and drop psychedelics together, wanting to share the experience of enlightenment. Cocaine changed all that. Generally speaking, guys shared their coke either to impress or to get laid. It was too expensive for a collective experience. It was anything but inclusive—it was the "all about me" drug, but we didn't see it that way. We believed coke would be to the 1980s what marijuana was to the 1960s. We were blinded by the snow.

Taking a Quaalude was guaranteed to pleasure you with a four—to six-hour "love trip."

All your inhibitions and fears disappeared and you were enhanced by a deep appreciation and love for music, sex, friendship, and all of humanity. It was glorious from beginning to end.

Then it wore off, you got tired, and you went to sleep. No hangover. Perfect!

The sexual revolution of the 1960s united with society's "on-again" love affair with cocaine and the love drug Quaalude of the 1970s to form the perfect storm. They unleashed an era of unbridled sexual behavior like nothing American society had seen before.

It was party time all across America.

Chapter Twelve:
Bombs Away

THE FIRST THING THAT went through my mind the morning after my grand reopening of Studio 54 was, "How the hell am I going to do this night after night? How do I maintain the same level of excitement and enthusiasm that I experienced last night?" Yes, it was outrageous and the people were dazzling, but every night? People were already comparing the new Studio 54 to the old Studio 54. Could I make the regulars—the crowd of the late 1970s—happy? I was committed. It would be my mission to maintain the charisma that made Studio 54.

The second thing that went through my mind was, "I'm going to need a shitload of coke."

Luckily for me, I had my Virgin Island connections. The coke in St. Thomas was of incredible quality, as close to pure as it got. St. Thomas was my source for the good stuff that got served to the celebrities at Studio. The fact that St. Thomas was an American territory allowed me to carry coke back into New York without passing through customs, and if I couldn't make the trip, I'd send an assistant who'd be thrilled to visit the islands.

In the months after the opening, that fall and winter, I kept my eyes open for party opportunities. Whenever I met a well-known personality—an artist, writer, Broadway actor, movie star, fashion designer, member of the Eurotrash set, or anyone with a following—I'd suggest that Studio 54 host a party in his or her honor. In the beginning, the guest of honor gave me a list of their friends to receive complimentary admission, but soon we were also printing up invitations that could be mailed or given out by the honoree. It meant a lot of free admissions, but served to keep us busy and prominently placed in the press.

Studio opened each night at 10:00 p.m., and on many nights I'd schedule one of these private parties, which we referred to as "Cut Drop Parties." Several hundred invited VIP guests gathered behind the scrim (drop), a semi-transparent heavy mesh curtain that descended from the ceiling and divided the dance floor. The invited VIP guests entered through our backdoor stage entrance on Fifty-Third Street, gave their name to security, then joined the other guests behind the curtain dancing and treated to complimentary drinks. By 11:30 p.m. the dance floor in front of the scrim would become crowded with patrons, some of whom had been selected by Marc Benecke. Selected guests then paid the cover and entered through the Fifty-Fourth Street front door entrance, and others who had gained admission by being on the complimentary guest list didn't pay. By midnight, when the dancing was at a feverish pitch, the curtain dividing the two areas of the dance floor would be lifted with much musical fanfare and electrifying theatrical lighting effects. The two parties would then merge into one huge celebration with everyone screaming while onlookers watched from the balcony. I orchestrated this scene every night during the first few months, and although I was having fun, it was turning out to be more difficult than I expected.

It didn't take me long to figure out that each night was going to be a delicate balancing act between great fun and total chaos, and, most of the time, the direction it took was up to me and my ability to protect the VIPs. In front of the scrim there was a mass of over a thousand people dancing, drinking, and enjoying a wild scene. On the other side were one to two hundred people, including the guest of honor and their friends, enjoying a private, high-energy, complimentary cocktail party. I was trained over many years in the hospitality industry to be concerned about every guest in my establishment, but this experience was beyond anything they taught at Cornell. I had security—big, burly, and tough but polite sons of bitches who guarded each side of the scrim between the main dance floor and the area holding the celebrities. These men could and would handle anyone who got out of control. I knew this, and yet I worried about the precarious balance between controlled chaos and an utter riot.

The VIP guests could see the throng of patrons on the other side of the sheer curtain, while still enjoying their private party, and they would inevitably ask if I could keep the curtain down longer, pointing out what a good time they were having just amongst themselves.

And they were having a good time, but like me, they were also a bit nervous about how things would go once that scrim was lifted and the party on the other side enveloped them. Often I would choose to indulge them in one more round of drinks and an extra half hour before getting on with the night's planned events. All this did was prolong my anxiety, but I knew it would make them more comfortable.

As we prepared for this nightly ritual, I scanned the room, making sure the women were alright and had grabbed their purses, and gave myself ample time to get any celebrity who was vulnerable out of the area and into a secure place such as my office or one of the protected silver banquettes. I couldn't assign everyone a personal bodyguard—nor did they want one—but I kept a discreet watch over any vulnerable partygoers as best I could. During one such party, we featured *Flamingo Road* leading lady Morgan Fairchild, who was a huge star at the time. She and I sat on a swing that was lowered off the bridge above the crowd as the scrim was raised. Morgan wore a shimmering silver dress, I wore an elegant tuxedo, and we were both slowly lowered onto the teeming dance floor in a move orchestrated by our creative general manager, Michael Overington. Morgan had a blast, hung out for the entire evening, and returned to Studio whenever she was in Manhattan.

On the other hand, New York Jets football star Mark Gastineau was one of my guests who you would think did not need protecting. He was a big, strong, five-time Pro Bowl linebacker who was famous not only for being part of the much feared and vaunted Jets pass rush (which had been dubbed the "New York Sack Exchange" by the press) but also for doing his signature "sack dance" whenever he brought down an opposing team's quarterback. One night, around 1:00 a.m., after a Cut Drop Party honoring several of the Jets, Gastineau decided to hang out at the main bar. He and friends enjoyed a round of drinks. Manager David Miskit instructed bartender Scott Baird to give Gastineau the next round, compliments of Studio 54. After Gastineau and friends finished their drinks, he requested another complimentary round. Scott explained that he couldn't do that and then bartender L. J. Kirby suggested that Scotty, who was much smaller than the football giant but vey muscular, arm wrestle for it. If Gastineau won, his drinks were on the house. L. J. had seen Scotty bring down some of the most powerful guys you can imagine. Soon, a crowd gathered and began to take sides, cheering for either Gastineau or Scotty. I was busy attending to something else, but I heard the match went on for some time and the two appeared to be in a dead heat until slowly and steadily Scotty took Gastineau down.

Not happy, Gastineau left the main bar and headed out toward the front door. That would have been the end of the story, were it not for a Jets fan who followed Gastineau out and for some reason started to heckle him. This man had to be either drunk or simply out of his mind. What else could have compelled him to behave in such a manner as to make fun of a drunk NFL linebacker? Gastineau turned around and smashed the guy in the face, inflicting significant physical damage. I was unaware of all this until I saw several security guards dragging Gastineau toward the front door. He was trying to fight them off, kicking and struggling to break free. Not realizing what was going on or what I was getting myself into, I blocked the pathway to the door and shouted at the guards, "Mark is my guest! Let him go!" Gastineau broke loose and there was much confusion. Now everyone was in it, and I ended up flying through the air and landing hard on my back.

Naturally, the newspapers had a field day covering the story over the next several days, including an editorial cartoon in *The New York Post* depicting two men being tossed out of Studio 54. The caption read, "Why go all the way to the Meadowlands when you can catch the Jets in action right here?" I don't remember how much it cost in legal fees, but it was probably worth it, except for my injury. Stories like that, as well as the daily celebrity sightings and photographs kept Studio 54 in the papers, which was always good for business.

Over the next three years or so, I exerted enormous energy orchestrating extravagant parties for the rich and famous, while entertaining illustrious actors, fashion designers, sports stars, and politicians with cocaine and champagne. The crowd on the dance floor was happy to be one with the music and thrilled to be a part of the phenomenon that was Studio 54. My small second-floor office wasn't designed to be a party room, but it became just that—a jam-packed replacement for the larger, more comfortable basement scene run years earlier by Steve Rubell. But nobody ever complained, and I think the intimacy of it all broke down the inhibitions of many celebrities, fostering sweet, touching moments.

Mick Jagger was a regular in my office. He was very fond of my assistant Hilary Clark. Both of them were from England, and they entertained us regularly, serenading us with songs from their homeland, especially the song people sing every November 5 on Bonfire Night. Prolific film producer

Lester Persky, nicknamed "Pester Lursky" (meant in the most loving way), would howl with laughter when Mick and Hilary put on their various skits, sometimes joined by *People* writer Peter Lester, another Brit. I remember the delight and laughter from Diane von Fürstenberg watching a very happy Liza Minnelli teaching Goldie Hawn some dance moves. Later that evening Liza invited George Martin and Hilary back to her apartment to see Judy Garland's red sequined shoes from *The Wizard of Oz*, which she kept on display.

Conversations could turn political—like the night that Desi Arnaz Jr. was in the office with Mario Van Peebles, Phoebe Snow, Nile Rodgers, and David Bowie. Denise Chatman walked in with Luis Somoza, the nephew of Anastasio Somoza (former president of Nicaragua) and Jose Ramon Lorido aka Monsi Lorido, named Miami's Most Eligible Bachelor on the cover of *Miami Magazine*. (His sister Marivi is married to actor Andy Garcia.) It didn't take long for Desi and Monsi, two Cubans, to immediately "connect," as Cubans do, and the conversation turned to Fidel Castro. Within minutes, courtesy of my guests, I was snorting some of the best cocaine I have ever had and laughing my ass off. Not that I found talk of communism and dictators to be that funny, but watching David and Desi and Monsi reminded me of *I Love Lucy*, with David in the role of Lucy.

Then, Rick James walked in and turned the room upside down with his presence. I told Rick we were talking about dictators and Rick responded, "Oh, you mean like the motherfuckers over at MTV who won't play my videos?" Rick was impressed with how David had taken on Mark Goodman (a VJ on MTV) in an interview. During that interview, Bowie started in on Goodman about how MTV didn't play black artists. Goodman tried to explain that MTV was founded as a rock format idea. Bowie wouldn't give an inch. And Goodman knew he didn't have a leg to stand on, as it was a hot topic amongst MTV's staff. Initially, everyone was on board with the rock format idea. But once the channel started playing Spandau Ballet, which was essentially a white R&B act, they felt there was no reason not to play black R&B acts.

Whatever went down in my office—it was never boring.

There was a method to my madness in managing it all. I always carried a leather card case holding three-by-five index cards in my pocket to jot down notes, ideas, and observations. Upon awakening each day, my assistants and I would review my notes and categorize them accordingly. People have told me that my note-taking inspired them to do the same. Denise Chatman told me that years later, when she was working for Logos and Promotions Inc., the three-by-five leather card case she designed and produced as a holiday gift for their VIP clients was inspired by me.

Shortly after reopening Studio 54, as proprietor of the nightclub, a typical evening for me would begin with a scotch on the rocks and a few glasses of champagne as I was out and about at dinner parties or various restaurants. By 10:00 p.m. it was time to begin adding cocaine to the combination as I was now entering that intense time period of about four hours of service to my special guests, some of the most interesting people in the world, and my mind needed to be razor-sharp. This served its purpose until around 2:00 a.m. when I would permit myself to relax and join the party with more cocaine, some cognac, and a Quaalude or two to level me out from all the coke and the adrenaline rush of the previous four hours. I was functioning at an insane level of intensity and loving it—I was the embodiment of the popular philosophy of the time: "better living through chemicals."

By the end of our first few months, Studio 54 was often filled to capacity, with up to two thousand patrons on many evenings. Regulars from the "old" crowd were partying with members of the "new," younger crowd and a fresh crop of even younger underage beauties were champing at the bit to get in. The drinking age was eighteen in New York, and many teenaged girls had excellent fake IDs. The whirlwind of guests from the old Studio crowd were there—Liza, Cher, Rod Stewart, Calvin Klein, Halston, Andy Warhol, Bianca Jagger, Farrah Fawcett with Ryan O'Neal, Truman Capote, Elizabeth Taylor, Gene Simmons, Paul Stanley, and everyone's favorite Rolling Stones, Mick, Keith, and Ron Wood—otherwise known as The Regulars.

But now Studio was attracting the next generation of young celebrities, including Prince, Madonna, Ellen Barkin, Steven Tyler, Ben Stiller, Christie Brinkley, Tommy Hilfiger, Drew Barrymore, Heather Locklear, Chris Atkins, and other up-and-coming actors visiting from Hollywood. It also attracted most of New York's top models, including Iman, Carol Alt, Stephanie Seymour, Paulina Porizkova, Kelly LeBrock, Linda Evangelista, Janice Dickinson, and a host of others. Most night people still wanted to be part of Studio 54. They felt safe and protected by everyone who worked there, especially the babes in the coatroom, who were a wild bunch that saw everything, and would never, ever tell.

The Harris Sisters—Jayne Anne, Eloise, and Mary Lou Harris—aka The Screaming Violets, were a welcome sight to Studio 54's original crowd on the night of our reopening. Jayne Anne recently told me: "Back in 1978, as a young girl, I was fresh from the closing of our Harris families' Off Broadway show *Sky High*, and needed, as actors call it, 'a survival job.' I applied for a job at Studio 54. I'd been hanging out there anyway and figured it would be a good fit as I was well-versed in society and celebrity from working at the very prestigious Park Avenue Antique Shows at the New York Armory. After making it through the scrutiny of the Studio 54 interview, I was told to show up later that night. The coatroom was run by Lisa, a tall, attractive blonde with hair down to her waist who liked to twirl to the music. The guys loved her and all the other girls in coat check who were beautiful, svelte, and liked to twirl to the music. Depending on the events of the evening, there could be as many as four or five coat check spaces running at once, in various locations throughout the club, which was great because a week or so later my sisters were hired as well, solving all of our financial and social problems. At some point Lisa decided to leave and my sisters and I took over the running of Studio 54's coatrooms.

The Harris Sisters aka The Screaming Violets—Mary Lou Harris, Jayne Anne Harris, and Eloise Harris (center). They saw it all, but would never tell.
Photograph by Nancy Brown, courtesy of the Harris Family Archive.

"Some nights were an endless parade of celebrities. Some showed up to make an appearance for the cameras and then left, some came in to party and some to party hard. We checked hundreds of coats, stoles, mink, fox, and sable furs, and any unique possession one could ask us to care for including a few dogs and a baby for twenty minutes. We were union actors and singers as well, sometimes burning the candle at both ends, working in the club at night and spending our days on movie sets, commercial sets, modeling, and soap operas. A nap station was set up under one of the back coat check racks and we all took turns napping. Celebrities often used our coatroom to take a break from the crowds. Cher would come in and spruce up—she was cool. Francesco Scavullo was one of our favorites, such a nice guy. Way Bandy was another sweetheart."

Steve Steckel, a member of Studio's security team, recently told me that security always jumped to it whenever André the Giant, the professional wrestler and actor, arrived at the front door. André was huge, seven feet five inches tall, weighed 525 pounds, and he always showed up with three girls on each arm so they had to open all the doors at the same time that led to the main room. Jayne Anne Harris went on to say, "André was an excellent tipper and very friendly. Most celebrities were very nice to us coat check girls, polite, sweet, and generous in their tipping. The coat check was very lucrative and some girls were very smart with their money. Some paid for college and others bought Manhattan apartments. The hours were grueling and the work was extremely physical. We're not sure how we did it."

It was exhilarating to play host to some of the most famous people in the world whenever they felt like dropping in to have fun and be seen. It was thrilling for me, personally, when King Juan Carlos of Spain visited. The king ended up in the midst of a scene with Carmen D'Alessio and Steve Rubell. Steve, who craved the company of celebrities almost as much as he did Quaaludes, and Carmen, whose native language was Spanish and also loved rubbing elbows with famous people, fought for the King's attention in front of his banquette. When I realized that the king was becoming uncomfortable, I was able to ease Steve and Carmen aside and engaged the King in a conversation about my studies at the Universities of Madrid and Santander. He was charismatic and appeared interested in my experiences in Spain. At one point in our conversations, he invited me to open a Studio 54 in Madrid—an offer I should have taken more seriously. Unfortunately, I was too caught up organizing each night at Studio 54 to think about anything else.

There was a lot of resentment about Studio 54 reopening so successfully, and we received several bomb threats, presumably from people who in the past had problems getting in. I hired a bodyguard as a police officer friend of mine suggested. I didn't mess around: I secured the services of a former FBI agent. Then, one Saturday night, we received the most serious of threats because of its specificity—the *New York Post* was anonymously called and told a bomb would go off that night in Studio 54 at 1:00 a.m. The NYPD bomb squad came in with their big bomb-sniffing German Shepherd and swept the place—in the middle of the party. Of all the crazy and outlandish things I witnessed over the years at Studio 54, nothing struck me as more odd than the sight of a German Shepherd sniffing the seats in the dark balcony.

Thankfully, the dog didn't find anything, and the cops gave me a choice: A) cause mass hysteria and possibly permanently damage the reputation of Studio by evacuating the club in a panic, or B) ride it out.

I decided not to tell the crowd, crossed my fingers, and let the revelry continue.

It was closing in on midnight, and my "brave" ex-FBI agent was sweating. He sheepishly came over to me after the cops left and gulped, "Mark, I have a wife and kids at home. I can't stay here just hoping there's no bomb." I looked at my watch, saw that it was 12:05 a.m., and I let him go—permanently. I decided personal private security wasn't for me and managed my life without it for the next three years. Rick James found it hard to believe that Mick Jagger bounced around New York City at night alone. I never saw any of the Stones with security. Whenever Rick was asked why he usually had somebody with him, he never failed to cite John Lennon. I couldn't argue with him..

At 12:45 a.m., I moved through the crowd to the center of the dance floor and lost myself in the beat of the music and the energy of the crowd. A navy man to the end, if Studio was going down, I was going with it.

Chapter Thirteen:
It's All About the Guest List

WITHIN A FEW MONTHS or so of our reopening, I hired some of New York's most attractive and socially-connected young women as assistants, which I did to cover both daytime and nighttime activities. Among those I hired was the charming Christina Oxenberg, sister of *Dynasty* star Catherine Oxenberg (their mother: Princess Elizabeth of Yugoslavia). Another of these fabulous women was the very young, beautiful, cherub-faced blonde, Gwynne Rivers. If the truth is to be told, Gwynne was fourteen years old the first time she saw the inside of Studio 54. She danced the night away with a much older gay friend who carried a tambourine everywhere and worked for Gwynne's father, artist Larry Rivers. One year later she met Mick Jagger for the first time at a Cut Drop Party at Studio while celebrating an exhibition of her father's art at the very prestigious Marlborough Gallery, which had taken place earlier that evening. Gwynne worked with Myra Scheer to guarantee the success of the event, calling all the right people in her father's circle of friends, ensuring a hot crowd and a fun time behind the scrim at Studio 54.

Gwynne's godfather, Earl McGrath, president of Rolling Stones Records, walked into the party with Mick Jagger, and sparks began to fly. Mick was immediately smitten with Gwynne—who was dressed in a long taffeta gown— telling her she reminded him of the debutantes he dated in London. When he put his arm around her neck and hugged her, the photographers went crazy. From then on, in addition to being the daughter of famous artist Larry Rivers, Gwynne was now known as the sometime companion of Mick Jagger—much to the chagrin of Mick's girlfriend (and later wife), supermodel Jerry Hall.

Gwynne had such good instincts about special events that I hired her to work for me at Studio. Gwynne recently reminded me of how sweet and protective she thought it was that, in spite of her being a streetwise kid, I made it a point to pick her up after school and take her to the office for her first day on the job. The rest of the week I sent my driver, Fred, and, after that, she made it on her own. She was smart and self-assured. Her fellow classmates were speechless when Gwynne told them, "I'm working at Studio 54." Mick and Gwynne continued to see each other off and on in subsequent years. Things came to a head on the night of Gwynne's eighteenth birthday party, which we hosted at Studio. While Larry Rivers played a short set with his jazz band, Mick and Gwynne ended up in an embrace that went on for quite a while until Jerry Hall managed to break it up—but not before a photographer for the *New York Post* captured Mick and Gwynne entwined. The picture made the front page of the *Post* the next day. Jerry later wrote of her irritation with Mick's interludes with Gwynne and others in her book *Tall Tales*.

Gwynne proved to be a valuable asset to me at Studio. She knew a lot of really cool people. I met Henry Eshelman through Gwynne and hired him to work in our mailroom. She introduced me to David Wallis, a sure-shot young promoter with a phenomenal mailing list, who knew Clint Smith, a childhood friend of Eddie Murphy, and through Clint booked several SNL parties for us. David was sixteen but looked twelve. When he introduced himself to my partner, Stanley Tate, and requested his check for a party he had booked, Stanley was in disbelief. He then called Denise Chatman, in my office, to verify David's claim, which Denise did. Stanley then screamed into the phone, "That's impossible! He doesn't even shave yet!"

Gwynne suggested I hire Victoria Leacock, daughter of the late film director Richard Leacock. I did and she proved to be one of my more serious daytime assistants. This is how Victoria remembers it: "I dropped out of Adelphi College when I was eighteen and had been going to Studio since I was fourteen. It was my home. Mark hired me to work as a daytime assistant at the Penthouse. There weren't too many rules. Some of the girls were as high as he was. I arrived for my first day at work and remember seeing a part-time assistant, with her face pressed onto the floor snorting the carpet, muttering, "Is this dust or coke?"

Back in 1965, when I was running the Forest Hills Inn, my father introduced me to Denise Chatman, a beautiful young blonde model. She was renting a charming turret room at the Inn. Her grandmother and my father had met through Rabbi Abraham Hecht from Brooklyn, whose endorsement was sought by almost every Democratic politician running for statewide office in New York. Her great aunt, Bunny Isador, was in the Ziegfeld Follies, her father had been a road man for Decca Records, and her mother a Walter Thornton model and a June Taylor dancer. She was steeped in the blues and jazz and loved The Rolling Stones as much as I did. Denise and I bonded immediately. When I invited her to see the new club I was opening, The Candy Store, she jumped at the chance to be one of the Go-Go Girls that danced on the tables. She tired of that within a few months and went on to make her mark in the music industry with the Cayre Brothers. She was a partner to Ken Cayre in the launch of Salsoul Records working in production, marketing, radio, and club promotion. It was now 1982 and Denise came to see me seeking a job at Studio. Having partied at Studio 54 from the very beginning, she understood the scene, had amazing contacts in the music industry, and shared my love of R&B music. I hired her immediately, and she was responsible for producing some of our biggest music events and parties.

My office was a very pleasant environment to work in, day or night. Even though the cream carpeting had seen better days, the wall-to-wall mirrors behind the desk area and the mellow recessed lighting gave the small space a comfortable vibe. It had a glow about it. The moment our doors closed at Studio 54 each night (early morning, really), the cleaning crew went into action throughout the entire club area and all the executive offices. By 10:00 a.m. the offices were cleaned and ready for the day staff to arrive. There was always a vase of fresh Stargazer lilies on my desk, giving the room a pleasant floral scent mixed in with a fresh breeze from the window, which the girls usually kept open. They could count on a lot of activity below on West Fifty-Third Street, as the back stage door entrance to the Roseland Ballroom was just a few doors away.

Denise Chatman worked out of my office at Studio 54, arriving Monday through Friday at noon. Shelley Tupper, one of my original hires at the Virgin Isle Hotel, had proven to be so good with celebrities and special events that I rehired her just in time for the opening of Studio 54 in New York. Shelley descended from Thomas Tupper, one of the founding fathers of Sandwich, Massachusetts, which was settled in 1637. Shelley's blood ran blue—but on the dance floor, she was all black. Shelley would join Denise at the office around 2:00 p.m. and Gwynne Rivers would arrive around 3:30 p.m.—right after school let out. The girls got along well and had many a laugh girl-talking about all the goings on at Studio. On more than one occasion Gwynne arrived with doodles drawn in black magic marker all over her legs—courtesy of Mick Jagger. Mick knew Gwynne's parents and, living close by, he would stop by their apartment and hang out—doodling on Gwynne's ankle as they all sat around the kitchen table.

One afternoon I called the office to speak with Gwynne and Denise picked up. I could hear a lot of laughing in the background and I asked her what was so funny. She said, "[One of the top models in the world whose name I am forbidden to mention] just arrived and she can barely walk. She just spent four days with Rick James at The Plaza Hotel—she said that his dick is the size of a Heineken bottle." Another time when I called they were flipping coins over who could keep Richard Gere's black sweater—left in the office the night before.

Hilary Clark, a very attractive teenager from England, with a mane of long blonde ringlets and an irresistible sense of personal style, became one of my key nighttime assistants. She was very sexy in an Edwardian way, short skirts, lace and epaulets on her jackets. Everyone loved her: she was so full of joy and always smiling. Shortly after I hired Hilary, she introduced me to her tweedy, straight-laced father, who asked me in his distinctive English accent for assurance that I would keep an eye on her. I promised him I would do my best to see to it that no harm came to her.

As my nighttime assistant, Hilary and I would entertain guests at the large square bar situated under the balcony adjacent to the dance floor, manned by the hunks behind the bar. It was always packed, sometimes with several hundred people, four deep, and served by some of New York's hottest guys—the Studio 54 bartenders. They were young, chiseled, and gorgeous. They weren't just eye candy—words often used to describe the head bartender L. J. Kirby, a Warren Beatty look-alike who was mesmerizing to watch. To our regulars, he could be a confidante at 4:00 a.m.; to a first-time guest he could be charming, seductive and flash the most welcoming smile. L. J. set the bar pretty high for the others. Bumping, grinding, taking orders, dancing, pouring drinks—you couldn't take your eyes off him. Women loved him, models ogled him, the queens worshipped him, and guys trusted him. Other than the dance floor, it was the hottest show in town. Sal DeFalco, Scott Baird, Cort Brown, Steve and Jonathan Learn, and Oscar Lopez were all there—doing it every night.

Hilary and I gave out free drinks as we entertained, moving and dancing from group to group, partying with everyone, squirting people with the soda guns, sometimes doing a line or two off the bar or throwing back shots with folks. We'd grab people, hug and kiss, create a scene together. It doesn't sound like work, but it was. It was imperative that Hilary be at my side so that when I needed a person on the spot to escort a VIP through the club to my office or the front door, or if I needed someone to clear out a banquette for a group of celebrities, someone could take care of it without interrupting the schmoozing.

Ian Schrager, always a ladies' man, soon developed a crush on Hilary. Ian of course knew his way around the club so he would take the passageway under the dance floor, come up the back steps, and open the service door at the back of the bar, where he'd yell to me in his raspy voice with a thick Brooklyn accent, "Hey Mark! Mark! Can I see ya for a minute?"

I'd respond, "Okay Ian, what do you need?"

Sometimes, he'd have something important to say—telling me there was an issue he spotted that needed taking care of—but more often than not he'd say, "Can you do me a favor? Can you let Hilary off early?" Ian had a lot of time on his hands since he was no longer running things at Studio 54.

I tried to accommodate Ian. We'd developed a relationship beginning with our time during negotiations in jail and then throughout preparations for the club's reopening, so as soon as I could, I'd let Hilary go, usually at 4:00 a.m. She'd tell me with a big smile, "I really like Ian!"

Then, a year or so later, Tony Curtis developed a crush on Hilary. The Tony Curtis of Studio 54 days didn't look like the tan and handsome Hollywood hunk with curly black hair and tight muscular body of the film *Spartacus*. He was drawn, pale, and sickly white. He often slurred his words, a result of his constant drinking, and he appeared to be stoned most of the time. Tony did a lot of coke. His reckless lifestyle really got the best of him. I don't remember who or what it was that finally convinced me, but I agreed to let Hilary accompany Tony to the Manila Film Festival. Tony had begged me for permission to take Hilary, saying, "I promise nothing will happen, I'll take care of her. She'll be safe—we'll be with Imelda and her husband Ferdinand Marcos, the president of the Philippines." I knew Tony was scheduled to be the Guest of Honor at the film festival, and I understood that he wanted to look good with Hilary on his arm. She was young and beautiful, a hot commodity. When Hilary personally begged me for the time off, I said yes. All I know is she didn't return with a drug addiction, pregnant, or ill. I had kept my word to her father.

While I was doing my thing at the main bar with Hilary or attending to a visiting celebrity in my office, my other assistant, Shelley Tupper, could be counted on to take care of whomever or whatever. Shelley said in a recent interview:

"Mark couldn't be in two places at the same time. Typically, I was out in the front of the club, close to the entrance hallway. I'd review the guest list with Chuck Garelick, our head of security and Marc Benecke at the front door, greet celebrities, get them situated, order their drinks, or I'd just show them around and introduce them to folks. They liked that. I'd keep the photographers at a distance, which made them feel safe and comfortable. They trusted me. Sometimes they just wanted to get out of the spotlight and chill, so I'd invite them up to Mark's office. After a while they'd go back down to the club and enjoy the scene. And then I could dance. I did a lot of dancing. Mark relied on me to run all over the club. I did a lot of running. I'd run through the basement under the dance floor to get to the front door to greet celebrities—then up to the Rubber Room, back down to the basement, up to the Cut Drop Party—out to the front door—back to Mark's office—down to the dance floor—all over the club and fast. I was Mark's buffer."

The lack of cell phones made it far more difficult to function, but it also made Studio 54's atmosphere of "no one will know tomorrow what you did here tonight" possible. Studio couldn't have existed in today's world unless we made it mandatory to check all electronic devices at the door.

Shelley continued: "One night, I was in the office with Mark, reviewing the guest list when Michael Johnson, owner of Studio Instrument Rentals, located just down the street from Studio, called me to say that Pete Townshend of The Who was with him at SIR and that he wanted to bring him over to Studio. 'But he's not into the disco scene, Shelley; you've got to make it interesting,' Michael said. Sylvester Stallone was expected at the front door at any minute and then Chuck called and told Mark, 'Stallone is here, he's walking to the main bar with Hilary.' I told Mark, 'You go take care of Sly and I'll deal with Pete.' Five minutes later I was waiting at the back door when Michael Johnson arrived with Pete Townsend. It was around midnight and the club was jumpin' hot and packed. I gave Michael a kiss and I introduced myself to Pete and told him, 'Relax and follow me…I'm taking you both to a place that's fun and quiet.' At that moment, Mark walked up with Sly and we all stood there for a minute talking and I noticed that Pete wasn't paying any attention at all—

he was mesmerized by the dance floor, which was visible through the metal mesh curtain separating us. Mark headed back to the main bar with Sly, while Michael, Pete, and I headed down the back stairs to the basement. I kept them both close to me as we passed through the busy mailroom and down another flight of stairs through another basement that had fake chickens hanging from the ceiling everywhere. Pete was fascinated. We went through a dark room and then down a ladder into another dark room and then into a recording studio, Charlie Benanty's Soundworks, Inc., under Studio 54. Pete looked dazed—this was not where he expected to land. Immediately he walked over to the baby grand piano, sat down, and played for me. No photos, no press, just a cool moment away from the spotlight."

The Sodom and Gomorrah scene at Studio 54 was made possible thanks to the many nooks and crannies throughout Studio which were perfect for sexual interactions: the backstage area, the basement (for those with access), the Ladies' Lounge, and the second-floor balcony were very popular. There was a small bar up there and Calvin Klein and Halston liked to hang up there with Steve. It wasn't as crazy as the main bar. The closet near the bar was a favorite secret spot of Steve's. The legendary Rubber Room was the dark balcony and bar area, seventy-five or so feet above the dance floor at the very top of Studio 54. It was decorated with high-tech industrial black rubber trim and flooring that could be easily washed down. Without fail, every night after all the lunacy, the busboys would find discarded rubbers, poppers, and panties all over the floor—a testimony to the night's fun and games. Alec Baldwin, who had worked there as a busboy back in the day when he was a struggling young actor, said he finally had to quit Studio 54 because seeing the sexual interplay night after night left him perpetually horny. No problem, there were hundreds of young hot boys waiting to replace him.

Then there was the famous DJ booth, adjacent to the second-floor balcony and partially suspended high above the dance floor. It provided a bird's-eye view of the entire dance floor.

The booth was a popular stop for almost every major celebrity and visiting DJ. I remember one particular night when author and acid enthusiast Dr. Timothy Leary tripped out in the booth. Earlier in the day when I heard he was coming I cooked up a surprise of Special K, a dissociative anesthetic that makes patients feel detached from their pain and environment. It's prepared by cooking liquid ketamine in a spoon with a lighter, which then turns into an off-white powder. You store it in a little glass vial until you snort it and then, BOOM! When Timothy arrived we hit the Special K first and then the dance floor. A few minutes later I saw Dr. Leary standing on the top of the DJ booth waving his arms, screaming, "This is the center of the universe!" as lights flashed wildly over his head. What a night!

The DJ booth was an oasis of sorts. It was a safe haven for Michael Jackson, who always danced to his own beat, and one night he did just that on the bridge with the crowd screaming for him below. Incredibly shy, he was the biggest star in the world and we did our best to make him comfortable; he often dropped in after attending such events as the opening night of Yul Brynner's Broadway revival of *The King and I*, the Broadway opening of *The Wiz*, and whenever else he felt like stopping by. Michael liked the DJ booth more than any other spot in Studio: that's where he felt safe and comfortable. He could see everything. It was his perch.

DJ Robbie Leslie, who played at Studio on occasion for Michael Fesco, had this to say: "Most of the celebrities had no clue as to the workings of the DJ booth. They'd park themselves right in front of the turntables to look down on the crowded dance floor. Halston was notorious for this and I honestly believe he did it on purpose to vex the DJs. They'd browse through your records while you were trying to pick the next song, oblivious to the fact that we were actually working. And the booth was the perfect place for them to pop a Quaalude or do a stealthy snort of coke if you knew all the sight lines."

DJ Leroy Washington had a different take: "I welcomed Halston in the booth. For years I did all the music for Halston's runway presentations during Fashion Week."

Many people liked to sit and watch the DJ work his magic. People hanging out on the second floor balcony or in the Rubber Room were offered unobstructed views of the DJ booth, making it very difficult, but not impossible, for the DJ to get a blow job once in a while—too open and exposed, not an enclosed booth off to the side, like at some other clubs.

The Ladies' Lounge was like no other spot in the club. The posh velvet chaise lounges and dimly lit atmosphere made you feel as if you had walked into another period in time. One evening I escorted a well-known Broadway celebrity to the ladies' bathroom. As we made our way through the Ladies' Lounge, crowded with tuxedos and gowns, we headed for the stalls. I saw Nile Rodgers just ahead of us as he slipped into a vacant stall. I could always spot

Nile, he loved black leather pants and beautiful women. I smiled to myself. He referred to this area as his office. I quickly grabbed the door of the next available stall and held it open for my gal, thinking I would then return downstairs to the hot brunette I left waiting on one of the silver banquettes.

But my Broadway gal surprised me when she said, "Please, don't leave," as she sat down on the toilet. "Do you have any coke?" she asked. I pulled out my gold spoon and gave her two heaping servings; then, as I was putting the spoon up to my nose, she began to slowly pull down the zipper on my pants, gazing coquettishly up at me with those gorgeous eyes and big smile. Trying to make no noise and stay discreet (there were dozens of people within earshot, including Nile who I could hear talking and snorting in the next stall), she gently began to tease me with her lips and tongue. Then she got more and more into the action, all the while looking up at me standing above her. Although I didn't plan on going that far, she was so fucking hot and the way she was looking up at me drove me so crazy, so I exploded in her mouth. She smiled. Together we returned to the main bar.

Henry Eshelman, who worked in the mailroom, wrote a short piece back in 1981 for a local publication, entitled "The Toilet." It stated:

> Wait a minute—do all those people have to go at once? Why, there's men in that line too... At Studio 54, perhaps the most potentially mundane activity one might perform in a club has been elevated to the status of high art. The Ladies' Lounge in the club is a scene upon which many personal dramas are played and is as exciting and convivial a gathering place as any in the club. You come into the outer lounge and feel like you're on the set of a Noel Coward play: men and women in black tie and evening dress exchange witticisms with an air of urbanity and sophistication.

In the first few crazy months after the reopening, I developed a routine that made the chaos seem "organized," at least from my point of view. Unless I was required to wear a tux, I almost always wore a sport jacket over a shirt or sweater, jeans, and my Adidas. My limo, which I shared with my friend and attorney Eric Rosenfeld (until Eric realized that, once I took over Studio 54, I needed it from nine at night until ten o'clock the next morning), would pick me up from my apartment and take me to Mortimer's, Elaine's, or Café Central, where Bruce Willis tended bar and Paulie Herman orchestrated a nightly scene with regulars Robert De Niro, Joe Pesci, Christopher Walken, and a then relatively unknown Kevin Spacey. They often ended up at Studio 54 after the restaurant closed at 3:00 a.m.

Sometimes I stopped at Le Cirque when it was still in the charming Mayfair Hotel on Sixty-Fifth and Park Avenue. And true to its name, it was a circus of the most dazzling sort. The jewels, fashions, pedigrees, and attitudes in one room on any given night were electric. I'd work the room, inviting people to Studio 54; sometimes I'd enjoy a light dinner and chat with Sirio Maccioni, the owner. Whenever he requested that I put some of his clients on our guest list, I would oblige, make the arrangements, and then head over to my office at Studio. I discovered in my conversations with Sirio that most people in New York were still afraid of being hassled and embarrassed at the front door of Studio 54. I would assure all the people I had extended invitations to throughout each evening that they would be on my personal VIP guest list. Upon my arrival at the club each evening, I'd review policy issues and other details for that night's events, including the all-important guest list, which closed at 6:00 p.m. but somehow kept evolving until 9:00 p.m. for mere mortals and never closed to the "chosen ones."

Life at Studio 54, for me and everyone who worked there, was all about the coveted guest list. Whether I was dining out and inviting people to stop by later that evening or monitoring anyone with access to it—it was all about the guest list. People would pay big to get on it. My assistants were offered cash, furs, drugs, plane tickets, use of private limos, tickets to sold-out concerts and Broadway shows, jewelry, and designer clothing. During the first few months at Studio 54, a former beauty queen and friend was my assistant. I trusted her to field the hundreds of calls coming in each day from hopeful guests. She would give me the requests for the list and at about 6:00 p.m. I would check off those that I approved, and she would then call those people back. One day, several months later, I noticed her office was full of orchids and unopened gift boxes from Bergdorf Goodman, sent by wealthy Arab princes who normally didn't make the list. I replaced her immediately.

Melina Brown, a young, smart, and very pretty brunette, with a take-no-bullshit personality, was the gatekeeper of the Fifty-Third Street stage door reception office during the day. She screened every person wanting access to the club through that door and personally answered every phone line coming in to

Studio—before the fourth ring. That was the rule. If a public relations person or manager or agent wanted their client on the guest list, they went through Melina. She would then transfer the call to one of my assistants working in my upstairs office at Studio or to one of my assistants at my penthouse. The backdoor operation was controlled insanity. It was the only way in or out during the day, and it was used by everybody for everything; employees, deliveries, people arriving for meetings with staff members, musical guests arriving for sound checks, models and actors answering casting calls, bartenders, busboys, DJs dropping off cassettes, liquor salesmen, food deliveries, painters, caterers, carpenters, agent, and managers. Everyone had a résumé to drop off, hoping for a shot at something at Studio 54. Around 8:00 p.m. it could get crazy. Sometimes Melina's blonde bombshell sister Snoogy Brown would help out. But Melina always had it under control, so whenever she called me at home we knew it was important.

Early in the day of a private party for Phil Collins, I sent a memo to my staff stating, "Absolutely no more additions to the guest list this evening." Phil Collins' smash hit record "You Can't Hurry Love," was burning up dance floors around the world and in heavy rotation on MTV. It was a hot invite. At 5:00 p.m. Melina called me saying, "Denise Chatman is requesting Robert Dalrymple plus three for the guest list tonight. She said please don't freak out, she'll explain when she arrives. She tried calling you several times at the penthouse but all the lines were busy. Mark, it's been insane here. What should I do?"

I soon found out the addition was Princess Farahnaz Pahlavi, the twenty-one-year-old daughter of The Shah of Iran. She would be accompanied by her date, Robert Dalrymple, a friend of Denise, and he needed a "plus-two" for the required security detail. Robert requested that her name not appear on our guest list, for security reasons. Much to her chagrin, the princess was prohibited by her family from venturing anywhere outside the family's Manhattan residence without a mandatory three-person security detail. Her father had died in 1980 after being overthrown and forced to flee the country with his family. She was a young and beautiful princess who just wanted to experience Studio 54, and possibly a twirl around the dance floor, and that she did. With confetti raining down and the Man in the Moon taking his hits of coke, the princess enjoyed her Studio 54 experience—the music, lights, and energy were off the hook.

Chapter Fourteen:
Hook Up the Promoters

MARC BENECKE, AND LATER other doormen, did the nightly picking and choosing at the red velvet ropes. The guest list, which guaranteed entrance, became a great way to measure status in Manhattan. Determining who got into the club on any given night, whether or not they were treated as a VIP, and how many guests they were allowed to bring with them, was a source of major power at the time. It made people grateful if handled properly, and vindictive if not. It was easy to make enemies.

I never liked the original front-door policy at Studio 54, but I understood why it was a necessary evil. It was an integral part of what created "the stir" from the very first night Studio 54 opened in 1977. As Andy Warhol liked to say, "It was a dictatorship at the door and democracy on the floor." Apparently Truman Capote agreed, because he was fond of saying, "It's totally integrated— both socially and ethnically. Anything goes. Boys and boys, girls and girls, girls and boys, nudes and fire hydrants." That's true. It was poor, rich, black, white, gay, and straight. Studio 54 was democratic.

As time went by, I developed my own sense of a pecking order at the front door. Most everyone who called to be on the guest list wanted to add an additional three to six friends to get in free, so I created a new rule of thumb. A movie star could bring unlimited guests, a prince or princess could invite five to six guests, counts and countesses four, most other VIPS three, and so on. Once the guest list was finalized and all other arrangements were set, I would make my way through the club, making certain everyone was in place and ready to go for that night's festivities. We'd dim the lights and unlock the front doors. If we had a Cut Drop Party, the backdoor host would be stationed at our

Fifty-Third Street entrance with the VIP guest list, a single security guard, and coat check, if necessary, depending on the weather.

One night, as we were getting ready to open, I was on my way back into the club after unlocking the front doors when I happened to glance over at the coat room and noticed the Harris Sisters were moving very slowly. They were huddled together, staring at the dollar bills they would use to make change throughout the evening. When they turned their heads or made any movement at all it was just like a movie in slow motion. They had the money so close to their faces—as if they were almost blind and they appeared to be talking to it—giggling and giggling some more and then they started kissing and hugging each other. I thought their behavior very odd but I admired how close-knit they were as a family. I had a lot on my mind and forgot about it until later in the evening when the bartenders started spraying each other with soda guns, full force. It looked like fire sprinklers had gone off—there was club soda everywhere—they were drenched and then they started spraying the customers. One girl grabbed a gun from Scott Baird and then, delighting herself to no end, sprayed herself in the face and then her friend. I was dumbfounded, but the crowd at the main bar next to the dance floor was loving it. We could do no wrong at Studio 54. I looked up at the DJ booth and Leroy appeared normal and then I saw the tech rail crew flying in their underwear. As Jayne Harris recently said, "'Close your eyes and try this' was the mantra back then. Sometimes it was exotic food or a pill. That night the entire staff, except for Leroy, had eaten dried hallucinogenic mushrooms. We had all received communion. The managers had no idea what was going on. We were never scolded—just told not to do it again in an office memo."

To get the early crowd going, DJ Leroy Washington would play moody mellow dance music like "La Vie en Rose" by Grace Jones. Uninhibited exhibitionist dancers in outlandish getups would begin prancing around the club and the dance floor. Occasionally, on nights when people were reluctant to get out on an empty dance floor, I would grab a couple of girls and start the dancing myself. Soon, the club would fill, the cut drop would rise, and the crowd would become a pulsating mass of one with the beat.

From the moment one entered the magnificent mirrored entrance hall, the magic took over. You felt glamorous, young, and beautiful, regardless of your age, style, or level of attractiveness. You were free to do whatever made you happy without fear of judgment. The dance floor was the heart of Studio 54, pumping life into everyone who danced on it. Wealthy danced next to poor, famous next to nobodies, straights next to gays, black and white together. The spotlights flashing on the dance floor made everyone feel like a star and when the red lights took over, chasing each other from one pole to the next with swirling police car lights at the base, it ignited a feeling that something exciting was happening within. Red lights would retreat and strobes pulsed on and off, causing the cast of characters on the stage/dance floor to glow in the dark for a moment, then disappear into the blackness only to reappear moments later when the blue neon reflecting panels were lowered. Fake snow and glitter might rain down from overhead or waist-high smoke might find its way in and around the dancers' feet as ever-changing scenic props dropped down behind. By then, the bridge, supporting as many as one hundred people partying above the dance floor, swayed while the famous spoon holding lighted cocaine flakes dipped toward the celestial body to carve some coke out of the "moon." The sheer theatricality of Studio 54 was defining, intoxicating, and liberating. Everyone danced, played, and indulged. We were in the moment. The Studio 54 mantra was, "Tonight is your time, so just do it!"

I too got lost in the music. I was the host and every night was my party; my first priority was always my guests, but later on in the evening after all the coke and Quaaludes and more coke and another Quaalude you could always find me on the dance floor, caught up in the rhythm that was Studio 54. But aside from all the playing around, I worked very hard to make Studio financially viable. I had no choice. As part of my deal to reopen Studio 54, I had agreed to pay the IRS a percentage of our gross, to pay down the back taxes owed by Steve and Ian from their Studio 54 days in the 1970s. Additionally, during my negotiations with them in prison, I had agreed to make monthly payments to Steve and Ian for "non-compete compensation" as part of the purchase price. Then Steve convinced my partner Stanley to pay for their office, their secretary's salary, and some additional expenses which all seemed doable based upon the operational numbers they presented to my attorney and me when we met with them in prison. But in reality, those numbers were out of whack, putting significant financial pressure on me.

I was forced to devise new ways to attract cool people to fill the club every night. I couldn't rely on celebrities and press alone and hope that paying customers would just show up. For one thing, a lot of people were still afraid to go to Studio 54 for fear of being turned away. I had to figure out a way to get the word and invitations out there and into the hands of patrons who would pay the twenty dollars admission, luring them to the club with fun events and celebrity happenings, thus guaranteeing much-needed paid admissions. My Cut Drop Parties were successful, but everything—admission, drinks, hors d'oeuvres—was complimentary. Yes, we got the desired press as a result of all the freebies, but in addition to that, I needed cool-looking people who would pay.

I initiated meetings with key figures, "pied pipers" from different social worlds with contacts in fashion, Broadway, photography, modeling, sports, the Social Register's young waspy preppies, the up-and-coming offspring of the rich and famous, the Eurotrash crowd, Yuppies, and the gay crowd. During the first few months of 1982, I created different themed evenings with my key figures, whom I dubbed promoters, as the hosts. I peppered celebrities into the mix on some invitations, which attracted patrons who were only too happy to line up outside and pay to get in with a guaranteed admission pay invite. The promoters invited their friends, and the friends of their friends (and so on), and most nights we achieved the number of paid admissions necessary to make the club financially successful.

Phone, mail, and handouts were the only means by which to promote in those days before the Internet. When Studio first opened, all the invitations were mailed and addressed by hand with a broad tip brush in beautiful calligraphy, but times changed, so at Michael Overington's suggestion, we hired his good friend from high school, Beth Ann Maliner. She took over and managed our massive basement mailroom. Henry Eshelman stayed on as director. After much effort, she was able to convert our guest list to the first TRS-80 desktop computer from Radio Shack, and we no longer had to keep a calligraphist on our payroll. Now, a computer did all the work. Beth Ann was Michael's right arm; he referred to her as his "lieutenant." She executed invitation design with graphic designer John Sex, purchased the mailing machines (postage, sealing, stuffing etc.), hired all the kids in the mailroom, maintained our mailing list of many tens of thousands of names, sourced supplies and props, and helped coordinate the hundreds of details involved in producing the level of events we were known for at Studio 54. One night the entire wall space of Studio would be painted white and the next night—hot pink or black. The details were endless. Beth Ann also assisted Sunday Night promoter Michael Fesco in coordinating the details involved in his parties as well.

To some promoters I paid money, while others did it for free drinks and front door privileges. Some were willing to work in return for backstairs privileges and occasional invitations into my office with guest celebrities, affording them bragging rights. Others ended up making a good living, getting a cut of the front door receipts for thousands of guests. Some of the first people to become promoters with me at Studio continue in that capacity at other clubs to this day. Most nightclubs now rely on promoters.

Initially when I took over Studio, come midnight, I moved around the big square bar as quickly as possible, ordering drinks on the house for VIPs, regulars, and attractive women. After a few months, Stanley, who loved budgets and controls, tried to rein in what he viewed as "Mark's extravagance with free drinks" and created a system using drink tickets. However, once all the promoters became aware of the new system, chaos ensued. They were all over me and Stanley to give them fists full of drink tickets for the guest hosts to share with their friends, reasoning it was the guest hosts who attracted the much-needed paying guests. Drink tickets soon became the norm in the industry, as did creating themes for each night of the week.

Monday night was set aside for paid, catered events to generate as much revenue as possible. Our catering department targeted Fortune 500 companies and the crème de la crème of New York charities. Steve and Ian had no time for charity events, according to Marc Benecke in an interview with Cathy St. George on *The Marc and Myra Show*. Marc responded to a comment made about Studio 54 doing so many charitable events under my reign: "[Under Steve and Ian] we were much too self-absorbed to do charity events." Well, under my reign we needed the charity events. Stanley and I were operating Studio on a very different business model. We were paying Studio 54's taxes on revenue we generated and paying off Steve and Ian's back taxes to the IRS, so we didn't have the mounds of cash they had in the late 1970s.

Our catering department was brilliantly managed by Shay Knuth, who was intelligent and beautiful enough to be featured in *Playboy* four times. Shay lived around the corner from Studio 54 and brought her buddy Pepe, a huge red Chow Chow, to the office every day. They were a sight walking across the dance floor during daytime meetings with prospective clients and on a few occasions Pepe could be seen prancing around at early evening events.

If on a Monday night we didn't have a catering booking, I might stage a special evening around a personal cause or specific celebrity, provided the occasion or celebrity was important enough. That was the case on the evening I agreed to host the famous—or shall I say infamous—singing debut of Elite model (the "world's first supermodel") Janice Dickinson, who recently claimed to have been drugged and taken advantage of by Bill Cosby. You've probably heard how Barbra Streisand gets crazy when the acoustics aren't perfect and the sound people aren't getting it just right, as well she should, given her extraordinary talent and attention to detail. Well, Janice fancied herself another Streisand. I did my best to accommodate her insane demands. Janice was beautiful, but she was also eccentric, which was on display as she was preparing for her big singing debut.

The best-looking crowd in town had shown up to see Janice, but after her first few songs, the guests started talking amongst themselves. People at Studio wanted to *be* the show, not watch one, unless of course the show was The Temptations or Lou Reed. At the end of her performance, I arranged for white rose petals to fall from the rigging. It was a terrific party. Janice's entire family was there to watch her. But it was obvious to everyone there, including Janice, that she had lost the attention of the room and she felt humiliated. Her sister Debbie, also a successful model, got on my case, demanding to know why this or that wasn't perfect. I wasn't thrilled about the dressing-down, as great effort went into the staging, but I understood that she was protecting her sister.

Other Monday night parties I personally hosted included debutante Cornelia Guest's twenty-first birthday party. (Back in the 1980s she was known as "The Deb of the Decade." *New York* magazine named her the ultimate Deb of all time in 2010.) That night, we transformed the dance floor into a winter scene depicting a European Alpine village, complete with authentic-looking shops that served local French, German, and Italian Alpine fare for a casual buffet dinner. The party was hosted by Cornelia's mother, C. Z. Guest, the doyen of New York society, renowned for her "April in Paris Ball." C. Z. invited a diverse A-list crowd, including Estee Lauder of Lauder Cosmetics, super agent Irving "Swifty" Lazar, renowned fashion designer Oscar de la Renta, Diana Ross, Bianca Jagger, then up-and-coming fashion designer Carolina Herrera, plus an assortment of A-list European and American royalty. Even some members of the Kennedy family, who didn't frequent Studio after having been mistakenly turned away from the front door years earlier by Marc Benecke, were there. After dinner, as *The New York Times* reported, I climbed onto the bridge, suspended high above the dancers, and, together with Millie Kaiserman, ex-wife of fashion designer Bill Kaiserman, belted out a rousing rendition of "Hit the Road, Jack." Everyone began to dance; the Alpine Village disappeared high into the rigging and fake snow fell over the crowd and blanketed the dance floor as Stevie Wonder sang "Happy Birthday" to Cornelia. Cornelia described it as "magical."

Because of C. Z. Guest and the caliber of the guests that night, we received an enormous amount of press in the society pages, including a major story in *The New York Times*—which almost never covers events at nightclubs—and another story with a picture captioned "Cornelia and Mom C. Z. at last night's Birthday Bash at Studio 54" by the *New York Post*'s Eugenia Sheppard, titled "Birthday Guests Galore."

Tuesday night was always a chic, waspy, preppy social night organized by a number of my assistants. After the first year, Baird Jones, an eccentric, well-connected social organizer who at the time covered the New York night scene for Page Six in the *New York Post*, joined the Tuesday night mix. He brought in some of my favorite people: George Plimpton, Prince Dimitri of Yugoslavia, and my good friend and traveling companion, the French beauty Countess Antonia de Portago, who performed at Studio with her band "Antonia and the Operators," dressed as Marie Antoinette.

During the three and a half years that I was at the helm of Studio 54, there were many promoters who contributed to its success, including Bill Jarema, the Beaver Brothers, and numerous others. Occasionally Junior International Club events organized by French promoters Ludovic Autet and Marc Biron were added to the mix, bringing in several hundred young wannabe European counts and countesses who hoped to meet a prince or two. On occasion, Prince Albert of Monaco and other lesser-known royalty acted as honored guests to attract that crowd.

One memorable Tuesday event was the opening of the new Prince Egon von Fürstenberg Boutique on Madison Avenue. We hosted a lavish party, complete with a sit-down dinner of roast pheasant and Fürstenberg beer, for 150 guests during the early part of the evening. We transformed the dance floor into a Hapsburgian dining palace, which we dressed up with heraldic banners carrying the von Fürstenberg crest, plus statues and elaborate floral arrangements. To add to the ambience, we arranged for ten Hungarian violinists to play during dinner. On cue, the tech crew made the night's set disappear and the dance floor opened up for a raucous party featuring two thousand revelers. No detail was spared that evening—except for one. Someone miscounted, leaving us with fewer chairs than needed for dinner. Fortunately, the guests took it all in stride, and in the spirit of the evening turned the potentially disastrous mishap into an impromptu game of musical chairs that everyone enjoyed. All except Egon's estranged wife Diane, who spent most of the evening nibbling on her escort's ear and commenting, "I don't understand who the guests are. I thought someone was a waiter and it was Egon's store manager," as reported in the Eye of *Women's Wear Daily*.

We also hosted a birthday party for Kathy Hilton, a beautiful young woman making a name for herself in New York society as the wife of hotel heir Rick Hilton. The press loved her then, and again years later as the mother of Nicky and Paris Hilton.

Wednesday night was a Business Networking/Wall Street night hosted by antiwar activist Jerry Rubin and his wife Mimi. Mimi's sister Burr Leonard assisted with all the promotional work necessary to make an event like theirs so successful. It was at one of these Business Networking Nights in New York that Bob Greene of the *Chicago Tribune* coined the term "Yuppie," which was a play on words from Jerry's "YIPPIE" (Youth International Party) days with cohort Abbie Hoffman back in 1968.

Jerry Rubin and Abbie Hoffman first gained national notoriety in 1966 as antiwar activists when they were called to Washington, DC to testify at the House Un-American Committee (HUAC) and while doing so caused a commotion when Jerry appeared wearing a Revolutionary War costume and Abbie showed up dressed as Santa Claus. In 1968 the Vietnam War was at its peak and the city of Chicago was hosting The Democratic National Convention where Senator Hubert Humphrey was nominated as the Democrat's Presidential Nominee. Ten thousand protesters arrived in the city for a peaceful protest against the war and were met by a very paranoid Mayor Richard M. Daley and his twenty-three thousand Chicago Police Officers and National Guard. A riot broke out. Mayor Daley blamed Jerry, Abbie, Tom Hayden (who became a California Senator and married Jane Fonda), Rennie Davis, David Dellinger, John Froines, and Lee Weiner; they were then tried as the Chicago Seven. Bobby Seale of the Black Panthers was tried separately.

When told they were being arrested for conspiracy, Abbie responded, "Conspiracy? We couldn't agree on lunch." During the trial, Jerry and Abbie made the most of every opportunity to taunt Judge Hoffman (no relation to

Abbie). They entered his courtroom wearing black judicial robes and when Judge Hoffman ordered them to remove them, they did so—only to reveal Chicago Police uniforms underneath. They were revolutionaries, pranksters, activists, and absolutely brilliant at working the media.

In 1980, Jerry Rubin began hosting "Networking Salons" at his apartment. He would invite people and "their two most interesting friends" to network and exchange business cards. Those were the days when it was impolite to ask people what they did for a living, and this newer kind of "networking" was considered at once both tasteless and fun. The parties caught on and were written up in *The New York Times* and *The Washington Post*. Maurice Brahms, the owner of The Underground, a large, struggling nightclub, invited Jerry and Mimi to host their Networking event at his new venue. I knew Jerry and Mimi through the Speakers Division at New Line Cinema and I immediately contacted Jerry when I heard about the big turnout at The Underground that February, about six months after I opened Studio.

Mimi later told me that Maurice, who had just gotten out of federal prison, had come to Jerry's and her apartment pleading with them to reject my offer and remain at The Underground. Maurice had appealed to Jerry, as a former moral crusader and activist, to think long and hard how someone of his ethical character could possibly enter into any business arrangement where the two men (Steve and Ian) who sent him to jail to get lighter sentences for themselves would benefit. No doubt Brahms was influenced by the astounding numbers of guests that had been generated by Rubin in his first foray into the nightclub world; 3,900 people showed up the first night. Perhaps Maurice still remembered the "curse" he had put on me two years earlier, at his opening of Bonds, a club that didn't last.

Not identifying with Brahms' battles, Mimi and Jerry moved the party anyway, understanding the much greater charisma of Studio 54. Combining Studio's magic with the Rubins' promotional skills allowed us to charge a cover at the door and still generate thousands of dollars of revenue every Wednesday night during the usually "dark" hours from 5:00 p.m. to 10:00 p.m. The atmosphere during the early hours of the Networking Salons was completely different from late-night Studio. Since it's impossible to have a business-related conversation amid thundering bass and flashing lights, we turned the house lights down to a warm glow, darkened the dance floor, and toned down the music. People could then hear each other speak. From 5:00 p.m. to 9:00 p.m. it was DJ Federico Gonzalez on the turntables playing mashups of jazz classics with standards from all of the jazz and blues greats like Lionel Hampton, Frank Sinatra, Tommy Dorsey, and Aretha Franklin. My man Leroy Washington would then take over the turntables at 9:00 p.m. and continue on in a mellow mood and then, at 10:00 p.m., he would phase in the dance music and the party began. Two thousand five hundred fans of Jerry Rubin's Networking Salons packed the house every Wednesday night, and enough of them stayed past 10:00 p.m. to the point that I didn't need any other promoters for that night. The Business Networking night was a huge success for all involved and attracted cohosts for the events such as The Beach Boys, Allen Ginsberg, and R. J. Reynolds' tobacco heir Patrick Reynolds, who became famous as an antismoking activist, among others.

One Wednesday night that will always stand out in my mind is when Reggie Jackson of the New York Yankees popped in. The Studio crowd went crazy—chanting "Reggie, Reggie." He was immediately greeted by model, Lynn Jefferson. As the *New York Post* reported, Lynn promptly plucked Reggie's cowboy hat "and wished him well." Reggie danced and partied all night long with one gorgeous girl after another. There was nothing to suggest that just a few hours earlier the Yankees had lost the final game of the World Series to the Los Angeles Dodgers. He was New York's "Mr. October," Reggie Jackson.

Abbie Hoffman decided he wanted to jump in the party game so he hosted a fundraiser, The River Rat Ball, in an effort to raise money to protect New York's waterways, a cause very close to his heart and that of his good friend, Pete Seeger. I agreed to do it on a Monday night as I could see it was going to be a star-studded affair. It was a huge success with the help of his good friend, Prakash Mishra, and committee members Meryl Streep, Mia Farrow, Susan Sarandon, and Harry Belafonte. Friends like Carly Simon, Jack Nicholson, Kurtis Blow, Joe Namath, Joni Mitchell, Warren Beatty, Joan Rivers, and others partied into the night. I remember a very mellow scene in my office that night, with a lot of candles, and seated at a small table was Grace Jones and Marianne Faithfull, deep in conversation. Mick Jagger was lounging on the couch with Gwynne Rivers on his lap. Marianne was the sex symbol of the 1960s as well as being the girlfriend of Mick Jagger. They were rock and roll's "it" couple for several years. Mick and Keith Richards wrote Marianne's hit "As Tears Go By." At one point Gwynne whispered to me that she was doing her best to remain "cool" in the presence of such music greats. The party was a huge success financially and in the press.

Chapter Fifteen:
Studio 54...a Way of Life

"**B**EAUTIFUL PEOPLE THURSDAY NIGHT Parties" were a favorite night with the modeling agencies.

It was an evening for models and photographers and parties like the *Sports Illustrated* Wet T-Shirt Night featuring Ford Model Christie Brinkley. We always invited a combined, gay and straight, crowd from the fashion world. John Blair, the owner of a popular gay gym back then and still a major promoter today, usually arranged those evenings, along with a young David Sarner. Together, they did a superb job of promoting Thursday Nights at Studio. We featured and honored the hottest models from Ford, Zoli, Elite, Wilhelmina, Sue Charney, Click, and some of the up-and-coming modeling agencies. Shelley Tupper booked a party for one of the new agencies in town on a Thursday night and they chose the theme "Girls' Night Out," which inspired Shelley to have our design team hang rows and rows of beautiful French lingerie on clothes lines across the main room entrance. The crowd loved it.

The party for Cathy St. George to celebrate her August 1982 centerfold in *Playboy* was coordinated by Steve Rubell's former assistant, Myra Sheer, who currently cohosts a retrospective talk show on SiriusXM Studio 54 Radio with Marc Benecke. It was so crowded that Timothy Hutton, who was friends with Cathy, was turned away at the door. That tidbit made Page Six of the *New York Post*, and the *New York Daily News* ran photos from the party. Also, Robin Leach conducted a visually captivating interview with Cathy for *Entertainment Tonight*. People on the dance floor screamed with joy when thousands of pictures of Cathy floated down from overhead.

Cathy also cohosted a "Save The Whales" fundraiser at Studio with Robert De Niro and Joe Pesci, and she celebrated the thirtieth anniversary of *Playboy* with a party at Studio 54. She was always very cool—everyone loved her. Cathy recently reminded me of a fun night we shared in New York. We were at a Yankee game with restaurant owner/sports groupie George Martin, who was friends with Yankees owner George Steinbrenner, and we were invited to sit in the Owners Box. Cathy stood up when spotlighted before the sold-out crowd and got a bigger ovation as a *Playboy* centerfold than the ballplayers.

One of the most unforgettable nights, for me, was the private party for *The King and I*. It was a Thursday night and the club was packed. Yul Brynner, Michael Jackson, and all the young children in the cast, entered through the Fifty-Third Street stage door entrance into their private party behind the scrim. The tables were laden with colorful cakes, candies, giant cookies, and huge cupcakes for Michael and the children, and fresh strawberries, cheesecake, and champagne for the rest of us. They were all having a good time stuffing their faces and then Frank Sinatra and Jerry Lewis walked in. My heart skipped a beat. Could Dean Martin be not too far behind? The children ran to Jerry Lewis—trying to be polite but all talking to him at the same time. I introduced myself to Frank and Jerry, and then Sinatra walked straight to the table with the cheesecake, ignoring Yul Brynner, his longtime friend and golfing buddy who was sitting with superstar Michael Jackson. Frank was hungry. He joked, "I have to take a bite of this cheesecake before I take a bite of my buddy Yul." Michael just sat there in his Royal Military–style garb—staring. Yes, he was the undisputed "King of Pop," but tonight he was in the presence of the chairman of the board and film and comedy royalty.

Mary Lou Harris said she'll never forget the party for *The King And I*: "It was in the back behind the curtain and security waved me in to give a guest her coat check receipt. Yul Brynner was there and Michael Jackson was seated at his table. Many of the children in the show were in attendance and one of the boys managed to slip past security into John Blair's gay Thursday Night party. On my way back to the coatroom I saw this small child running around and then he disappeared. I returned to the coatroom and a few minutes later the same little boy ran past the coatroom laughing and giggling. A few minutes later he ran past again, laughing and giggling. And then again and again. Every few minutes he'd run by giggling and laughing to himself. I became concerned and stepped out to see what was going on. He was trailing a guy in cowboy boots and chaps with no pants on—his ass hanging out. Thank God I got to him before he made his way up to the balcony or Rubber Room. I laughed and then sternly asked, 'Where is your mother?' He pointed to the back of the club and I returned him to the private party."

Frank Sinatra and Jerry Lewis didn't hang around very long. I was told Frank had a recording session the next day and Jerry was doing work on *The King of Comedy*. I am all male and I love my women, but I was swooning like a schoolgirl for the rest of the night. Yul Brynner and Michael Jackson hung out in the DJ booth for a while to the delight of the crowd, and then left through the back door.

Friday night was an expanded preppy event that became known as "Second Generation Night," so called because it was often frequented by the offspring of major celebrities. Regulars included Maria Burton, daughter of Elizabeth Taylor and Richard Burton; Cecilia and Anthony Peck, children of Oscar-winning actor Gregory Peck of *To Kill A Mockingbird*; Ben Stiller and his sister, Amy, children of comedians Jerry Stiller and Anne Meara; Gwynne Rivers, daughter of artist Larry Rivers; Victoria Leacock, daughter of late film director Richard Leacock; Frazer Pennebaker, son of D. A. Pennebaker the celebrated documentary filmmaker who helped make the "cinéma vérité" style of filmmaking popular; Rip Torn's son Tony; Mario Van Peebles, son of actor, director, writer, and composer Melvin Van Peebles; Amy Lumet, daughter of Sidney Lumet and granddaughter of actress/singer Lena Horne; and actor Francesco Quinn of *Platoon* and *The Young and The Restless*, son of the Oscar-winning actor Anthony Quinn from *Viva Zapata!* In October 1983, *People* ran a story with a picture of many of these young partygoers titled "At This Studio 54 Bash The Right Names To Drop Belong To The Parents." One of our most successful Friday Night Preppy parties was produced by second-generation member Gwynne Rivers: "A Night of Polo—Celebrating the Piaget Cup." Gwynne did a great job. She contacted the ten most social people at Brown University, put their names on the invitation, and made them part of the committee to promote the event. She rented polo mallets and our interior design team decorated the main bar in a polo theme. We were packed. Girls showed up hoping to meet a boy from Brown and the guys showed up for the girls—and a whole lot of fun.

Marc Benecke, who had started as our doorman, came to me early in 1982 and made it clear that he was no longer comfortable in the front door position. He was a valued employee and so he switched gears and moved into promoting. He helped me organize some of the preppy crowd for Tuesday and

Friday nights. He did that very successfully for several years and in the process became a celebrity himself, this time inviting people to the door rather than sending them away. Despite his reputation among some who had been turned away by him, Marc was a decent, charming, good-looking, and intelligent guy. He was always on time, never had a drug problem, went to the gym every day, and always looked great outside the door to "54."

One Friday night, we celebrated Shelley Tupper's birthday. It drew a large preppy crowd of hardcore partiers. The invitation said, "Please Join Rick James and Chuck Zito of the Hells Angels in Celebration of Shelley Tupper's Twenty-First Birthday." The club was packed because, black or white, all the kids loved Rick James and his album *Street Songs*. They went wild, packing the dance floor, whenever Leroy played "Super Freak" and "Give It To Me Baby."

In the words of Shelley Tupper:

> *I was not going to have a typical coming out party...my twenty-first Birthday Celebration was going to be wild. At twenty-one I wasn't on the track my parents would have liked. The only thing waspy about me was my upbringing but I still wanted my parents, especially my Dad, to think I was doing something with my life. The fact that I worked at Studio 54 might have been cool to me and my friends but it was totally unacceptable to my parents. They were constantly asking what my plan was and why didn't I consider getting a job on Wall Street. My Dad would say 'You'd be a fantastic broker.' 'But I'm bad at math,' would be my reply and it went on like that over and over. But for me, I was living the high-life. Popular doesn't begin to describe it. Here I am working in the world's most famous nightclub where everyone wanted to be my best friend, mess with my hair, dress me up, do their drugs, and sleep with me! What twenty-one-year-old at the time wouldn't think that was cool?*
>
> *My big entrance at my party was on the Bridge. Two shirtless, hot-bodied bus boys are at one end of the Bridge with a HUGE heart shaped pink birthday cake and I am at the other end, wearing a fancy sparkly designer dress by Pinky and Diane, feeling pretty cool in the spotlight of it all. On either side of me*

are two Hells Angels who escort me to the middle of the Bridge where my good buddy Rick James is singing Happy Birthday. Below the bridge, on the dance floor looking up, were all my friends, and my very waspy parents. I will never forget the look on the faces of everyone below, all smiling–EXCEPT my parents. They had a look of utter disbelief on their faces. My poor southern-belle mother was probably thinking "this is our precious daughter's coming of age party?

Once the singing and the cake presentation were over I made it down to the VIP area. So there we are, all the cool people and me, Queen of the Night, the Hells Angels, Rick James, and my parents. The party is heating up and I'm trying to take it all in but I keep seeing my parents out of the corner of my eye. My mother is bopping gently to the disco beat and my father is seething. This guy goes up to my Dad, and I can hear him slurring his words and he says 'Shelleeeey is reaallleeey special—I really mean it.' My Dad looked like he was about to throw up his dinner. When the guy turned around to talk to me I saw why….his nostrils were rimmed in white powder.

It wasn't long before my parents had enough. But before they left my Dad walked over to me, got in real close to hug me goodbye and whispered 'this was a great party Shelley, when are you going to get a real job?'"

Saturday nights were usually jammed with returning people from some of the previous nights' groups, plus good-looking out-of-towners and some of the cooler young people from the boroughs. I liked Saturday nights, they were unpredictable, especially if we had an after-party booked for the cast and crew of *Saturday Night Live*.

I remember one Saturday night, soon after our grand opening. Studio was so crowded that the only place you could move was on the dance floor. Word had gotten out that the cast and crew of *Saturday Night Live*, and musical guest Rod Stewart, would be at Studio 54 on October 3, the first show of the new season. Studio had been closed for so long and New Yorkers just wanted to get a glimpse of Belushi, Aykroyd, Gilda, Eddie, Bill Murray, and some of the other characters we adored so much. But after an intense week of organized chaos before the live broadcast every Saturday night, the cast preferred to keep to themselves and just relax. The Rubber Room was the perfect spot for the *SNL* "after-parties." The *SNL* cast enjoyed dodging the crowd of fans waiting for them at the front door, choosing instead to go around to the back of the building and climb the ladder to the fire escape and then another five flights up to the fifth-floor balcony entrance door where security was waiting to let them in. One night at an *SNL* party in the Rubber Room, John Belushi complained to me that he was hot and needed some air. He bolted and left by the back door to the fire escape. He showed up in my office a few minutes later and took over the scene dominating the room with his antics...until Rick James walked in with two absolutely gorgeous black girls and threw a bag of white powder down on my desk and announced, "I'm Rick James...say hello to my bitches... LET'S PARTY." John was speechless.

The Rubber Room was the perfect place to host parties for people who preferred a more laid-back atmosphere than the one downstairs in the Main Room. Shelley became friends with Jo and Ron Wood of The Rolling Stones and arranged a birthday celebration for Jo and friends. Jo requested that her guests enter by the fire escape and make the five-story climb on the outside of the building dressed in skimpy dresses in the freezing cold of March. It was cool, sexy, and scary. Jo loved carousels, so Shelley arranged for a cake that looked exactly like the beautiful carousel in Central Park. Jo loved it.

Sunday night became a dedicated gay night hosted by the legendary Michael Fesco, and the club was always jam-packed with gorgeous gay boys. Michael did his own thing and didn't need me, so I tried to take Sunday nights off to decompress, but if Peter Allen or someone special was performing, then I was as excited as everyone else to be there. Celebrities, male and female, gay and straight, showed up unannounced without fanfare wearing jeans and tees, preferring the Sunday night gay crowd and music that made you want to dance your tits off. Michael appeared on Broadway for fourteen years in various productions then turned to producing and brought Patti LaBelle to Broadway. He was the first to present Tea Dance at his club, The Ice Palace in Cherry Grove, and later at Flamingo, his club in Manhattan. He also created "Black Party," inspired by New York's West Side leather bars. Michael orchestrated and managed every project he took on flawlessly, recently saying, "Give a Queen a staple gun and some fabric and the job gets done."

On Michael's opening night at Studio 54, 3,700 men waited on a line that extended two city blocks. His Sunday nights would be considered off the hook had you never been to a gay club before. The offerings at Studio 54 were tame compared to The Anvil, MineShaft, or The Toilet. The gay crowd has their look and signifiers. Back then it was Levi's 501 jeans, white sleeveless T-shirts, flannel shirts, Converse or Adidas sneakers, and brown leather bomber jackets with sheepskin collars. They had an ingenious way of communicating their sexual preferences. If a gay man wore a blue handkerchief in his right hip pocket, it meant he was into the passive role during sexual intercourse, the left pocket meant he took the active role of the male. The same went for keys on a chain or earrings. The placement of these items, when worn in the straight community, would signify absolutely nothing.

Michael Fesco's Sunday night theme parties were off the hook—WILD.
Amyl nitrate, Quaaludes, pot, and sex...RULED!!
Photograph by Andre Landers.

At a Sunday night party, if you ventured up to the second-floor balcony you might see two men making out and jerking each other off. Up in the Rubber Room, a man would be grinding to the beat while being penetrated from behind and a very good-looking older man would be getting sucked off by a very young beautiful boy. Over in a corner a man might face the wall, legs spread apart with his hands up against the wall and another very macho looking guy spits on his own cock then penetrates him. Nothing unusual. Men, beautiful young boys, dancing and loving and having a good time. The entertainment, usually arranged by Billy Smith, included Grace Jones, The Weather Girls, and Eartha Kitt, among others. Michael Fesco handpicked the hottest DJs to compliment his outrageously themed parties. Michael knew his crowd and his music. He would choose DJ Richie Rivera from The Anvil when he needed "down and dirty" for his "Black Parties" and DJ Howard Merritt or maybe Robbie Leslie when he wanted a lighter mood with buoyant disco for his "White Parties." As Michael put it, "my crowd obeys the power of the beat."

The coatroom could get wild, as told to me by Jayne Anne Harris: "Michael's 'Tea Dances' at Studio were always jam-packed with fun and gorgeous gay boys there to dance the night away. In cold weather the coatroom was filled to the brim with identical brown leather bomber jackets with sheepskin collars. Euphoric boys would saunter up to the counter and say, 'I can't find my ticket,' and because all the coats looked exactly alike, we'd respond, 'Can you identify anything in your pockets?' The answer was always the same, 'poppers in one pocket and pot in the other.' No help there, so we'd scan the coats, confused by the overwhelming sea of possibilities. One night while my sister Eloise was performing one of these 'pain in the ass' searches of coat pockets, a vial of liquid amyl nitrate fell out and broke all over the floor of the coatroom, permeating the air with pungent smelling fumes and sending us into a world of kaleidoscope colors. We were floating four feet off the ground for the rest of the night."

To this day, after seventeen years, Michael's "Sea Tea" is America's only gay sailing Tea Dance which departs from Pier 40 in Manhattan and is still packed every Sunday from June until the end of September.

Chapter Sixteen:
A Cast of Characters

As Truman Capote liked to say, "Studio 54 was a character study." Allow me to introduce you to a few of my favorites.

Philippe de Montperreux was a pushy, thin, balding Algerian who reminded me of Peter Lorre in *Casablanca*. I met him early on, when he approached me in a shadowy corner at Studio, whispering in his thick French accent with a hand over his mouth, "Mark, I got ze best coke in New York." Naturally, I tried it—and he was right. It usually was. He became a regular in my office and at the bar, but he was also a fixture at many of the private parties of celebrities including Calvin Klein, who also must have gone for "ze best coke in New York." Nobody really knew who Philippe was or where he came from, but he was a character, and got along with most everyone, so that was good enough to make him (and his coke) a part of our crowd.

Recently, I had dinner with Rick Ferrari, a Hollywood agent and manager who frequented Studio as an underage companion of Bill Aucoin, manager of some top rock groups including KISS. He told me that Philippe continued on in his role as a druggie court jester for many years after Studio. I found Philippe to be most entertaining but some of our key employees—particularly the bar manager Skip Odek—couldn't stand him because he was always telling the other bartenders, "Mark sez I can have free drinks." I always made sure Philippe had drink tickets, but he didn't like to use them. He preferred to order "on the house" and that didn't fly with our accounting system at the bar.

Couri Hay was a fast-talking, flamboyantly gay gossip columnist writing for the *National Enquirer*. He was handsome, charming, and witty and always befriended important avant-garde people including Jay McInerney, Bret Easton Ellis, Tama Janowitz, Michael Musto (*The Village Voice*), and Anthony Haden-Guest. He hosted a number of fabulous parties at Studio; some would begin at his funky but elegant townhouse off Central Park West, then continue onto the dance floor at Studio. It was great fun and he was always an animated and entertaining host. I often told Couri that if anything happened to me, he would be my chosen successor.

Disco Sally was a sprightly thing in her late seventies who danced like a thirty-year-old, and was accompanied by a handsome young man named John on her arm. She was a retired Jewish lawyer who became a judge and suddenly went crazy due to the combination of cocaine and the Studio 54 Effect. But back in the day, she would dance nonstop—from midnight to 5:00 a.m. many nights a week, taking only bathroom and cocaine breaks. As *New York* magazine reported in 1991: "A tiny, seventy-seven-year-old lawyer named Sally Lippman was mourning the death of her husband when she happened upon the disco scene and changed her life. Dressed in tight pants and high-top sneakers, she became Disco Sally, a star at Studio 54 and Xenon who'd draw an audience of adoring fans as she got down on the dance floor." Celebrities lined up to be her dance partner. She ultimately married John, going on a crazy Virgin Isle Hotel trip for their honeymoon.

Nikki Haskell was a stockbroker during the early 1970s. She was a well-dressed, good-looking professional club-goer who made the scene everywhere. She was born and raised in Beverly Hills and got her feet wet at all the hot clubs in LA in the early days, including The Daisy. She also became a regular at Studio 54 in 1977. I met her at the Cannes Film Festival in 1978 when she was just starting to shoot her entertainment news magazine show, which was on some obscure cable station in New York. She always seemed to be surrounded by lights and cameras, which helped her to create a scene, and she always managed to be at the "most important party" in any city she was living in. Nikki was smart, Jewish, and very aggressive; so much so that she ended up knowing and becoming best friends with numerous major celebrities, including Donald and Ivana Trump, Jeremy Irons, Billy Idol, and others. You could always tell who the most important person at the party was, because Nikki would be standing next to him or her whenever a photographer was taking a picture. Since the TV show wasn't making any money, Nikki began creating events for extra cash, as she did for me on numerous occasions at Studio including a fabulous themed party for the premiere of Alan Carr's remake of *Where the Boys Are*; it turned out to be much better than the movie.

We decorated the entrance hall of Studio to look like the beach in Fort Lauderdale. Michael O. and his crew brought in tons of sand—it was at least six inches deep—covering the entire floor area of the entry hall. Then, they built a huge wooden boardwalk for guests to walk over the sand. There were surfboards and boats, tanned bikini-clad girls and surfer boys mingling amongst the patrons. It was spectacular. At the parties Nikki hosted, she always saw to it that there were enough celebrities among "the shleppers," as she referred to the less important people, to guarantee good press. She remained in my life, working together again, years later. Currently she is recreating her show to stream on Amazon.

George Paul Roselle was a flamboyantly gay French man and a great party promoter. He was attractive, in his fifties, slender, partially bald, and always beautifully dressed in French designer suits. George had impeccable taste and a great sense of humor. He was one of a kind. His specialty was creating parties and events around such illustrious women as Anne Eisenhower, the great-granddaughter of President/General Dwight D. Eisenhower; Ruth Warrick, former wife of Orson Welles and the costar of his American Film Classic, Citizen Kane; and Ann Miller. With guests like this, we made the social gossip columns of Eugenia Sheppard and Aileen Mehle (aka Suzy Knickerbocker). Somewhere along the way, George convinced me to hire him, on occasion, to host dinner parties for these celebrities at my penthouse, after which they'd make a short appearance at Studio and garnered the desired press. Before any one of these events, I recall George literally flying around my apartment, placing rose petals here, white orchids there, and dropping goldfish in the water goblets on the dinner table. His unique touches worked and became another reason for the press to report four or five times a week on all the happenings at Studio 54. After watching me blow cocaine up my nose every night for several years and listening to me insist I wasn't addicted and could stop immediately if I chose to, George Paul would give me that look of his with one eyebrow raised and quote actress Tallulah Bankhead: "Cocaine isn't habit-forming. I should know, I've been using it for seventeen years." Tragically, George Paul Roselle died a few years later of AIDS.

Carmen D'Alessio was another one of our mainstays. I briefly described Carmen earlier when Steve and Ian introduced her to me in their Manhattan jail cell. However, Carmen was such an interesting and loveable character that she deserves further mention. She was a very good-looking Peruvian woman with a great body and dynamic personality. She was a pioneer as a party promoter and possessed an amazing ability to remember thousands of names. Carmen's background was in fashion, having worked for Valentino and Yves St. Laurent. Somewhere along the way, she got to know every major designer in the world and started throwing parties for them at some of the early discos in Manhattan, long before Studio 54 opened. She was the person who originally told Steve and Ian to open in New York after hosting a party at their Queens nightclub, Enchanted Gardens. She also found the building for them at 254 West Fifty-Fourth Street, which would eventually become Studio 54.

Carmen was born into a wealthy family of attorneys in Peru, some of whom I've met and who know members of my father's family in Lima. She speaks five languages, which landed Carmen her original job in New York at the United Nations. She met all the beautiful people in the world who like to party and enjoy the nightlife—from Europe and South America, to Miami and LA.

As Carmen did for Steve and Ian, she introduced me to key members of the fashion crowd as well as her European group of counts, countesses, dukes, duchesses, rich European businessmen—the Eurotrash set and assorted hangers-on who air-kissed, said "darling," and made a party successful. They knew all the *right people*, spoke with foreign accents, wore expensive suits, checked the time on heirloom watches, carried designer handbags, and refused to pay for anything. They would say, "I am a VIP, I don't pay." In reality, some were shoe salesmen, pharmacists, dog walkers, waiters, and stock boys. The Dupont Twins were welcomed by all of New York society, especially by Andy Warhol who had a thing for twins regardless of lineage and welcomed them to his entourage. Truth is, they were the Laskos brothers, two high school kids from Fairfield County, Connecticut. On-demand fact checking was unheard of back then. Confirming a person's title or lineage before adding them to a VIP guest list involved phone calls and research. But the twins were cool and everyone liked them.

Carmen did a great job—she knew most of the people personally on her various lists as she had been at this for a while. She was in her mid-forties and spoke with an elegant Spanish/Italian accent and could rattle off fifty foreign names of people who were on her guest list in one sentence. Carmen usually produced two major events per month at Studio 54. She had a card file with thousands of party people that she maintains to this day. Now in her early seventies, Carmen is still arranging some of New York's chicest parties.

Fran Boyer was a valuable asset when she wanted to be. She was a good-looking former model and nice Jewish girl from Brooklyn who knew everyone in the fashion industry after working for Calvin Klein—and others—for years. Her problem was she liked coke too much—she was so thin, she looked like she had spent time in a concentration camp. Somewhere along the way she came into my life, and I gave her part-time work organizing fashion events with well-known models and designers. As time went by, and when she was straight enough to work, I increased her hours and she became an almost full-time assistant working by day out of my apartment. Fran was intuitive as a personal shopper, keeping my wardrobe stocked with fabulous comped Calvin Klein shirts. She'd go to Calvin's warehouse and return with exactly what I wanted. She had great style. Whenever I saw her, usually the first thing out of her mouth was, "Do ya' have any coke?" in her thick nasal Brooklyn accent. We spoke on the phone back in 2011, when I was in New York for the Sirius XM Studio 54 "One Night Only" Launch Party. She sounds exactly the same thirty years on.

Lynn Dubal, a very attractive and successful Seventh Avenue runway model, assisted Fran on some of the fashion shows at Studio. Lynn was a long-time favorite model of designer Tracey Mills and she had great connections. Lynn and Fran saved me tons of money in wardrobe expenses for all my assistants. They arranged to borrow "samples" from New York's top designers, which wasn't a hard sell to them given that beauties like my assistant Hilary Clark would parade around the main bar of Studio 54 at my side wearing their creations. Denise Chatman attended many formal music industry events in the name of Studio 54, dressed in formal designer gowns on loan from Tracy Mills, arranged by Lynn Dubal. It entailed a lot of work and talent, making the selections and arrangements, and for that I was beyond grateful. These days, Lynn can be found at one of New York's favorite celebrity hangouts, Serendipity, home of the patented Frozen Hot Chocolate. Always at the center of fashion and entertainment, Lynn works alongside her good friend and Serendipity owner, Stephen Bruce. I laugh when I think of Lynn and Fran sending cocaine back and forth via messenger, hidden in Calvin Klein hosiery packages. "Girls just wanna have fun" was their motto—they had to make it through another work day before heading back to Studio and partying with the hottest boys in town.

Shelley Tupper always looked "hot" in the photographs taken of her attending to A-list celebrities at Studio. She had her own sense of style but Janice Dickinson and Billy Tootsie treated her like a play doll, styling her hair and dressing her up in clothes borrowed from top designers who were only too happy to loan Janice anything she wanted for Shelley Tupper at Studio 54. Janice Dickinson was the original "supermodel" and one of the highest paid models in the world during my reign at Studio. She graced the cover of *Vogue* thirty-seven times and the cover of *ELLE* seven issues in a row.

The following are excerpts from several staff meeting minutes to provide you with a view of Studio's internal operations and to demonstrate what a pain in the ass the bartenders found Philippe de Montperreux to be.

STAFF MEETING—MINUTES FROM
January 24 and February 8, 1983

1. Skip's quote of the day: "If Philippe ever comes to the bar and demands complimentary drinks and then refuses to pay or to use drink tickets and then hassles the bartender, I will personally call security and have him ejected from the club."

2. The Penthouse (meaning Mark's apartment) staff must try harder to keep Studio staff aware of changes, additions to schedules, etc. Improvement to communications can only help.

3. George Martin is taking parties of people downstairs to do you-know-what— no one should be allowed to park down there. It is simply a thoroughfare for those people that have keys. It is especially bad to be down there at 4:00 a.m. when the night manager is putting money in the safe. Please people, use your heads.

4. Conference room was destroyed Sunday night—the people who populate it on Sundays are animals—let's get keys for the conference room.

5. All décor decisions should be checked out with Michael Overington first— don't go directly to David Lees—he can't make budget decisions. There is usually a concept being worked on for the week and ways to tie your party in with someone else's. Remember a little bit does not go a long way in Studio—it's often better to do nothing than a little something that gets totally lost in the room.

6. Michael Overington again reiterated that Shay is the key to scheduling. All new parties, changes, or confirmations should go through Shay. At the first sign of a party, fill out a party fact sheet roughly and distribute it immediately.

7. *Chuck Garelick (Head of Security) requested that the Guest List be rewritten to double space between names—Beth Ann will take care of that.*

8. *Denise requested real wine glasses at the bars—all the managers violently disagreed—they take up too much room at the bar and in the kitchen.*

9. *Security at Cut Drop Parties seems to be a problem especially with the coat check at the back door entrance—the suggestion was to tape the scrim down so that people can't get behind there.*

10. *Complaints that Sunday night security is lax and arrogant—seems to be because Chuck isn't around—He says he'll take care of it and it won't happen again.*

11. *Day crew complains that night security and night crew are searching the furniture at the end of the night for "goodies"—David Miskett (night manager) says nonsense—the busboys beat everyone to it.*

Now I'll tell you about my crew—my drug buddies. The first was Gustavo Novoa, the very talented artist from Chile. In 1977 he published *Jungle Fables*, a book of his paintings and poems on the theme of "vice and virtue" conveying a deep commitment to ecology, wildlife preservation, and a more humane world. He gave his creatures human characteristics and made them philosophical. I treasure the painting he gave me, one of his well-known animal reflection paintings of leopards, which has followed me for years and hangs behind my desk. His paintings have been collected by the First Families of Reagan and Bush, Prince Charles of England, Sylvester Stallone, and designers Valentino and Versace. Gustavo was happy, very charming, and always looking to have a good time. One late night, prowling in an abandoned building while getting high, he said, "I think of myself as a black panther in the body of a well-travelled painter."

Another hard-partying buddy was Guy Burgos. He was handsome with slicked-back hair and was always impeccably dressed. He was a South American socialite and the ex-husband of a niece of Winston Churchill, Lady Sarah Spencer-Churchill. As Lady Sarah liked to tell it, she was newly divorced and breaking out of her conventional life as a housewife and mother in her early forties when she met Guy Burgos, twenty years her junior. "It was our first date and Guy made love to me not once but five times—at the door, on the stair, in the drawing room, etc. in the first half hour." She said the experience was an awakening, and it changed her life forever. Their marriage ended after only nine months, with Sara filing for divorce after she caught Guy in Capri cheating on her with another man. Guy was always up for anything, with a big smile and his charming Latin accent. Nothing was too outrageous. He knew everybody from the Rio/Punta del Este/South American crowd to the chic Europeans. He could party nonstop for days and loved massive amounts of cocaine and champagne—we really got into some shit.

Any night spent with my wild friend, Prince Egon von Fürstenberg, was always full of surprises. He was a direct descendant of German/Italian royalty from the Hapsburg family on his father's side and the Agnelli Family (Fiat) on his mother's. Egon was baptized by the future Pope John XXIII. He must have truly loved fashion, because he did not need to work and earn money, yet he worked as a buyer for Macy's and attended classes at the Fashion Institute of Technology at night. He married the Belgian-born Diane Halfin, daughter of a Holocaust survivor. His family didn't approve of the marriage, as Diane was Jewish and pregnant. She kept his last name after the divorce and, at his urging, opened her own fashion house and went on to become the designer Diane von Fürstenberg, creator of the "Wrap Dress." She married Barry Diller in 2000. Egon was bisexual and the ultimate party person. He knew everyone, always had a beautiful woman (or man) on his arm, and was always smiling, laughing, and telling jokes in five different languages. On the occasions that I would leave Studio and make the scene at other clubs, I would frequently go with Egon, Guy, and Gustavo. We might do Regine's or, if it was close to closing time at Studio, we'd venture downtown to a party in some abandoned building. But one thing is for certain—I'd be fucked up on a shitload of alcohol and exotic drugs, laughing my ass off.

One night, Gustavo handed me what he said was a very special joint. I lit it with a match and took my first hit. It was Angel Dust and it blew my mind. I felt invincible and experienced a level of euphoria well beyond anything I got from cocaine, yet I could still function. It was fucking incredible. I urinated from the balcony off Studio's five-story fire escape into the courtyard, with Guy and a crowd cheering me on.

After that, Angel Dust became the star of my show and my drug of choice, with an endless supply of cocaine and Quaaludes waiting in the wings.

Chapter Seventeen:
Bono and Bowie on Elvis

B Y THE END OF the 1970s, pop culture had decided "Disco Sucks." It was declared dead in a crazy vinyl record burning, public relations stunt promoted by radio DJ Steve Dahl in Chicago's Comiskey Park during a doubleheader between the White Sox and the Detroit Tigers in July of 1979. The time for disco-driven music and arrangements supporting the four-on-the-floor and eight-on-the-hi-hat sound was over. No longer would it dominate the radio station playlists and the focus of record companies.

But I knew that Studio 54 was not a disco. It was a venue for dancing, a dance club, a dance hall, call it what you will—but to me it was another version of Small's Paradise, a place where I had become acutely aware at a very young age that extraordinary things can happen on a dance floor. Dancing has the power to break down barriers and bring people together. When you strip it down of any formalities, dancing is the basic act of moving rhythmically to a beat or music. It is primal, spiritual, and tribal. If you've ever really gotten into a beat, you know what I mean. If you haven't—it's never too late. When people dance for hours on end they often go into a trancelike state that encourages a sense of community with the other dancers. Particularly so when enhanced by alcohol and drugs. I felt it at Small's and I felt it in Brazil. There is something about doing the same thing at the same time with other people that forges a bond. Military drills apply this theory, with repetitive chants, a cadence, which is repeated over and over in step with marching troops, something I saw a lot of while at Officer Candidate School in the navy. It's a high of the highest order because it fosters group affiliation: we come to think of the group as part of us.

Throughout history, civilizations have participated in dancing, from the whole-body convulsions of African dance to the stiff posture of Irish jigs, and we all appreciate the sensual hip action and sexy flair of Latin dance. Some cultures promote dancing as part of their religious observance while others use dance to communicate within courtship and mating rituals. Some men dance to show strength and fearlessness, to intimidate—like New Zealand's rugby team, "All Blacks," when they perform a Haka, the Maori challenge, before each match. Unforgettable are my nights dancing with wild abandon at Le Jardin in the mid-1970s where Truman Capote could be found seated in one of the rattan fan chairs in back by the mirrors holding court next to the dance floor watching the boys—and the few females granted entry—dancing for joy to some of the best dance music ever recorded. Dancing oneself into frenetic ecstasy has been going on for centuries throughout the world. The Haitian people participate in Voodoo dances and the Brazilian people have Macumba. I still remember the heavy bass, rhythm, and unity on the dance floor of my youth, at Small's Paradise, where my mind was transported into an altered state just as it would years later in Brazil.

Many of the rhythms that Brazil celebrates today originated in the 1550s when African slaves were imported to Brazil. They were permitted to summon their gods by playing drums and this new sound in percussion combined with the existing rhythms of Brazil—and thus the Samba, the rhythm of the saints, was born. I have returned to Brazil on a number of occasions, and I always find myself drawn to the trancelike state inspired by the continuous rhythm of the Samba bands and Batucadas. In America, many slave owners refused the slaves their drums, believing the instrument to be a tool of communication that could be used against them in an uprising. Fortunately, the percussion and rhythms of American slaves survived, then mated with our existing American rhythms, adding to it the music configurations from Eastern European Klezmer music (sometimes called Yiddish jazz) and then borrowed from some of America's other cultural influences, and BOOM this glorious mash-up gave us the Jazz Age and the Birth of the Blues.

The Hebrew people have a long and rich tradition of spiritual release through dance as well, dating back to King David's ecstatic dance before the Ark of the Covenant as it was being carried into Jerusalem in 875 BCE. A kind of circle dance is still practiced in Hasidic Jewish communities today, where the Rabbi will dance on his own within a circle formed by a group, creating new movements for the circle to pick up and integrate into their dance. As a child, my father occasionally took me to synagogues in Brooklyn and I watched the men dancing for hours, often stimulated by wine or schnapps. Now, years later, I still remember the energy.

In the 1950s I was listening to Perry Como on the radio one minute, and the next minute I went WILD—feeling the rhythm in my soul of Little Richard, Chuck Berry, Sam Cooke, Bill Haley and His Comets, and Elvis Presley. Alan Freed played all this great new music on his radio program. It made me wild—it moved me—it changed the way we danced and dressed and felt about music. Freed gave this new sound a name—rock and roll—and he hosted hops at The Brooklyn Paramount Theater for teens like me to see and hear it. He played all the stuff that many white radio DJs either couldn't or wouldn't play because it was "race music"—as it was referred to in the 1950s. Parents, teachers, churches, and public officials referred to it as the devil's music, presumably because it was mixed with black music which many white people were prejudiced against at the time. And then it became too big to ignore.

It all exploded in the form of Elvis Presley—a hip-shaking, hot, handsome white boy. U2's Bono summed it up best when describing the effect Elvis had on the world: "Elvis Presley was the 'Big Bang' of rock and roll. It all came from there and what you had in Elvis Presley is a very interesting moment because, really, to be pretentious about it for a minute, you had two cultures colliding. You had the white, European culture and an African culture coming together—the rhythm of black music and the melody chord progressions of white music—coming together. That was the moment. That's really it. Out of all that came The Beatles and The Stones, you can't underestimate what happened. It all goes back to Elvis."

One night, David Bowie was hanging in my office and said: "The first time I heard 'Tutti Fruiti' by Elvis, I knew I'd heard God."

Elvis was a white boy possessed by black music, a fact of huge importance. Through his music, Elvis exposed America's sheltered young white teenagers to black American culture. The boundaries between blacks and whites were now challenged.

That was the sound that changed music history and then came the move that changed dance history, the most liberating of all moves—the twist. It set a revolution in motion and paved the way for disco.

Traditionally, people in America danced together in very specific choreographed movements of dance—a man and a woman, holding and facing each other, the man leading and the woman following. The twist changed all that, with repercussions felt way beyond the dance floor. A woman was now free to move to her own beat. She was no longer required to follow a man or to be led by a partner. It was very liberating, and however insignificant it may appear to be today, trust me, it helped to crack open the door to the women's movement and sexual liberation.

David Mancuso was the pioneering spirit, DJ, and owner of the world famous Loft in Manhattan. Carmen D'Alessio was an early devotee of The Loft. David believed the twist was introduced at rent parties in Harlem. Rent parties were gatherings for people to pool their resources to help a friend. People brought food and music was provided by a record player or musicians donating their time and talent. The host charged admission and the money collected was then donated to a friend in need of money to pay their rent. Some of these parties were real happenings where the music and dancing was wild and innovative. But more than that, it fostered a strong feeling of community, family, and support. Eldridge Cleaver, member of the Black Panther Party, agreed with David because he is often quoted as saying, "The twist was a guided missile, launched from the ghetto, right to the very heart of suburbia."

Frankie Crocker explained it to me this way: "The twist was a form of African American dance that exploded into pop culture consciousness because it was so easy for white people to do. You know that specific hip and pelvic movement like drying yourself off with a towel—and then the ball of the foot putting out a cigarette movement? Well that definitely can be traced to the black community, back many years to slave plantations, and further back to Africa." I agree with him that the twist permeated the American scene as it did because it was so easy for white people to do it. The number one record in America by Chubby Checker was "Let's Do The Twist," and all the nightly reporting of celebrities at the Peppermint Lounge in New York City definitely added to the craze of it all. It was a pop culture happening bringing the masses to the dance floor. Parents, children, politicians, garbage collectors, factory workers, and socialites—everyone was doing the twist.

This newfound freedom of movement encouraged people to develop their own style and do their own thing, laying the groundwork for many changes to come. As we moved deeper into the 1960s, a premium was placed on feeling free, not being uptight. It was about taking drugs and surrounding yourself with a loving community of peers. People were at odds with themselves and their country over the Vietnam War. The horror broadcast nightly on the evening news was inescapable, but it didn't stop people from dancing. It mirrored a new way of living and loving, a newfound freedom of expression in the length of our hair, psychedelics, protest movements, manner of dress, and, of course, Woodstock. We were all consolidated by this new force called rock and roll. It begged you to move to the beat of your own drum, hit the dance floor, and do your own thing. It prepared America and people around the world for what was just around the corner, a movement that would bring millions out onto the dance floor once again—the disco craze.

Back in 1972, history was made once again at The Peppermint Lounge when it closed and then reopened as Hollywood, a dance club catering to a gay clientele offering the best dance music in the city. Two girls I knew that loved to dance would invite me to go with them from time to time. The club was packed seven nights a week. Hollywood is credited as being the club where most of the now legendary, but then unknown, DJs played 45s and albums, experimenting and fine-tuning a new craft whereby they extended and changed the structure of a record—making cuts, editing, and blending the records together to the delight of the people on the dance floor. The significance of what went down at Hollywood and the effect these very young DJs who played there had on the music industry and the future of dance music cannot be overstated.

The five original resident DJs who played Hollywood and then moved on to New York's historic clubs of the disco era were: Tony Gioe to the Copacabana, the Copa's only resident DJ until 1982; Bobby DJ Guttadaro to Le Jardin and The Continental Baths; Tom Savarese to the Ice Palace and 12 West; Joey Palminteri to Sound Machine; Richie Kaczor to Studio 54.

Steve D'Acquisto, Francis Grasso, Michael Capella, and Alfie Davison hung out at Hollywood, fine-tuning their craft, sharing music and technical ideas with the DJs playing at Hollywood. Other regulars who moved on to the clubs of that time period were: David Rodriguez to The Limelight in Greenwich Village; Tony Smith to Barefoot Boy, Xenon, and now on Sirius XM Studio 54 Radio; Tee Scott to Better Days; John "Jellybean" Benitez to The Funhouse, Madonna, and now Sirius XM Studio 54 Radio; Bobby Gordon to 12 West and the recording studio The Hit Factory; Joey Madonia to Disco II, The Garage, and now his very own DJ Heaven; Bacho Mangual to Revelations and Plato's Retreat. Two DJs opened their own clubs downtown: David Mancuso, Owner of The Loft; and Nicky Siano, Owner of The Gallery where his now famous understudies, Larry Levan and Frankie Knuckles worked and hung out. Galaxy 21 would later become the new DJ hangout where they would learn from the now legendary DJ Walter Gibbons.

Tom Moulton, a hero to thousands of DJs around the world for his brilliant mixes on some of the best dance records ever recorded and immediately recognizable by his logo "A TOM MOULTON MIX," remembers the time period very well and had this to say: "By the mid-seventies DJs had demonstrated the power they had over the record-buying public. I will never forget the following full page commentary in *Billboard* magazine by its editor Bill Wardlow."

WILL SOMEBODY EXPLAIN TO ME

HOW GLORIA GAYNOR'S "NEVER CAN SAY GOODBYE"

CAN SELL 10,000 COPIES IN ONE WEEK

AND NOT ONE RADIO STATION IS PLAYING IT

People heard it on the dance floor and not the radio. These young kids were breaking all the rules and making hits out of songs that the record companies absolutely failed to *hear* as hits. Record executives took notice and for the first time ever chose to work with some of these talented guys and listen to their innovative ideas on this new sound in dance music. The DJs were thrilled to be included in the creative process. Receiving payment for their time and skill was a whole other story, one of the greatest rip-offs in music history.

Billboard magazine labeled it disco.

The sound exploded and the hustle was on.

From 1974 to 1979 it was four-on-the-floor, that galloping feeling of the 4/4 time, the drum and snare, lush violins, and soulful horn sections. The beat was faster, the dance floors wilder, and the song lyrics more suggestive than ever before. Donna Summer made it all about the orgasm, celebrating hers for eighteen minutes on "Love To Love You Baby"; Anita Ward let everyone know you can "Ring My Bell" if you do her right; The Salsoul Orchestra told you over and over that "You're Just The Right Size"; and Barry White, the Maestro of Love, wanted us to know that—no matter how hard—he just "Can't Get Enough."

John Travolta, The Bee Gees, and the film *Saturday Night Fever* took it to a whole new level of popularity, selling forty million records—more albums than any other soundtrack in history at that time. Everyone tried to cash in on the craze, prompting artists like Arthur Fiedler and the Boston Pops to release the album *Saturday Night Fiedler* and Johnny Mathis and Ethel Merman to record disco-themed albums as well.

And then it was over.

Chapter Eighteen:
Disco to Dance Club

Radio personality Frankie Crocker became my go-to music guru. I first met Frankie at Mt. Snow in the early 1970s. A six-foot-three black man in a silver ski suit shushing over the ski trails was impossible to miss back then. Frankie had become the program director at WBLS, the number-one radio station in New York City, and a trailblazer in radio broadcasting. It was unheard of back then for a black DJ on a black-owned radio station with an R&B format to play early Rolling Stones or Jimi Hendrix, but Frankie Crocker did. His outsized ego, handsome movie-star lifestyle (he owned a home next door to Cary Grant in the Hollywood Hills), and knack for self-promotion were legendary. A typical intro from back in the day as a young jock making a name for himself in radio would go something like this: "Good Afternoon, New York. You have heard of the Seven Wonders of the World. You are about to witness the Eighth. This is yours truly, Frankie Crocker."

In early 1981 everyone was asking me, "Mark, why do you still want to own a disco? Haven't you seen the 'DISCO IS DEAD' stickers plastered all over the city?" It became a mantra, steadily repeated by my colleagues, friends, and family. But I saw Studio 54 as a dance club and I truly believed that people would always love to dance. Frankie Crocker told me, "It's all going back to R&B-influenced productions like Blondie's 'Rapture' and the sound of Chic sampled in The Sugarhill Gang's 'Rapper's Delight,'" both of which I really liked. It made no difference to me what you called it or what label you put on it—rap, new wave, or euro—I was hearing some great new music on the radio and in other venues and I wanted it played at Studio 54. I was determined to make it happen.

I asked Denise Chatman if I should give DJ Leroy Washington extra money to buy all the new records I wanted to hear played at Studio, but she said it wasn't necessary, that working club DJs like Leroy belong to Record Pools. Prior to working for me at Studio, Denise was director of national club promotion at Salsoul Records. She went on to explain: "The term 'record pool' was coined by David Mancuso but the concept was conceived of by Tony Gioe while working at Club Hollywood. Tony envisioned it as a service, operating out of a central location in Manhattan, that would provide DJs with free copies of new releases from participating record companies. DJs would listen to the records and if they liked what they heard, they'd play the new releases in their respective clubs. The DJs at Hollywood were paid forty dollars a night to play from ten p.m. to four a.m., if the bar went over a thousand dollars, they were paid an extra twenty dollars. By the time they returned home to get some sleep it was nine a.m. A record pool would save them time and money. Tony organized a meeting at Club Hollywood, inviting all the DJs he knew and some record company executives, to discuss his concept. It took a while, with all the queens and egos involved, but eventually the first-ever record pool found a home with David Mancuso at Ninety-Nine Prince Street, The Loft. Soon after, Record Pools all over the US were organized, serving several thousand DJs across the country and around the world."

This made perfect sense to me: before the advent of the Internet and sharing music files, if I was in a club and heard a song that I liked I'd ask the DJ the name of it and then go out and buy it. Record stores were everywhere back then. I was buying albums for my personal enjoyment and they cost me $3.49 and 45s were $0.49 apiece, so I understood how it really did add up to be quite an expense for the DJs.

Changing the music format at Studio 54 was a must. I met with resistance—much of it from Steve Rubell, who was entitled to some creative input, based on papers we had signed while he and Ian were in prison. They received no money down for the purchase of Studio 54, and they were rightfully concerned about Studio's future and their payout.

The friction started when I began spending time with Rick James, giving him and his entourage the super VIP treatment. Steve thought that Rick and his dreadlocked entourage were "too black" for the scene and very different from Andre Leon Talley, Diana Ross, and some of his other guests. I was crazy about Rick's album *Street Songs*, which contained one of my favorite dance cuts, "Super Freak," which had just come out the summer before my reopening. I appreciated what a great talent Rick was. He was also a very smart guy and we'd become good friends, so I refused to budge.

It all came to a head with Steve on a Saturday night—November 7, 1981. Rick James was the musical guest on *Saturday Night Live* and Lauren Hutton was the host. Rick got me great seats in the front row of the audience. It was thrilling to be there and see all the set changes and goings-on that are off camera to the audience watching at home. Eddie Murphy was classic as Velvet Jones in his sketch "How To Be A Pimp." After the show we all went back to Studio 54 and waited for Rick to arrive. I told Leroy to get "Super Freak" ready to go. Rick was "full-blown Rick James" when he made his entrance into the main room—and why not? He'd just rocked his performance on *SNL* and was ready to party at Studio 54 with his band and thirty-person entourage. They were all about leather and dreadlocks, suede and braids, boots and glitter, and a whole lot of black and white tits and ass. They danced their way into the club and over to the main bar. It was wild. The crowd loved Rick and went crazy. Steve Rubell wasn't too happy and he told me so. It was so ridiculous that I had to laugh, especially around 3:00 a.m., when Rick was still holding court at the main bar and out of nowhere, my man DJ Leroy Washington played "Love Man" by Otis Redding and Rick went crazy. Rick grabbed my pen, pretending it was a microphone, singing along with Otis Redding about how pretty he was while his entourage went crazy too, dancing around Rick, grabbing girls and other people at the main bar. It was the kind of wild atmosphere Rick brought to any space he was in—which is why jaded Hollywood A-listers and the guys in the street both loved Rick. When the song ended everybody clapped—Rick took a bow and then looked at me and said, "Mark please ask L. J., that Warren Beatty–lookin' motherfucker over there (pointing to bartender L. J. Kirby) to pour us some drinks. I'm thirsty."

Rick was a great talent and so much fun to be around. I just couldn't understand why Steve Rubell was giving me shit.

But that was all about to change.

The next day Steve decided to consult with someone whom he had great respect for and he called David Geffen, founder of Geffen Records, one of the hottest and most successful record executives in the music industry back then and to this day. David listened and then he told Steve, "Rick James is a huge talent—his album *Street Songs* just sold three million copies." Steve backed down. Steve thought Studio 54 had a lot of soul under his watch, but it was about to get a whole lot more soulful under mine. I extended VIP treatment to include friends like Jimmy Cliff and Soul Train creator Don Cornelius. I welcomed promotions with WBLS Radio personality Frankie Crocker and the young, up-and-coming urban promoter, Dahved Levy, of present-day Caribbean Fever fame, whom Denise Chatman introduced me to.

Bringing a very talented DJ back from earlier Studio days and the Virgin Isle Hotel was important. Steve tried to get my business partner Stanley to nix it, referring to my chosen spinner—Leroy Washington—as a "shvartze" (Yiddish for black person). I know Steve didn't mean it in a racist way because he personally chose the DJs for Studio 54's reopening night in '81 and they were both black. I don't have a clue why he made that remark. Leroy had played at Studio under Steve's reign back in 1978. He and Richie Kaczor were friends, and Richie had agreed to let Leroy play at Studio if Leroy could find him a much-needed copy of Marvin Gaye and Tammi Terrell's "If This World Were Mine" on a 7." Leroy found it, and he got to play the following night at 4:00 a.m. It worked out perfectly for Leroy. He would hit Studio after playing from 10:00 p.m. to 3:00 a.m. at Marco's on Forty-Third Street on the East Side. From that night on it was agreed that Leroy would play at 4:00 a.m. and Richie was free to leave and hit the other clubs.

Leroy was from Detroit, Michigan—a Motown Man—and he became my DJ of choice. His record collection, purchased from DJ Jonathan Fearing, and from owning High-Tech Records on Bleeker Street, was unlimited, as was his knowledge of and appreciation for every genre of music that might be needed at Studio 54. It was in his brain and at his fingertips at a moment's notice—and I knew that I could count on Leroy to go with the dance floor—not his ego. That was crucial to the success of my plan. Leroy came through for me night after night for over three years. If I asked him to play a special occasion on a Monday night, he would. My instincts proved to be right on. Our early evening straight crowd loved Leroy's selections and they packed the dance floor, taking breaks to go to the bar and spend money. There's an old saying: "If you're sober enough to drive you're not drunk enough to dance." It all worked together and our bars started doing more business. Leroy had the music under control and now I could get as fucked-up-high as I wanted.

The music varied, depending on the night and the time. It was always different, determined by the event and the crowd invited. On the designated straight nights from 10:00 p.m. until about 1:00 a.m. the music was up for grabs.

Usually the early evening crowd was happiest when dancing to what they heard on pop radio, such as ABBA, Human League, The Go-Go's, Devo, Van Halen, Men At Work, Eurythmics, and Blondie, with a couple of disco classics thrown in. The crowd loved it. The emphasis changed from formulaic disco and R&B to pop-oriented dance music. New Wave, which some well-known DJs didn't like very much, was in heavy rotation. At around 1:00 a.m. the music became decidedly more R&B with the sounds of James Brown (past and present) in heavy rotation along with The Temptations; Ashford & Simpson; The Detroit Emeralds; The Gap Band; Earth, Wind & Fire; Marvin Gaye; and Ray Charles, though Leroy always managed to throw in some Rolling Stones too. I've always loved the saxophone and it doesn't get any better than Bobby Keys on The Stones' "Brown Sugar" to get me going in the wee hours at Studio 54. Whatever else Leroy knew the late-night crowd would like he'd put on the turntable. We continued to make room for some Studio 54 disco favorites, like Gloria Gaynor's "I Will Survive," of historical significance to the club and its founders, but disco was no longer the emphasis for hours at a time. I was always pushing for more R&B to be mixed in late at night, and that worked, so I was happy, but Leroy did what he had to do and kept the popular music of the day on the turntables to keep the crowd happy. I know for a fact that Leroy's emphasis on the New Wave sound early in the evening and Motown late in the evening was one of the reasons so many rockers enjoyed Studio during my reign. Keith Richards once told me he could never get enough of Motown. Studio 54 went from a disco to a dance club.

Thursday night—our popular gay influenced "models and fashion photographers" night—still needed an influx of new blood, so I brought in DJ Frank Corr from Crisco Disco, and he completely lit up Thursday nights. Once or twice Larry Levan from the Paradise Garage played on a Thursday night; he and Joey Madonia liked to hang out on Sunday nights. Robbie Leslie played a couple of times as well; he currently hosts a slot on Sirius XM Radio's Studio 54 channel, keeping the memories of Studio 54 alive. He recently shared this, and I quote, "Can I tell you what it was like to be at the controls of one of the best sound systems in the world? It was like having your finger on the red button somewhere in Washington and Moscow."

Music was important; it was the essence of the club. Studio 54 may have started out as a disco, but as I ushered it through a change in direction, it became a dance club just like my favorite, Small's Paradise in Harlem. I was gratified when I spotted the December 22, 2003 issue of *New York* magazine's cover story: "100 Years Of New York's Hottest Scenes," on which Studio 54, Small's Paradise, and The Copacabana were featured in the top ten.

A major innovation was introduced to Studio 54 when I had a giant video screen installed in late 1982. Seeing Michael Jackson play out on the big screen dancing to "Billie Jean" at Studio 54 created quite a stir. Music videos and MTV were a huge deal at the time and we were the first club to present music simultaneously with video images on a big screen. But nothing prepared us for the joy and pandemonium that broke out one night in December of 1983 when we showed Michael Jackson's thirteen-minute video "Thriller" for the first time. We were the first club to show it, and the night it premiered at Studio 54 Michael Jackson made a surprise visit. Frank Corr was on the turntables that night and remembers it this way: "The crowd went 'dancing crazy' when the video appeared, but when someone screamed 'Michael!' and pointed to the DJ booth and everyone saw Michael Jackson in the flesh, it was as wild as wild can get in a very happy way. Everyone was cool, but I had to tell the tech crew to move the bridge back to the DJ booth when it came time for Michael to leave. There was no way to take him through the crowd in the club." Michael then danced on the bridge and out the back door. Every night after that, the screen would be lowered three or four times per night to show "Thriller" and the crowd would go out of their minds, screaming and dancing along with Michael, and they always wanted more. The video presentation was always a real showstopper. In addition to the large screen, we installed several video monitors at the main bar making it one of our most exciting visual effects.

I also tempered the prerecorded music and video wall with live performances by Lou Reed, The Temptations, Four Tops, Chubby Checker, and The Beastie Boys, to name a few. Stevie Wonder recorded on our dance floor, taking advantage of the great acoustic quality once we were able to drill a hole and connect to Charlie Benanty's recording studio, Soundworks, located below Studio. I was happy with the events we had on our schedule as a result of my new hire, Denise Chatman.

Studio was "the" place to have a party, so Ford Modeling Agency decided to host their "Face of The Eighties" party at Studio 54. The Ford Agency had been number one in the industry since the 1950s when they discovered Suzy Parker, Dovima, and Carmen Dell'Orefice, who is still stunning and modeling in her eighties. She had no choice but to continue with her career, as she was another casualty of Bernie Madoff, with whom she invested her life's savings. In the 1960s, Ford signed the luscious British import Jean Shrimpton, and then Ali McGraw, and remained number one in the world into the 1970s representing Cheryl Tiegs, Christie Brinkley, Jerry Hall, Lauren Hutton, Rene Russo, and Kim Basinger, and in 1975 they signed nine-year-old Brooke Shields.

Early in my reign, Eileen Ford asked Joey Hunter, President of Ford Modeling Agency, to contact Studio 54 and see if we could get either the Four Tops to sing their big hit "Sugar Pie Honey Bunch" or The Temptations to sing "My Girl." I was thrilled. Joey Hunter was a standout in the world of modeling. A handsome, hard-working guy who, to this day, takes his profession very seriously, earning him a stellar reputation in a cutthroat business. He was instrumental in the development of Model Wire, the software used today at most modeling agencies. I liked and respected him. Roy Cohn hosted Joey's fortieth birthday bash at Studio 54. I was determined to get one of the groups Eileen Ford requested, as the relationship between Ford and Studio was of paramount importance to me.

The Ford Agency was legendary for the lengths to which Eileen and Jerry Ford would go to protect the models. Most girls lucky enough to be signed by the Fords were very young and not from Manhattan, so they were eager to experience New York City at night, and that meant one thing—Studio 54. Some girls actually lived in the Ford family townhouse and had to abide by strict rules and curfews and some of the girls were legendary in their determination to party while Eileen believed in good manners and white gloves. Joey Hunter told me the girls living with Eileen and Jerry would hide their dancing shoes in a downstairs room used by the housekeepers next to the back service entrance. They'd then put on their pajamas, yawn, and fake a "goodnight, I'm going to sleep now," and after Eileen and Jerry were tucked in bed and sound asleep, the girls would tiptoe back down the stairs, change clothes, stash their pajamas, and head to Studio 54, hopefully returning to their bedrooms before the Ford family awoke. I was familiar with Eileen's rules, and anything I could do to please her other than babysit, I would try to do, but I also had a club to run.

Ford had a lot of competition by the time I reopened Studio. Elite, Zoli, Wilhelmina, Sue Charney, Click, and other boutique agencies were all in the game now. At Ford, it was all about eating your vegetables and getting your beauty sleep; over at Elite Models it was about drinking champagne and hanging out with the very handsome John Casablancas at Studio 54 into the wee hours of the morning.

John defected from Ford to start Elite Models and he was a force to be reckoned with—and so the model wars began. I remained neutral, hosting parties for all the agencies. John developed his girls into celebrities and pitched them very successfully as the new stars of music videos and presenters on MTV. He guided the careers of Iman, Heidi Klum, Paulina Porizkova, Cindy Crawford, Linda Evangelista, Claudia Schiffer, and Gisele Bündchen, making the successful ones very, very rich. John is credited with turning models into idols and creating the supermodel moment by driving modeling rates to a new high. It was said that he acted more like the manager of a rock band, encouraging his young charges to embrace a lifestyle of champagne, wild parties, and massive paychecks. Linda Evangelista summed up this new attitude when she was quoted in *Vogue*: "We don't wake up for less than $10,000 a day." I have many good memories of partying with John, and I was very sad to hear of his passing in 2013.

Booking The Temps or The Tops would not only please the Fords, it would also fit in perfectly with the changes I was making to the music. My plan was to present more live R&B music in addition to performances with prerecorded music tracks. I asked Denise Chatman to make some calls, and within a few days we were booked with The Temptations. The night would be a huge success with gorgeous models everywhere dancing to the tune of "My Girl." When Rick James found out about the upcoming Ford Models party he got very excited. He planned to surprise everyone, especially his uncle, Melvyn Franklin, the famous deep bass voice of The Temptations, and suddenly appear on stage and sing "Super Freak" live with The Temps, just as they did on the original album recording. We will never know how Eileen Ford might have reacted to Rick singing about "a very kinky girl, the kind you don't take home to mother" because, just as we were about to go to print on the invitations, we were informed that The Temptations were embarking on a European tour and due to schedule changes in Europe, they would be ever so grateful if we could change the date.

As it turned out, we couldn't change the date but we were thrilled that Eileen Ford's other choice, the Four Tops, were available; what could be more all-American and wholesome than hearing the sounds of "Sugar Pie Honey Bunch?" Jerry Ford was the onstage Master of Ceremonies for the evening and the models surrounding him were the hottest new faces on the scene. The crowd went crazy when he crowned Tricia Helfer, Ford's New Face Of The Eighties. (Tricia is still as beautiful as ever. Check her out in *Battlestar Galactica* and the 2013 series *Killer Women*.) Frankie Crocker then took the stage to wild applause and introduced the Four Tops who hit the stage singing "Baby I Need Your Loving;" they brought the house down and followed with "Standing In The Shadows Of Love" and "Reach Out, I'll Be There." Levi Stubbs, the lead singer, one of the greatest voices ever in R&B music, tore it up.

Everything was picture-perfect—until the party inadvertently moved into the basement. Based upon the document I signed with the ABC, I could lose my liquor license over this potential misunderstanding. I could see the headline: "Parties In The Basement—Business as Usual at Studio 54." That's all the State Liquor Authority and ABC would have to hear.

The Four Tops had just finished their performance. They were using my office as a Green Room, and it was packed to capacity. So I snuck out and headed down to the basement, taking Levi, Lawrence, Duke, and Obie—all Four Tops—with me. Along the way, Nile Rogers and then Frankie Crocker joined us with several beautiful women in tow. I figured it would be quiet down there. Wrong. Keith Richards and Ronnie Wood were heading up the stairs as we were heading down the stairs and once The Stones saw The Tops it was "party time." Years later when I read *Life* by Keith Richards, he summed it up best with this reference to himself, Mick, Charlie, and Bill, on their first US road tour back in 1964: "We waited for each new release by The Temptations and the Four Tops to keep us going while we were on the road. Motown was our food, on the road and off, we just wanted to be black motherfuckers."

So there we were in the basement of Studio 54, and as I looked around, it definitely did look like I was hosting a party in the basement. At first, busboys were running back and forth under the dance floor, trying to avoid the crowd, saving time bringing drinks to the VIPs upstairs, but soon they were bringing drinks to us in the basement. Models were everywhere, giggling and dancing, everyone had a drink in hand, and chairs were already set up for us. We had used the area earlier as a dressing room for the band and it was all quite comfortable. There was a lot of hand-slapping, laughing, champagne, and cocaine. Had I been raided, it would have looked like I was "operating a VIP lounge" in the basement. I had to make a move. I told security to clear all guests out my office, the stairs, and every nook and cranny leading to my

Welcome to Studio 54

The Forest Hills Inn—my first business venture after the navy.

"Miss Perpetual Motion"—Candy Johnson and her band (Mickey, Larry, and The Exciters) tore it up onstage at The Candy Store, my first nightclub venture in Manhattan. Candy appeared in the Beach Party *movies.*

March 1972/60 cents

Signature

*Olympic skier and model Suzy Chaffee with me on a chairlift
at my Mt. Snow resort.*

I was riding high in the early 1970s with an eighty-three-foot, all-teak Chinese Junk and amateur ski racing with Olympians.

Roy Cohn with Ian Schrager and Steve Rubell at a press conference after the bust.

Roy Cohn and I worked the phones in the jailhouse lobby—negotiating with Steve and Ian to buy Studio 54.

The Virgin Isle Hotel before the hurricane.

Wild things were always happening in my private cabana next to the Virgin Isle Hotel pool deck.

The dance floor and DJ booth amidst the chaotic renovations as we prepared to reopen Studio 54 in 1981. Photo by Adam Scull.

In my office at Studio 54 with Carmen D'Alessio, we were reviewing plans for the VIP dinner and reopening night party. Photo by Adam Scull.

*Mimi and yippie/yuppie Jerry Rubin host their very successful
Wednesday Networking Night.*

*Yuppie Abbie Hoffman thanks committee members Karen Black and Carly Simon
for making his Save the River benefit a huge success. Photo by Adam Scull.*

Michael Jackson used to hang out in the DJ booth, his favorite spot high above the crowd. Studio 54 Head of Security Chuck Garelick is in the background. Photo by Richard Manning.

Splash

Larkin Arnold of Columbia Records, recording artist Rebbie Jackson, and Studio 54 resident DJ Leroy Washington hung out in the DJ booth while promoting the album Centipede. *Photo by Richard Manning.*

Gay danced next to straight, rich next to poor, black next to white...the dance floor was democratic. United by the power of the beat.

A few of the Studio 54 bartenders:
L. J. Kirby, Bob Farrell, John Bello, and Oscar Lopez.

The cocaine in the Virgin Islands was as pure as it gets. My good buddy Rick James and I got very high in Rick's suite at the Virgin Isle Hotel.

eddie murphy
nick ashford bill jarema valerie simpson
cornelia guest milan millie kaiserman
cordially invite you to a
birthday celebration for

MARK FLEISCHMAN AND RICK JAMES

at

Studio 54

254 West 54th Street

10:30 pm.

COMPLIMENTARY ADMISSION FOR TWO

WITH THIS INVITATION

It was a wild and wonderful night. We got so fucked up. I remember nothing.

Denise Chatman, her father W. D. Chatman, and attorney Robert Leighton enjoyed
an early evening of jazz and conversation at Jerry Rubin Networking Night.
Photo by Richard Manning.

I had the honor of introducing Bill Clinton on saxophone at Tatou New York.

TATOU

Tatou Supper Club. Tatou New York pictured left,
Tatou LA pictured above and below.

The red-hot upstairs dance club at Tatou LA.
Photos by David Rockwell.

I walked down the aisle with my dream girl Mimi during our wedding at Tatou LA in 1994. My best man and brother Alan is pictured behind us. Photo by George Leonard.

President Ronald Reagan enjoyed the antics of Tony Curtis when hanging out at Tatou LA. The former first lady, Nancy Reagan, didn't appreciate Tony's humor.

Ski bum staff of Tatou Aspen.

Tatou Tokyo.

Above: A recent picture taken while skiing with my daughter Hilary.

Right: A photo of me, Mimi, Adam, and Juliet— my new family (after Jerry Rubin was killed in an auto accident in 1994).

office, and I was finally able to move the party out of the basement and to my office upstairs.

As nervous as I had been, I should emphasize that it was moments like this that made it all worthwhile. I was spending time with people I held in high esteem. Nile Rodgers is a genius, from his early productions with Chic and David Bowie, to his more current work with Daft Punk and Pharrell on "Get Lucky." The sound of my youth was Levi Stubbs and the Four Tops, Frankie Crocker on the radio, and The Rolling Stones. They were all there, taking such obvious delight in each other's company, doing lines and talking trash…and it was all happening right here, at my club. The State Liquor Authority would never have believed that I didn't plan this. I respected my agreement with the State Liquor Authority, and I abided by the rules, but on this night and at that point in the game my attitude was "fuck it, this is my club" and I took another hit of coke. Since that night, the Four Tops, Frankie Crocker, and The Rolling Stones have all been inducted into the Rock and Roll Hall of Fame.

Chapter Nineteen:
Walk on the Wild Side

MY FORAY INTO THE world of R&B music continued when Denise Chatman walked into Studio 54 late one night wearing a formal gown and a big smile and asked me if I would work with her on a party for Marvin Gaye, who had just released the very, very hot "Sexual Healing." I said, "Yes, of course! Let's do it." She had just come from the annual T. J. Martell Foundation Dinner at The Waldorf Astoria, where Walter Yetnikoff, President of CBS Records, was holding court with Morris Levy and friends. Walter asked Denise to help him plan something special for Marvin Gaye at Studio 54 in celebration of "Sexual Healing" and Marvin's week of sold-out performances at Radio City Music Hall. Walter was thrilled with "Sexual Healing," but irate after listening to the new tracks Marvin had just finished recording for his new album release. The title track was origianlly named "Sanctified Pussy." Marvin reasoned that if a James Bond film could succeed at the box office with a character named Pussy Galore he could do the same. Marvin was highly intelligent but there was no reasoning with him when he was eating cocaine for breakfast.

I was ecstatic at the thought of a party at Studio 54 for Marvin Gaye, but Denise told me that Walter Yetnikoff confirmed what she already knew, having met with Marvin when she worked at Salsoul Records—the man was charming but oh so difficult. Even though he was back living in the USA after ducking the IRS for several years (his IRS debt is now settled) and freed from his contract with Motown and had a new recording contract with Columbia Records, and even with the smash hit "Sexual Healing," Marvin was as troubled as ever—coked-up and out of it, twenty-four seven.

This was to be Walter's party for Marvin, but Walter had a record company to run, and so it was up to Columbia Records' Amy Strauss, manager of Artist Functions at Columbia Records, and Denise to put it all together.

Locking in a date was every bit the nightmare Denise predicted it would be, but she knew she had my support. Marvin would agree to a date and then cancel it the following day, creating havoc on our event schedule at Studio. At one point I had to send Denise down to the Virgin Islands to relax. Shay Knuth and Shelley Tupper joined her. I arranged some excursions and snorkeling time for them on The Calypso, the Jacques Cousteau boat. The girls played in the sun during the day and at night the phone calls continued between Denise and Amy. After several months of back and forth with Marvin, nothing had been finalized.

And then it all came together—the date was agreed upon.

I was in my Jacuzzi when my assistant, Victoria Leacock, knocked on the door. "Denise wants you to know, Mick Jagger just called her for the guest list, he'll be there. He wants Marvin to know." Word had leaked out about the party, but Columbia Records wanted to keep it intimate. Was I surprised that Mick Jagger had personally called to be placed on the guest list for a party honoring Marvin Gaye? Hell no. Mick, Keith, and the other Stones were steeped in R&B. The number one single from their 1965 album was "Little Red Rooster," written by Willie Dixon and previously recorded by Howlin' Wolf in 1961. Since the age of ten, they all knew everything there was to know about America's rhythm and blues artists. To the Rolling Stones, Marvin Gaye was a god.

The "behind the scenes" planning at Studio was always a challenge in an effort to be creative, and the Marvin Gaye party was no different. Columbia Records came up with a brilliant idea that was sure to please Marvin. A few months back, on February 13, 1983, Marvin sang the National Anthem at the NBA All-Star Game, hosted by the LA Lakers in Los Angeles. He sang it with a simple drum track, in his inimitable style, and he brought the house down. It was one of his proudest moments. And so on the night of May 16, 1983 Marvin Gaye entered Studio 54, and as he walked the long, beautiful mirrored entryway into the main room, DJ Leroy Washington cut the music and blasted Marvin singing the National Anthem, which was simultaneously visible on all the video monitors and the huge screen over the dance floor. Tall, dark, and handsome, wearing sunglasses and looking every bit of the rock and roll royalty that he was, Marvin Gaye entered the main room of Studio 54 to wild applause. After some time spent saying hello to friends and the record/ radio industry people in attendance, Walter Yetnikoff and his girlfriend Boom Boom, Marvin Gaye and Mick Jagger disappeared into my office. At one point Marvin made an appearance from the second-floor balcony outside my office that looked out over the dance floor and the entire club. It was a moment to remember for those who experienced it—he truly was a musical genius. He was the voice for a generation; the haunting and timeless "What's Goin' On" is as relevant today as it was in 1971 when it consumed America's airwaves, heard everywhere—college campuses, office buildings, car radios, and the battlefields of Vietnam.

Marvin Gaye and Mick Jagger spent most of the night holding court behind closed doors, as royalty are known to do.

Studio 54 would go on to present some of the most diverse and exciting music ever staged at the club. When Denise took a call from Eric Kronfeld, who represented Lou Reed, she could hardly contain herself. After all, this was the cofounder of The Velvet Underground. She thought having Lou Reed perform at Studio would be over the top, while I thought it might be *too* over the top. We'd never done an advance-sale event before, and I was nervous when she asked—no, begged—for my approval. Essentially, I'd be agreeing to close my doors to the regular clientele without any guarantee. Would Lou Reed's crowd come to Studio? I wasn't sure, but I finally agreed to give it a shot. Lou Reed Live at Studio 54 sold out in three hours. The night of the performance, I stood there listening to Lou Reed sing "Walk On The Wild Side," and it all made perfect sense to me. The song is his affectionate salute to the misfits, hustlers, and transvestites who once inhabited the orbit of Andy Warhol. Lou Reed will be missed. His words will forever remind me that, once past the red velvet rope, Studio 54 was a definite walk on the wild side.

Henry Eshelman, Director of our Mailroom Operations, was on top of it when he asked me for permission to book the Beastie Boys at Studio 54 for another advanced-sale event. I had not heard of them, but I trusted Henry; plus, the success of Lou Reed at Studio 54 inspired me to be more open about the genres of music to consider. I was totally unprepared for this group of three white Jewish kids from New York City, and in that I learned a valuable lesson. Keep your mind open to the power of another beat. Our crowd went insane and so did I. I couldn't sit down. I was hooked on this new sound, a harbinger of things to come when, twelve years later, I would present rap and hip hop at The Century Club in Los Angeles.

In the years that I owned Studio 54, we presented some of the most diverse and exciting music ever staged at the club. Some of the acts performed on the dance floor during TV productions. Earth, Wind & Fire; Joni Mitchell; The Sugarhill Gang; Teddy Pendergrass; and everyone's favorite on The Match Game, Charles Nelson Reilly, stand out in my memory. Others performed from the spectacular and versatile moving bridge twenty feet high in the air above the dance floor, spanning the entire length of the dance area. It could be moved stage front and stage rear. It was constructed of steel and strong enough to safely accommodate one hundred screaming, dancing, jumping people, powered by a motor and operated by our tech crew. There was an entrance to the bridge directly outside my office door on the second-floor landing, so my office often functioned as a green room. When visiting artists came off the bridge or stage after a performance, it was my pleasure to make them feel welcome and comfortable. I usually had coke, champagne, and Quaaludes waiting—whatever their pleasure—for them and their entourage of friends to enjoy. In an effort to promote their records and careers, many appeared without compensation, so this was my way of showing a little gratitude for their performances—plus, I got to hang out with many interesting and talented people.

The bridge served as a concert stage for the beautiful Laura Branigan, who was proudly showcased by the great Ahmet Ertegun, chief of Atlantic Records. The Weather Girls, aka Two Tons o' Fun, brought the house down when my good friend, songwriter Paul Jabara ("Enough is Enough" and "Last Dance"), directed and choreographed the girls and a slew of dancers for the debut of his and Paul Shaffer's now-iconic disco song "It's Raining Men." The Studio 54 Sunday night gay crowd went wild upon hearing it for the first time. Disco queen Gloria Gaynor entertained us royally from her perch on the bridge, singing "I Will Survive," her ever-popular number one record from *Billboard*'s Hot 100 chart in 1978.

To this day, it still irks Tom Moulton that some DJs take the credit for breaking "I Will Survive" and making it a number one record. I will set the record straight here and now with the following quote from Tom:

> *I was in the booth at Studio 54 when Richie Kaczor first played the 12" of 'I Will Survive' and they all walked off the dance floor.*

Richie stuck with it and over the course of a few weeks it caught on. Richie liked it when no one else was into a record. It was the B side of 'Substitute' and that's the one Polydor was pushing. Richie can take full credit for the success of 'I Will Survive.'

Studio 54 provided a new venue for The Harris Sisters and their band, Hibiscus and The Screaming Violets. I remember at one of their performances, Hibiscus and George Harris III (brother of the Harris Sisters) descended from the ceiling on a swing, joining his sisters on the moving bridge, which scared the shit out of all of them as it lurched forward and backward. The Screaming Violets were dressed in purple sequined gowns, purple marabou jackets, and four-inch spiked heels. The crowd loved it.

Other entertainers who performed for us included Tito Puente, who caused a commotion like no other in a packed-to-the-rafters house one night. The crowd demanded encore after encore of his Latin rhythms and percussion, and Tito obliged them, playing with that unforgettable smile on his face. K. C. and the Sunshine Band were so hugely popular, it didn't matter which night it was, as were The Village People whenever they performed—people screaming for more "YMCA." Everyone loved Cyndi Lauper, a hometown Brooklyn girl, beloved by New Yorkers especially when MTV always had her in heavy rotation with video hits like "Girls Just Wanna Have Fun." Flock of Seagulls performed at a private party and the club was packed with invited guests, much to the dismay of the crowd outside that couldn't be admitted. Duran Duran created an Elvis-style girl pandemonium when they performed to a packed Studio 54. Bobby Brown and New Edition packed the house with very young girls, each one in possession of a flawless fake ID, and Boy George and Culture Club agreed to appear but only if Frankie Crocker would introduce them. Grace Jones was so loved by all that no one ever missed one of her appearances or performances at Studio.

KISS performed live for an unforgettable 1982 New Year's Eve event that was simulcast in Italy for the San Remo Film Festival. Talk about wild happenings. We had a stage set up for their performance, and it was quite a challenge controlling the fans, both male and female, who were, and still are, obsessed with them. Studio was a scene that night and Gene Simmons and Paul Stanley were forced to hang in my office to escape the crowds below. They were warm and friendly and we had a good time. Somehow fans figured out they were in my office on the second floor and managed to find a ladder and tried climbing up, hoping to get in or have a peek at the dynamic duo. We had to post security at the base of the fire escape to prevent fans from climbing up the five stories to the Rubber Room door, hoping to get in.

Madonna, then a virtual unknown, appeared on The Bridge in 1983 to perform "Holiday," as Halston, Steve Rubell, Billy Smith, and Seymour Stein of Sire Records watched from the second-floor landing. Earlier on the day of her performance at Studio, I witnessed firsthand the beginning of her diva behavior. I was walking across the back of the dance floor by the famous brick wall heading to a meeting in my partner Stanley Tate's office when I heard, "Well, where the fuck is he then? I'm waitin' here for close to forty minutes already." It was Madonna, a nobody, complaining that Frankie Crocker, the number one radio programmer in the US, was keeping her waiting. She'd arrived at the appointed time to do her sound check—nothing was happening and she was pissed. She was probably tired, as Billy Smith who'd arranged for her to sing that night told me he'd found her downstairs in a makeshift dressing room, where she'd spent most of the afternoon sleeping before her performance.

This was before the British accent and platinum records, but she was already in possession of the diva attitude—from birth, probably. But on that afternoon, as I watched this scene go down, the chutzpah—the balls—of an unknown was thrilling. I was secretly hoping that Frankie Crocker would show up and I could watch two divas go at it. After her performance that evening, local radio station Z100 added "Holiday" to the playlist, as did WBLS. In a matter of months Madonna would release her first album, which would go on to sell five million copies that year. She was on her way.

As time went on, Studio 54 was more in tune with the 1980s and doing better financially. It was time to relax, have a good time, and get really fucked up.

There was still some semblance of a relationship with Laurie Lister at the beginning of my reign at Studio 54 but my behavior was taking its toll, and then I crossed a line and did something on that past New Year's Eve that delivered the definitive blow to any hope she may have had that I was going to straighten up and behave like a mensch. I was en route from Miami to New York City on New Year's Eve day, with Dodi Fayed on his private jet. Dodi loved Quaaludes, good quality coke, and hot women, and he always had plenty of all three. We were celebrating the critical acclaim of "Chariots Of Fire," for which Dodi had an executive producer credit and which went on to win the Oscar for Best Picture in 1982. We were being entertained by some very attractive "hot to trot" flight attendants. I lost track of what day it was, forgot about my plans for later that evening with Laurie, and partied through the night in a suite at the Plaza Hotel with Dodi. After that, Laurie decided to move on and forget about me. I wish I could remember some of the details of that night. I know it was one hell of party, but I remember nothing, only the consequence I suffered—losing a truly incredible woman who I had been crazy about.

On August 31, 1997, Dodi Fayed lost his life in a car crash in Paris that also killed the beloved Princess Diana.

As the owner of Studio 54, I was considered by some to be a very eligible bachelor, but as it turned out, I was a lousy date. After a nice dinner out at some chic restaurant, I'd invite my date to join me at Studio 54 for an evening of fun and dancing. But there were always details to be addressed upon my arrival at the club each evening, so I'd settle my date in on one of the VIP banquettes, assign a busboy to look after her, then excuse myself and promise to return shortly. I'd go to my office, attend to the guest list, and then decide how much coke should be divided up for the evening and who should be assigned to do it—both of which were very important. I will explain.

When guests were invited to my office, they were greeted with a gold straw or a crisp rolled up hundred-dollar bill and invited to partake from one of the many lines of coke laid out on my long curved desk. It was very time-consuming to divide three or four grams of coke into thirty or forty lines of equal proportion—tedious, but a much-loved task for one of my trusted assistants to perform. Making the lines relatively even was important. I had no patience for such stuff, unless it was 5:00 a.m. and I was entertaining an intimate group—then I would gladly do it. Anyway, it was one of the very important details that I had to personally attend to. So, after the guest list was finalized and the coke was divided, I would then start on my party high for the evening. I'd take a few hits of my really good coke, drop a Quaalude or two, then head back downstairs to my date, waiting for me on one of the banquettes.

And that's when I would invariably get into trouble—walking through the club. People wanted to say hello, dance with me, meet their friends, meet my friends, ask for my card, give me their card, give me a résumé, promise me the best blow job ever, give me a cassette, solve a staff issue, get them high or get me high. I always intended to return to my dates within thirty minutes or so but there were times that I was gone for as long as one hour. Some women put up with this behavior, but many didn't.

One woman who was having none of my nonsense was Chen Sam, the very attractive publicist to Elizabeth Taylor. To put it simply, in order to get to Liz, you had to first go through Chen. I invited Chen to dinner and then we went to Studio 54 and several times I was forced to excuse myself to attend to other matters, leaving Chen alone at a VIP banquette, making her vulnerable to people who knew she was the conduit to Elizabeth Taylor. By 1:00 a.m. Chen let me know that she was furious with me. I apologized profusely as I walked her to the stage door exit and out to my waiting limousine to take her safely home. Before Studio 54, I had always dated women I considered to be my peers—intelligent, ambitious, and attractive women. After the Chen incident, I concluded that any attempt to date a woman like Chen was a mistake. I made it easy on myself and started picking up random, late-night strays.

Each night around 3:00 a.m. I had the freedom to start looking—that's when I was able to relax, have fun, and hit the dance floor. A flood of women came on to me. I was having sex everywhere—my office, the locked reception area, the liquor storage room, and the dark corners of the balcony. As the nights went by, the sex, drugs, and never-ending pressure to keep Studio 54 hot night after night consumed me. It was my life and I loved it. I forgot about friends like Bob Shaye, who told me years later, that on several occasions when he wanted to come to this or that event at Studio 54, I didn't return his phone calls. I was surrounded by a new group of good-looking, well-dressed, famous and not so famous people who loved Studio and became my new best friends. It's all so obvious to me now. I was living in a bubble of my own design, insulating myself from my former world.

To compliment that late-night feeling we were becoming known for at Studio 54, I would usually hand DJ Leroy Washington my list of personal requests for the remainder of the evening, always heavy on the R&B and other stuff that I really liked dancing to. Some personal favorites: The Rolling Stones' "Sympathy for the Devil," The Stray Cats' "Stray Cat Strut," The Weather Girls' "It's Raining Men," Barbra Streisand and Donna Summer's "Enough is Enough," ABBA's "Lay All Your Love On Me," Ray Charles' "Hit the Road Jack," Marvin Gaye's "Sexual Healing," Stevie Wonder's "Master Blaster," Lime's big hit "Babe We're Gonna Love Tonight," Eurhythmics' "Sweet Dreams," Nile Rodgers' "Le Freak," James Brown's "Papa's Got A Brand New Bag" and "I Feel Good," Rick James' "Super Freak" and "Give It To Me Baby," and Wild Cherry's "Play That Funky Music White Boy," which sort of became my theme song. Leroy would work his magic finding the perfect way to put it all together—playing my requests—while keeping the others on the dance floor happy, too. I'd be out there, in the midst of a thousand people, dancing and interacting with almost everyone, strutting my stuff, and I was pretty good at it. I loved music so much, I'd cruise around by myself moving to the beat, meeting folks, giving hugs, checking out women, hoping to set myself up for a sexual encounter either in my office, some obscure dark spot in Studio, or perhaps later that morning in my apartment in the hot tub. Women of all sizes, shapes, and nationalities were invited to my bed—often two at a time. It was the 1980s, and it was all about excess—not "less is more." The man of the 1970s was a sensitive hero type and the 1980s man was an unapologetic man of action. I dove into every sexual adventure with reckless abandon.

Potassa was a transvestite and a regular at Studio 54. She was tall, exotic, and absolutely gorgeous, with a thick Spanish accent, long fingernails, tight dresses, and a penchant for mentioning that she was a protégé of Salvador Dalí. She was always pestering me for a bottle of champagne while digging her sharp nails into my arm, reminding me, "Mark, Dahling, Stevie always took care of me." And it's true, Steve was known to tell the bartenders and managers, "Give Potassa a bottle of champagne whenever she wants it." Steve delighted in watching her take unsuspecting, straight guys up to the balcony and blowing their minds and their dicks with her very talented mouth. The girl could swallow. Potassa made the rounds of all the hot nightspots in the city. She was a regular in the entourage that Salvador Dalí was known to travel around town with. Dalí always had a lot of "women" with him. Trader Vic's was his favorite bar to begin his forays into the night. He and his girls loved the rum-laden concoctions, The Scorpion being a favorite, as it was for me a few years earlier. Sometimes my good friend Antonia de Portago would join them and they would all arrive at Studio with fresh gardenias in their hair, a telltale sign of where they'd been.

One night we were all hanging around the main bar and Potassa introduced me to Daniella, a real beauty. At about 5:00 a.m., she and I left Studio 54 and went to my apartment. After some champagne, I started fondling her magnificent breasts, concentrating on her nipples that reminded me of luscious strawberries. She pulled down my zipper, smiled, then knelt before me and started to suck me off. Damn she was good, but I didn't want to come just yet, so I dropped down to the floor and, pacing myself, I slowly removed her panties and then, Oh shit! What the fuck—a tiny curled-up penis! Mood kill!

Fortunately, "she/he" had the good grace to make a joke about it: "Oh, honey, I thought you knew what you were getting into," waving her hands in an effeminate way. It cut the tension, diffused my embarrassment and made things considerably less awkward for me as I called her a taxi.

As 1982 progressed, I ended up with two sex kittens living in the guest room of my penthouse. The first was Bobbie, a strikingly pretty blonde with a great body. Billy Smith, who booked up-and-coming recording artists like Madonna—before she became "Madonna"—and performed to prerecorded tracks on Studio's famous moving bridge, introduced her to me. Always smiling and moonfaced, Billy was a slippery character, but he got the job done. And when he heard I was looking for a secretary, he introduced me to Bobbie.

She was a nice Midwestern girl from Chicago. I told Billy that I wanted someone who was smart, could take dictation, type, and answer a very busy phone—politely. Bobbie could do it all with great efficiency. I needed a secretary because, during the day, I worked out of my duplex penthouse surrounded by an assortment of people, often finding that my schedule had me booked almost right to the minute before I had to leave for Studio 54. On the day I interviewed Bobbie, it was at my apartment. I dictated a letter to her and she typed it perfectly. Because there were other people and employees in the reception area as well as the living room upstairs, and I wanted to speak privately with Bobbie about hours and salary, I thought nothing of moving the interview to my bedroom suite. We sat on my bed to discuss everything as there was nothing else to sit on.

Things were really different in those days. Today, if I even suggested moving an interview with a woman or a man, for any reason, to a room with a bed in it, I could be sued for sexual harassment. I'd already told Bobbie she was hired and sex with me was never a prerequisite for any position offered by me in any of my business ventures over the years, but during the course of our conversation, her demeanor became more than a bit flirty. Then she mentioned she was looking for a place to stay. I did have a guest room but it's one thing to have someone work in your house—it's quite another to have them live in it. I had to think about that.

Some women, back then and now, are comfortable with and take pleasure in using sex to get what they want. So I was not surprised, and went with the flow, when Bobbie leaned over toward me, rubbing her breasts against me. I put my arm around her and kissed her. It was slow at first—deep, explorative, sensual—but as her breathing began to quicken and my hands found their way to her breasts, I felt her hand between my legs. She had the most incredible natural breasts—perfectly well-proportioned and soft. After that, it didn't take long to get to the main event. I stripped off her clothes while she peeled me out of mine, and when I got inside of her, it was lush and heavenly. I loved it. I rolled over and thought about her being in need of a place to live and said, "Yes, you are welcome to stay in my guest room. Absolutely." It was unintentional and with no real forethought that this new arrangement would work out to be an alternative to bringing home strangers at five o'clock in the morning.

Bobbie worked as my secretary in the afternoon, and also became a part-time bartender in the VIP area at Studio 54. It was a good spot for Bobbie—it didn't demand the furiously fast pace of the main bar, thus it gave her the opportunity to experience the scene without the pressures of being in the thick of the action, service-wise. She sold some drinks, but mostly accommodated people with drink tickets, which was always a good gig for tips. She was very happy. One night when we were playing after-hours, I asked her, "Do you like other women?"

"I've tried it," she said coyly, "and I liked it."

I kept that in mind when, a few weeks later, I met Sara in the VIP area, a nice Jewish girl with a wild zaftig body type. She was rubbing against me as we talked, and I may have kissed her—the details are a little fuzzy. I do remember that it was a Friday night, because I invited her to come to my apartment the following Saturday afternoon. During the week, my place was always sheer pandemonium. Promoters, secretaries, and assistants would be running around, in and out, between noon and 8:00 p.m. Those that worked nights would then change clothes and continue on to the club. But come the weekend, both Saturday and Sunday, my apartment was off-limits. I needed a place to retreat into for some kind of down time, to recharge from the mayhem that surrounded me all week.

Anyway, Sara came over early Saturday afternoon. Bobbie was in her room on the lower level. I brought Sara upstairs to the living room, where we immediately started going at it on the couch. We were kissing and things were getting really hot, so I started undressing her. She looked at me, eyes wide, and said, "But your secretary is downstairs! What would she say?"

"Don't worry about it," I said, and continued to strip both of us naked.

I got on top of her and we had sex on the large curved couch. Being inside her was divine. I loved her curvy body and her large breasts. I loved her smell and the way she moaned.

After we were done and putting our clothes on, she told me she was looking for work. "I'll be a domestic—I'll do anything," she said. I thought it over—it wasn't an unreasonable request. I was always hiring people but still in need of additional help around the apartment with all the entertaining I was doing. Then she added that, in addition to work, she was looking for a place to live. There was an extra bed in the guest room, but first I wanted to see if she and Bobbie would get along.

"Let's go downstairs and see if Bobbie is into a threesome," I suggested.

Sara was horrified. She'd briefly met Bobbie on her way in and mistakenly perceived her to be, in her words, "high falutin," since she was an "executive secretary." But I assured her everything would be fine, and I called Bobbie on the intercom to invite her up. When Bobbie arrived, I formally introduced the two of them and we all did some coke and as an afterthought we dropped some Quaaludes. I then said to Bobbie, "Would you like to join us for a threesome?"

Lucky me—Bobbie was game.

The three of us went into my bedroom suite where I had a big Jacuzzi tub. I suggested that we all get undressed as I filled the tub, and once I got the jets going, we all hopped in. Our tub play was pretty mellow—getting acquainted in the new scenario. We then dried off in big, fluffy bathrobes and went into the bedroom, where we all climbed on my California King Bed. I ensconced myself between them and said, "Let's do it."

Bobbie then licked her fingertips, pulled her knees up, spread her legs, and said, "Let's go."

On the nights that I was flying solo, I have to say it was nice to know that I had a good, solid option waiting for me at home. Actually, they were both at the club, so sometimes we'd all hop in my limo at 5:00 a.m. and stop for gyros in Times Square. We'd fuel up with food, then fuel up with coke. It helped give us all a reboot, tired from working, drinking, and partying all night. When we arrived home we'd shower, melt into terrycloth robes, jump into my bed, have sex, and pass out. I didn't have to entertain them or call them a taxi in the morning. We'd get it on and they'd return to their room. I was grateful. It was an easy, peaceful way to end it all and surrender to sleep. I was insanely happy.

Chapter Twenty:
Roy Cohn Brings the Feds to My Door

MOVIE PREMIERE EVENTS WERE always exciting and fun to host and we did a lot of them. *Conan the Barbarian* starring Arnold Schwarzenegger was memorable. Arnold was adored by the press from the very beginning, especially after earning a Golden Globe for his role in the film *Stay Hungry* with Sally Fields and Jeff Bridges. He followed that with *Pumping Iron* costarring Lou Ferrigno. Word leaked out earlier in the week that Arnold was scheduled to be at Studio after the premiere of *Conan the Barbarian* so the club was packed to capacity. Michael O. once again created an unforgettable scene inside Studio 54 to entertain our guests and enhance the theme of the evening. The club was decorated with huge styrofoam mountains and good looking guys in loincloths walked around and Barbarian women circulated at the bar and on the dance floor. Michael O. installed several huge cages in key spots throughout the club. Inside each cage was a beautiful girl, practically naked, struggling for freedom like a caged animal.

The vibe was electric in anticipation of seeing Arnold live in the flesh. Outside, on Fifty-Fourth Street, his crowd of hardcore fans waited, hoping to see him get out of his limo. Arnold always made a point to acknowledge them. I was in my office, in my private bathroom, doing a quick hit of coke when security informed me that Arnold had arrived and was being escorted via the underground passage to my office. A few minutes later, there he was, standing in front of me, larger than life—and I mean larger than life—with Maria Shriver on his arm. They were all over each other, very affectionate. Arnold was in the mood to party and wanted to take Maria down to the dance floor. He requested that he leave his jacket in my office. "But of course," I said. They took off with security and I was left standing alone, holding a sport jacket the size of a small country.

My lawyer, Roy Cohn, asked me to host (and pay for) a birthday dinner party in his own honor. Given all that he had done for me over the years, and all that he could do to me if I got on his bad side, I of course graciously agreed. Roy invited a powerful group, including Barbara Walters (who cohosted), Donald Trump, the infamous socialite Claus von Bülow, and dozens of judges and politicians, many of whom had never been to Studio. The dinner took place on the dance floor. Everything was black, including the walls, tablecloths, napkins, balloons—the enormous gold candelabras held eighteen-inch black tapered candles. The dinner was bathed in a deep blue and purple light, accompanied by selected classical music with a few arias mixed in, making it feel like a party for a Mafia Don. It was very dramatic, and very Roy. He loved it. It was low-key in the beginning, almost somber, but after many toasts and much good wine the laughter grew louder. Moments after dessert, our tech crew quickly and silently removed the tables and chairs, replaced by our comfortable banquettes. Everyone was startled at first, but before long they were all on their feet and dancing to the spectacular music and light show.

While Roy's party was typical of many of our high-profile black-tie dinner events, the evening proved to be problematic, as a result of the enormous amount of press coverage it received. Several months later, two large, no-nonsense G-Men showed up at my apartment, flashing badges and identifying themselves as agents from the Treasury Department: "We're here to investigate" is all I heard, and I almost shit in my pants. "Yes, we're here to determine the value of Roy Cohn's dinner party with regard to his taxes and whether you intend to send him a ten ninety-nine form. He is required to declare the value as income."

I couldn't believe my ears. I invited them in and excused myself to call Roy from another room. Roy said, and I quote, "Tell them to go fuck themselves."

I smiled to myself, but unlike Roy Cohn, I was not blessed with brass balls (and besides, as shrewd a lawyer as he was, I still remembered the sight of Steve and Ian stewing in jail), so I took a more diplomatic tack. I explained to the Feds that because Studio 54 didn't advertise, it was important that we give free parties for celebrities to keep our name in the press. I then showed them numerous press clippings from Roy's birthday dinner event, including a drop in Earl Wilson's column in the *New York Post* that described Roy's birthday as having both class and comedy. Ethel Merman sang "Everything's Coming Up Roses" and Cindy's husband Joey Adams, now deceased, was hilarious as the emcee. One of his jokes was, "Roy's a good lawyer. I got a traffic ticket and he got it reduced to manslaughter." I also showed the agents the picture story in the *New York Post* that showed Roy with Claus von Bülow who had just been released on a $1-million bond following his arrest for attempting to kill his wife, Sunny. He was still making the scene at all the best parties. Luckily, my explanation appeared to convince the federal agents that it was a legitimate marketing expense and, more importantly, that I had done nothing wrong. The Feds left me alone after that, but the IRS and other federal agencies never stopped stalking Roy until the day he died on August 2, 1986, of AIDS.

The key to keeping us hot was making certain that the name Studio 54 was featured in newspapers and magazines as often as they were published. To achieve this, I gave permission to key photographers (now called paparazzi) to hang out in the club, provided they abide by the cardinal rule: *never* take a picture of a celebrity unless they had my explicit consent (or that of the celebrity). Back then, and the same holds true today: some celebrities liked being photographed, while others didn't, and some got into it only once they'd loosened up with a few drinks. We respected their wishes. Our guests felt secure enough to dance, party, and get high openly. Unflattering photos were never published, and believe me there were plenty. After a night of partying hard, some of them looked zonked out of their minds. They were never photographed in uncompromising situations either, like the night one of the world's most famous designers passed out, her face in the planter of a palm tree.

Jayne Anne Harris shared this with me: "My first night working at Studio in the coat check was spent in the smaller VIP coatroom in the back of the club by the offices, which catered to guests attending private Cut Drop Parties, entering at the stage door entrance on Fifty-Third Street. Besides checking and guarding the coats, one of my duties that night was to help the world-famous wife of a world-famous rocker, up off the stairs where she lay, passed out in her fur coat, after having a bit too much fun. I took her to the back door to where cabs were always waiting to take celebrities home. She was put in a cab and arrived home safely. The next day there was an envelope with my name on it, left with Melina Brown in the reception office, and inside was a fifty-dollar tip." No photographs. No gossip. Studio 54 was her playground.

These trusted photographers included Robin Platzer and Sonia Moscowitz of *People* magazine, John Roca, Dick Corkery of the *New York Daily News*, Felice Quinto of Associated Press, Doug Vann of *The Village Voice*, Robert Roth of UPI, Richard Manning (RPM) of the *New York Post*, Rick Bard copublisher of *Studio 54 Magazine*, a few others covering international publications, and the up-and-coming Adam Scull and Patrick McMullan.

Some parties at Studio 54 were just for fun, and in many cases word of mouth could be better than press. For instance, Michael Fesco continued his tradition of Black Parties with "A Night Aboard The Titanic." Everyone wore black—our guests and the entire staff. The balcony, bars, walls, and DJ booth were covered and wrapped in black gauze. The invitations for the evening, as well as the swizzle sticks and cocktail napkins, were emblazoned with the Cunard White Star's original logo. That's the kind of detail a master party-thrower like Michael Fesco would pay attention to. At midnight, Peter Allen appeared on the catwalk above, showering everyone on the dance floor below with a fire hose. The crowd went crazy, attempting to get under the stream. When the lavish Titanic set sank, another set opened to reveal Eartha Kitt and a six-piece orchestra. The Diva began her thirty-minute performance with "I Want To Be Evil" and then disappeared to thundering applause. There were no inhibitions at this party. As it was every Sunday at Studio 54, the writhing bodies danced all night amidst the overwhelming aroma of amyl nitrate, emanating from small canisters worn around the neck. Contrary to rumors, I cannot take credit for pumping amyl nitrate through the air conditioning ducts at Studio.

Marci Klein celebrated her sweet sixteen at Studio 54. The details were overseen by Ian Schrager, and much of the design was a collaboration between florist Robert Isabell and our General Manager Michael Overington. Each of Marci's dinner guests received an invitation, hand delivered by one of our very good-looking employees working in the Studio 54 Mailroom. They each arrived wearing a white tuxedo and were driven to their destinations by limousine. The invite was a clear plexiglass box with "Marci" printed on the outside and inside were sixteen white candles.

Marci's guests entered through the main entrance on Fifty-Fourth Street hours before we opened to the public. When they stepped inside they saw six gorgeous guys dressed in tuxedos, seated at and playing six white baby grand pianos, lined up one after another down the grand entrance hall. Upon entering the main room and to the delight of Marci and her guests, they were treated to a vision of seven-foot-high birthday candles lighting up each of our twelve-foot-long banquettes, which were wrapped like giant birthday packages in huge swaths of ribbon and enormous four-foot bows. Everywhere, except the dance floor, guests walked through thousands of gift bows—the kind you peel off the self-adhesive backing and put on a present. Guests were sticking them on their faces, all over their clothes, and all over each other. The dance floor was set up with dinner tables, draped in white and illuminated from underneath. It was gorgeous. Upon arrival at 5:00 p.m. the bartenders, busboys, and waitstaff were taken out the back stage door entrance to an eighteen-wheeler truck, the inside of which had been transformed into a makeup studio. The makeup artists did their thing on each of them—they then changed into white tuxedo shirts and ties. It was all very dramatic. After dinner and some time around 11:00 p.m., the mirrored mylar back walls parted, and thirty female dancers in top hats and tails performed, like a Busby Berkeley musical, on a steep plexiglass staircase. It was so over the top. Marci's guests watched in wonder as Marci and her father, Calvin Klein, appeared on the staircase above the dancers and descended down the steps together. One thousand friends and acquaintances sang "Happy Birthday" as tons and tons of white sparkling confetti rained down twelve-inches deep and hundreds of balloons floated around from above. It was wild—and then the dancing began. It was breathtakingly beautiful, dramatic, and a very sweet sixteen birthday party. Earlier in the week, bartender L. J. Kirby asked Calvin Klein, "What are you going to give Marci for her birthday?" Calvin smiled and replied, "A party she will never forget." Marci went on to become a senior producer at *Saturday Night Live* and then an executive producer at NBC's *30 Rock,* winning four Emmy Awards for her work on both.

Sometimes, a celebrity would insist upon a dinner being served in their honor at my penthouse before their party at Studio 54, and rightfully so, if we were going to use their name to garner publicity. Typically, I would host one or two of these dinner parties every month, ordering cases of expensive champagne from the club. This became a source of irritation for my budget-conscious partner, Stanley Tate. Even though he was probably enticed into the Studio 54 deal because of the celebrities and glamour of it all, he never stopped kvetching about my spending on celebrity-driven events. In spite of the fact that I usually prepared the modest buffets myself to both keep costs down and to personalize it, Stanley still objected. My guests enjoyed these parties immensely, but Stanley pointed out that the costs for the good champagne, food, and cocaine were mounting. I responded, "So is our gross." Events such as these were a significant part of our marketing budget, as we did no advertising, not even a listing in the Nightclub section of *New York* magazine, like many other venues did.

I pointed out to Stanley that Steve and Ian actually paid cash to PR people who delivered celebrities to Studio 54. I had read the Henry Post article in *Esquire* a few years earlier that confirmed Steve had secured stars using a sliding scale. Publicist Joanne Horowitz was quoted as saying, "Cher and Sylvester Stallone are one hundred dollars each, Alice Cooper is less, but Stevie gives me more if it makes the papers." They provided unlimited amounts of cocaine and Quaaludes for the private VIP parties, a practice I continued, though not as openly, not in the basement, and not with as much coke. While I always tried to placate Stanley by keeping the costs of the food, beverages, and cocaine down, I never thought twice about spending money on celebrity events, because I knew that the name value of A-list or even several B-list stars was always good for business.

Stanley was a numbers-man by nature, and even though the sales numbers proved me correct, he couldn't accept the fact that my methods to attract and maintain our relationship with celebrities and the press were responsible for Studio 54 making money. It was a constant battle. However, he loved beautiful women and made exceptions for his favorites. Whenever Liliane Montevecchi walked into the club, Stanley was all eyes and served her and her guests our best champagne, on the house. He was crazy about her. And whenever Elizabeth Taylor was our guest he could not have been more charming, always offering her and her guests Dom Perignon. He had met Elizabeth previously, when she was the wife of Senator John Warner, at one of the many social events he attended in Washington, DC.

Sweet and irresistible with a fresh and natural all-American look describes supermodel, Shaun Casey. She graced the covers of *Harper's Bazaar* and *Glamour* many times. She was one of Calvin Klein's first models and the Estee Lauder girl from 1979 to 1984. Stanley was crazy about Shaun Casey and enjoyed being in her presence; she enjoyed conversation with him as well. He was a very good-looking, successful businessman, always impeccably dressed in a suit and tie; he'd travelled the world and lived an interesting life. One night Shaun walked into the club with some girlfriends and Stanley spotted them at the main bar. Shaun introduced Stanley to her friends and Stanley then said to L. J. Kirby, "Champagne please for Shaun and her friends."

Shaun then put her hand on Stanley's shoulder and very sweetly said, "Thank you Stanley...but not the cheap shit. I'd rather pay for the good stuff myself."

Stanley laughed and said, "L. J., a bottle of Dom Perignon for the ladies' please."

Stanley reminded me of my father, who likewise never understood many of the marketing decisions I made. The conflict with Stanley over my so-called "extravagant" spending reached a point where he actually asked my father to help keep me in line. I never knew about this until just a few years ago, when I interviewed Stanley in Miami for this memoir. He told me how distressed my father was, seeing me so out of control—a meshuggener (crazy), not just about reckless spending, but so deeply involved with drugs and alcohol. It saddened me to hear that, because the truth is, I did give my father tsuris (trouble), as he would put it in Yiddish, instead of nachas (joy).

Convinced that I was on a roll, stubbornly, I wouldn't listen to any of Stanley's arguments, which caused a rift between us over the years. Even when actors with the stature of the great Peter O'Toole were on the receiving end of my largesse, it was an issue with Stanley. Peter was attending a cocktail party at my penthouse one evening when he discreetly found his way into my bedroom, just as I was separating the pure cocaine from the not-so-pure. I heard someone enter, looked up and saw a tall man with flashing blue eyes. Before even saying hello, he politely asked me in his refined English accent, "May I have some?" Should I have said, "Oh, hello Lawrence of Arabia, I am the new owner of Studio 54, no you may not have some of this very expensive coke because my partner believes that celebrities like you are not worth it— even though Studio is going to get a shitload of press tomorrow thanks to you hangin' with us tonight?" Peter and I got high and partied through dinner, then into my limo and on to Studio for hours. "Peter O'Toole at Studio 54" hit the newspapers the following morning, capturing the attention of all. Peter was so interesting and sweet and had an outrageous sense of humor. We had a lot of laughs that night. It was a great honor to host him at Studio.

Christopher Atkins, an up-and-coming actor who had just starred in *The Blue Lagoon* with Brooke Shields, often attended parties at my home and soon became a real drinking and drugging buddy of mine. Studio 54's male bartenders and female staff all had crushes on him—two of which claim to have spent one glorious night with him in a threesome they will never forget. He was a wild man, and then he had the good sense to give it all up and has been sober ever since.

Robert Duvall was at one party and I remember him and Tanya Tucker deep in conversation for the entire evening. Robert wanted to know everything there was to know about life as a country and western star before filming began on his movie *Tender Mercies*. Tanya must have given him some great insight into his character because Robert Duvall went on to win the Oscar for Best Actor at the Academy Awards in 1984.

While reviewing issues of various *Studio 54 Magazines*, I came across a blurb about a dinner party at my penthouse I had completely forgotten about. It was for Clive Davis, who had recently published his memoir, *The Soundtrack of My Life*. The magazine went on to say:

> *Key figures in both the film and music business gathered at Mark Fleischman's Manhattan home to honor Clive Davis, the legendary music figure who helped launch the rock era, signing Janis Joplin, Jimi Hendrix, Billy Joel, Santana, Aerosmith, Chicago, and many others... The party went on to a resplendently turned out Studio 54 and the performance of one of Clive's new groups, 'A Flock of Seagulls.'*

In the last chapter of his memoir, Clive tells the story about his first gay sexual experience with a man he met at Studio 54. Studio 54 was liberating to many.

The dinner parties held in my apartment often culminated with a quick ride to Studio 54 in a big yellow school bus, arranged by a friend of Carmen D'Alessio, where the party would continue on. Ahmet Ertegun did the same, years earlier, picking up friends and taking them down to The Peppermint Lounge in a big yellow school bus to twist the night away. Our guests loved every minute of the ride to Studio. We usually made the morning papers after one of these celebrity events. My ideas were in place and working. We were attracting the right people and the right press; people were paying to get in and

I was having the best sex ever. I know I was burning it at both ends but I was having so much fun. I was dancing and getting high with people I had always wanted to meet and here they were in my club, hanging in my office till six in the morning, telling me *their* stories. I was spending a shitload of Studio 54's money on drugs for these people but the truth is, not all of them were worth it to Studio in press value—but hearing their stories was worth it to me. Some were totally full of shit—unknown, hangers-on—unaccomplished leeches. But they were attractive, well-mannered, and cultured characters—essential to the *magic* that was Studio 54. I rationalized, justified, and defended my behavior to myself and to my partner, Stanley.

The positive and negative effects of Studio 54 were a part of the nightly offering. Both played with the psyche. Some people were attracted to the positive. I embraced the path promising the wild and kinky. I fueled my journey with cocaine, alcohol, Quaaludes, and any other exotic combination of drugs I could get my hands on. Had I been given the chance to go back to the night I reopened Studio 54 and do it differently I would have shouted "No way, I'm having too much fun!"

Chapter Twenty-One:
Studio 54 Magazine

I N EARLY 1983, I introduced *Studio 54 Magazine*. Rick Bard, who published a nightlife magazine in New York, approached me with the very creative concept, suggesting that advertisers would be interested in placing ads with a magazine that used Studio 54 as its hook, rather than just focusing on generic nightlife as a whole. He was right—the advertisers loved it. The magazine always opened with great stories, gossip columns, and nightlife pictures. There was even a Mark After Dark gossip column, which I cowrote with Rick. Parts of the magazine are reproduced at the end of this chapter.

Rick, a creative publisher/photographer/writer who held a BA from MIT and an MBA from Harvard, had the idea of having each issue feature a celebrity guest host that I was to secure to act as a concierge into the world depicted on the pages of the magazine, and it worked. He now publishes the successful *Manhattan Brides* magazine.

Each issue would open with the host sharing their greeting, and the two I remember most clearly were Morgan Fairchild and Peter Allen. When Peter was the magazine's host in 1982, he said, "You'd think New Yorkers would be so tired after getting through a New York–day that they would just want to go home to pass out for tomorrow. So how come Calvin, Halston, Liza, Patti, and so many other New Yorkers stay up all night and still make millions the next day? It's because it's just more fun to go out than to stay in. I like Studio 54 because they give me free champagne. My favorite bartender is Paul. He keeps promising to take me up in his plane. I always promise to play tennis with him. What I like most about Studio 54 is you can go there and be quiet—sometimes the most interesting people are in the offices—or you can go there and be wild."

Meanwhile, when Morgan Fairchild hosted the magazine in 1983, she opened the magazine with, "New Yorkers are always celebrating, having fun, and going out all night. In New York I always get into trouble because I stay out until all hours. In California, I never do. As a dance maniac, I especially love New York because it's the center of the world for modern dance and ballet. I love to dance all night, which I can't do in California because it shuts down so early. So it's always fun to go to Studio and let myself go. The music, the nonstop excitement, and interesting people make me feel great, and Mark always gives me such a warm welcome. It's like a house party."

The magazine created a community, and people loved it. They were in the pictures, they saw themselves being photographed with celebrities, and they saw their life and culture reflected in a magazine that was made just for them. It became incredibly popular.

The following is taken from the July/August 1982 Issue of *Studio 54 Magazine* with Peter Allen on the cover and our guest host for that issue.

There were also gossip columns and here are a few quotes from Rick Bard's Midnight column:

Music...

In our last issue Peter Allen talked about possibly doing a play with Bob Fosse. Now it's definite. The two are scheduled to start collaborating after Bob finishes work on "Star 80," the film biography of Playmate Dorothy Stratten, starring Mariel Hemingway and Eric Roberts.

David Bowie's MGM/UA film "The Hunger" is scheduled for February 1983 release. He costars with Susan Sarandon and Catherine Deneuve. David—now in Switzerland cutting his next album—also begins his first tour in six years once the album is completed. The tour will take him to all corners of the world, but not before he lends his support to the January 31 fund raiser at Studio 54: Abbie Hoffman's "Save the Rivers Ball", aimed at cleaning up the Hudson, the St. Lawrence, and other rivers. Among other friends also lending their support are Dick Cavett, Mia Farrow, Harry Belafonte, Jack Nicholson, Susan Sarandon, Joseph Papp, Joan Rivers, and Dan Aykroyd.

Studio After Hours... Sometimes Studio 54 shines brightest during the day. The Studio recently became a job clearing house from 9:00 a.m. to 4:00 p.m. as Vietnam Vets got together with prospective employers at an event attended by Mayor Ed Koch who quoted from his Veteran's Day speech: "We are establishing in New York City a memorial for Vietnam Veterans. One part of it is stone, and the other is a living memorial. And the best living memorial for these veterans is a job."

Tinkerbelle was a regular contributor to Andy Warhol's *Interview* magazine in the early 1970s and *Studio 54 Magazine* in the 1980s. Tinkerbelle's Party Lines was another gossip column that went like this:

Party Rap Up... Just in case Carmen D'Alessio is wondering where all those presents come from, Carmen, Dear, you had a birthday party at Studio. Remember? The party was hosted by Lester Persky (escorting Valerie Perrine) and Mark Fleischman who started the evening with cocktails at Lester's magnificent Central Park penthouse, continuing to Mark's brother Alan's Tennessee Mountain Restaurant in Soho for a dinner of ribs, chicken, and chili... Carmen always had soul.

People are still talking about the Peter Allen party. Studio's interior was transformed into a festive Mexican Village with the food catered by Caramba, which is hailed as one of the best restaurants in town, and just opened Caramba II.

Also in swerving abundance were Tequila sunrises served, not shaken, by 54's drop-dead bartenders who always seem so less available than their beverages. Well, why ask for the moon when you can have a tequila sunrise?

Photos from several of the 1982 and 1983 issues of *Studio 54 Magazine*, hosted by Peter Allen and Morgan Fairchild, which I am providing with Rick Bard's permission:

6

7

1

Photos left to right: Rick and Kathy Hilton; Christie Brinkley and Olivier Chandon; me, Elsa Martinelli, and Christiana Martinelli; Tony Danza, Cathy St. George, and Rick Bard; Farrah Fawcett and Ryan O'Neal.

2

Photos left to right: Marci and Calvin Klein; Olivier Chandon, Christie Brinkley, and Chris Atkins; Bianca Jagger;
Jenny Lumet and Timothy Hutton; Maria Floria Miller and Carter Cooper.

Photos left to right: Chris Barker, Arlene Dahl, and Pierre Cardin; New York Governor Hugh Carey; Laurente Giorgio and Olivier de Montal; Anthony Quinn; Carolina Herrera; Brooke Shields and Valentino; Evangeline Gouletas-Carey; Ivana and Donald Trump.

Photos left to right: Massimo Gargia and Francine Crescent (French Vogue Editor); Yanet Cuevas; Susan Blonde; Gloria Gaynor and Ahmet Ertegun (Atlantic Records Chairman); Toni De Marco and Halston; Sherry Slonim.

5

Photos left to right: Me, Lorna Luft, George Martin, and Ron Wood; George Stamas and Slim Mellon; Diane and Egon von Fürstenberg; Jaques Morali and Harold Stanegl; Geoffrey Holder; Mimi and Jerry Rubin; Stanley Tate and Laurie Lister; Givenchy.

6

Photos left to right: Denise Gentile, Ty Smith, Brigid Nunez, Nigel, Sue Charney, and Collin Bernsen; Gwynne Rivers and Mick Jagger; Genie Francis; Audrey Landers (Dallas); Larissa and Thierry Mugler; Lester Persky, me, and George Martin in his Dawn Patrol jacket.

7

Photos left to right: Mr. and Mrs. Nick Nolte; DeDe Ryan, George Paul Rosell, and Eve Orton; Britt Ekland; Iman and John Casablancas; Betsy Gonzales, Clovis Ruffin, and Phyllis Hyman; Nona Hendryx, Peter Allen, and Patti Labelle; Peter Allen and Ellen Greene; Andrew Stein.

8

Photos left to right: Penthouse Pets; Debi Monahan; Jacqueline Bisset and Alex Godunov; Patty Oja and Jerry Brandt (owner of the Ritz); Cathy St. George (current Playboy Playmate) and Shay Knuth (former Playmate); Raquel Welch.

9

Photos left to right: Jack Lemmon; Farrah Fawcett; Carmen D'Allessio and Andy Warhol; Luis Malle and Candice Bergen; Tony Curtis; K. Smith, Baroness P. Von Karkoch, Debbie Dickinson, and Pamela Cooper; Suzy Chaffee; Patti Hansen and me.

Photos left to right: Pamela Palmedo, Stacey Purchase, and Susan Dalton; Andy Gibb; Cher dancing with Liza Minelli; Shelley Tupper; Pat Cleveland.

11

Photos left to right: Jamie Lee Curtis; me, Cathy St. George, Cornelia Guest, and Lester Persky; Josy Nowack and Debbie Leitner; Mario, Maria, Megan, and Melvin Van Peebles; Arnold Schwarzenegger and Maria Shriver; Tony Danza, Cathy St. George, and Rick Bard.

Studio 54 Bartenders—Sal DeFalco did more interviews about Studio 54 than any other bartender.
Top row, left to right: John Bello, Scott Baird, Dave Burns, and L. J. Kirby.
Bottom row, left to right: Sal DeFalco, Randy Kelly (middle right), and Dave Dickerson.

Chapter Twenty-Two:
Scandal Hits Studio 54

W E WERE ALWAYS PUSHING the envelope to create unique event concepts that would garner the press we needed to sustain the paying customers necessary to cover the cost of the celebrity hosts, their friends, and the drinks and drugs it took to keep them happy. It was a party train—get onboard. The pressure was on to outdo the other large clubs that were opening in Manhattan, like The Red Parrot, Limelight, and, more significantly, Area. When we were running low on ideas, we came up with a new, never-before-celebrated category— "Scandal" parties. Until then, people involved in scandals weren't celebrated as they are today; some hid in shameful isolation. Studio 54 changed all that in the 1980s. The most memorable of the "Scandalized" parties we hosted were for the Mayflower Madam Sydney Biddle Barrows and Rita Jenrette.

The Mayflower Madam became infamous when her high-end escort business was busted in 1984. Cachet, as it was called, focused on delivering classy prostitutes to the wealthy and powerful. Though she opened under the pseudonym Sheila Devin, *New York Post* reporter Peter Fearon discovered Sydney's true identity, including the fact that she came from an upper-crust family—descendants of passengers on the Mayflower, hence her nickname the Mayflower Madam. Sydney was a beautiful woman and unique in that she managed to exist in the middle of the firestorm of one of the biggest sex scandals ever to hit New York City, without an iota of remorse or shame. Her attitude inspired our "Scandal" parties and paved the way for the "fifteen-minutes of shame" scandalized people enjoy today. Sydney is currently a management consultant and writer with several successful books in publication.

Rita Jenrette was our guest of honor at another Studio 54 "Scandal" party. Rita was a winning combination of beauty and brains. She was a model for

Clairol Inc., and then in 1973 she became director of research for the Republican Party of Texas. In 1976 she married US Congressman John Jenrette of South Carolina. The film *American Hustle* is based on the ABSCAM scandal of 1980 in which Congressman Jenrette is depicted as having been convicted of taking a bribe in an FBI undercover operation, investigating the trafficking of stolen property. It ultimately led to the conviction of a US Senator, five members of the House of Representatives, and other city, state, and INS officials. Paulie Herman, a frequent guest at Studio 54 and the host of Columbus Restaurant, played the part of Robert De Niro's attorney in the film.

During the investigation, Rita turned on her husband, talked to the media, posed for *Playboy*, and alerted authorities to the $25,000 in cash she found in her husband's closet—telling them it was the ABSCAM money. Rita courted publicity. She announced she was seeking a divorce and began to disclose the salacious details of her sex life with her former husband—specifically the time they had made love on the steps of the US Capitol. Rita was thrilled to be the guest of honor at one of Studio 54's Scandal parties. She was appearing on stage in *The Philadelphia Story* and a huge crowd came out to meet her in New York. Rita moved on to become a successful author, on-air personality, and real estate agent. She is currently married to Prince Nicolò Boncompagni Ludovisi of the Italian province of Piombino.

Once I was in the driver's seat at Studio 54, I had to regularly come up with quality celebrity events that would guarantee the press we needed, keep our regular guests coming out during the week, and attract new people to the club. Every morning the four-page Celebrity Bulletin from Celebrity Service was placed on each of our desks. It was the first thing we looked at when starting our business day. We scoured it, then hit the phones, networking within our individual areas of expertise. Our survival depended on it. It was our Bible.

In 1939, Earl Blackwell, a Southern gentleman and impresario to the stars, founded the very lucrative New York-based Celebrity Service, an information and research service which reports on the comings and goings of celebrities in the arts, politics, sports, and business. Celebrity Bulletin was delivered to us five days a week, providing us with such valuable information as: which celebrities were coming to town that day, the reason for their visit, which hotel they were staying at, and their contact information. Bill Murray was our contact at Celebrity Service. He is a good and kind man, who was great to work with and never missed a good party.

The following pages of Celebrity Bulletin have been reprinted from the archives of Celebrity Service, illustrating why it was so crucial to our success in planning many of our events.

THE   NEW YORK EDITION

CELEBRITY BULLETIN

PUBLISHED DAILY • 171 W. 57th ST. • NEW YORK, N.Y. 10019 • 212-PL 7-7979

NEW YORK ARRIVALS:
ELIZABETH TAYLOR

TUESDAY, MAY 25, 1982.
arrives the 1st week of July from London after completing her limited engagement in "The Little Foxes;" remains here for conferences regarding The Elizabeth Taylor Repertory Company with co-producer ZEV BUFMAN. PR: Chen Sam & Assoc.(Dolph Browning), 628 5915. Agt: The Lantz Office, 586 0220.

RICHARD GERE

, whose new Paramount Pictures film "An Officer & A Gentleman" opens July 30, has returned from West Coast meetings and conferences. Agt: Wm. Morris(Johnnie Planco), JU6 5100. PR: P/M/K(Catherine Olim), 759 5202. PR Con(Par.): Tamara Rawitt, 333 4902.

JOHN DENVER

arrives from his major-city concert tour to appear on 6/2 @ Meadowlands & 6/3 @ Nassau Coliseum. PR: Rogers & Cowan(Joe Dera), 490 8200. PR Con(RCA): Barbara Pepe, 930 4000.

THE   NEW YORK EDITION

CELEBRITY BULLETIN

PUBLISHED DAILY • 171 W. 57th ST. • NEW YORK, N.Y. 10019 • 212-PL 7-7979

EARL BLACKWELL
President

NEW YORK ARRIVALS:
AUDREY HEPBURN

THURSDAY, MAY 6, 1982.
arrives 5/8 from Europe to be one of the fashion models at the Fashion Institute of Technology's gala benefit on 5/10 honoring HUBERT DE GIVENCHY with a 30 year retrospective of the designer's couture fashions. At the Pierre. PR Con(F.I.T.): John Latham, 760 7614. Agt: Kurt Frings, (213) 274 8881.

PETER O'TOOLE

has returned from Mexico vacation; in town for an indefinite period for meetings and project conferences. At the Plaza. Agt: Wm. Morris(Carmen LaVia), JU6 5100.

THE — NEW YORK EDITION

CELEBRITY BULLETIN

PUBLISHED DAILY • 171 W. 57th ST. • NEW YORK, N.Y. 10019 • 212-PL 7-7979

CELEBRITY
INFORMATION
AND RESEARCH
SERVICE
INC.

EARL BLACKWELL
President

NEW YORK ARRIVALS:

MONDAY-TUESDAY, MAY 31-JUNE 1, 1982.

LIV ULLMANN
arrives 6/12 from Norway to begin rehearsals for a new production of Ibsen's "Ghosts" w/JOHN NEVILLE which the Kennedy Center will present at the Eisenhower Theatre beginning on 7/12 prior to Broadway. PR: John Springer Assoc., 421 6720. Agt: The Lantz Office, 586 0200.

WARREN BEATTY
has returned from Paris & European visit. At the Carlyle. Agt: Wm. Morris(Stan Kamen) (213) CR4 7451. PR: Rogers & Cowan(Pat Newcomb), 490 8200.

LINDA RONSTADT
arrives to perform at a special concert for Nuclear Disarmament on 6/9 & 6/10 @ Nassau Coliseum. PR: Mahoney/Wasserman(Geraldine McInnerny), 751 2060. PR Con(concert): David Fenton Communications, 489 5630.

JOHN CARPENTER
, director of Universal Pictures' "The Thing" starring KURT RUSSELL, arrives 6/6 from Los Angeles for a few days of interviews and promotional activities for the Turman-Foster Company prod. which opens 6/25; in town thru 6/12. PR Con(film): P/M/K(Michele Smith), 759 5202. PR Con(Universal): Suzanne Salter, 759 7500.

THE — NEW YORK EDITION

CELEBRITY BULLETIN

PUBLISHED DAILY • 171 W. 57th ST. • NEW YORK, N.Y. 10019 • 212-PL 7-7979

CELEBRITY
INFORMATION
AND RESEARCH
SERVICE
INC.

EARL BLACKWELL
President

NEW YORK ARRIVALS:

MONDAY, JUNE 21, 1982.

JOHN TRAVOLTA
has arrived from the West Coast for a brief visit for meetings and conferences. At the United Nations Plaza Hotel. Agt: Creative Artists Agency, (213) 277 4545. PR: M/S Billings Publicity, Ltd., 581 4493.

RYAN O'NEAL
has arrived from Los Angeles for a private visit; here thru 6/21. At the Pierre. Agt: ICM(Sue Mengers), (213) 550 4000.

KURT RUSSELL
arrives 6/21 from L.A. for interviews to promote his starring role in JOHN CARPENTER's "The Thing." The Universal Pictures film opens here on 6/25. PR Con(film): P/M/K (Michele Smith), 759 5202. Agt: Wm. Morris (Ed Bondy), (213) CR4 7451. PR Con(Univ.): Suzanne Salter, 759 7500.

FARRAH FAWCETT
has arrived from the West Coast for a personal visit. At the Pierre. Agt: ICM(Sue Mengers),

MATT DILLON
has returned to town after completing a major city promotional tour for his new Walt Disney Productions film "Tex;" remains here for interviews & tv appearances. PR Con (Tex): Nancy Seltzer & Assoc., 593 3352. Mgr: Vic Ramos, 473 2610.

Nobody was better at booking events at Studio 54 than Michael Redwine. He was a valued member of my staff, booking many of our most successful nights, garnering great press, paid admissions, and bar action. The following four parties were just a few of the events produced by Michael in 1983.

We hosted many parties in celebration of movie premieres and one of my personal favorites was the night we honored Anthony Perkins and the 1983 release of *Psycho II*. Perkins attended with his beautiful wife Berry Berenson and cast members Meg Tilly, Robert Loggia, and Vera Miles who appeared in Hitchcock's original Psycho as well as in *Psycho II*. Michael O. set up twenty bathtubs in the entrance hall, complete with shower curtains and water, to create the famous shower scene from the original *Psycho*. Instead of Janet Leigh behind each curtain, our guests found a scantily clad male or female model. Perkins declared it to be "the most incredible party ever given to launch a movie"—a sentiment echoed by many of the guests that night. The list included such luminaries as composer and former conductor of The New York Symphony Orchestra—Leonard Bernstein, Patricia Kennedy Lawford, Ursula Andress, Arianna Stassinopoulos, jewelry designer Kenneth Jay Lane, New York Mayor Ed Koch (who in the past had been against Studio reopening), and his famous commissioner of cultural affairs, Bess Myerson, the former Miss America of 1945.

"Tony Award Winning Actor Michael Moriarty Invites You To Celebrate Raquel Welch in *Woman of the Year*" is how the invitation read. This night was one of my favorites for the obvious reason that I got to hang out with and look at Raquel Welch all night. Hosting her party at Studio 54 was a truly memorable experience. She was so sweet, inviting me to see her performance in *Woman of the Year* as her guest. I went and she blew me away. I had seen Lauren Bacall in the production and she was wonderful, but Raquel took it to another level of enjoyment. I had never heard catcalls in a Broadway theater before—but she brought the unthinkable out in men. Her costumes did justice to her magnificent body and, just in case you haven't heard, she can really sing and dance, kicking those beautiful legs sky-high. The crowd at Studio went wild upon her arrival.

"*Playboy Magazine* Invites You To Celebrate the Thirtieth Anniversary Playmate Search and Debut of 1983's PLAYMATE of the Year—Marianne Gravatte." She was Playmate of the Month in the October 1982 Issue and then Playmate of the Year in 1983. She was so hot and so was Studio 54. As usual on nights like this, we were packed. Hundreds of guys came out for Playboy Parties and so did hundreds of girls, wanting to be where the guys were that night. It was always a fun crowd. Once again the overflow of people stopped traffic on Fifty-Fourth Street. As much as I appreciate beautiful women, I spent most of that night in my office getting high with Don Cornelius and James Brown, determined to get a commitment from Don to do a monthly broadcast of *Soul Train LIVE from Studio 54,* and I wanted to lock in a date for a James Brown concert. At one point, Robin Williams joined us, and the interplay between Robin and the Godfather of Soul was unforgettable. Robin danced and sang, doing a manic impersonation of James Brown, for James Brown. I only wished I'd had the means to record it.

Around 3:00 a.m., after James and Don left, I decided to head up to the Rubber Room. The Rubber Room was not a room at all but the third-tier balcony of The Gallo Opera House, now Studio 54. It was seventy-five feet above it all, offering an unobstructed view of the dance floor and all of the goings-on below. The walls, ceiling, bar, and rubberized floor covering were all black. The two black leather banquettes and a small bar area made it very intimate. I felt like relaxing on one of the banquettes so I climbed the stairs with Luciana, a very tall, stunning, short-haired Italian brunette I had just met on the dance floor a few minutes earlier.

When we reached the Rubber Room I immediately caught a whiff of amyl nitrate and then my eyes took it all in. At least twenty-five to thirty very hot, scantily clad young ladies wearing bustiers and lingerie were dancing and moving to the beat of "Feel the Need In Me" by The Detroit Emeralds.

I recognized some of the girls from Tropicalia, a club I went to several times with Frankie Crocker before I bought Studio 54. It was on the Upper East Side, a cool little spot, with lots of mirrors, and a good DJ—Jay Negron. Frankie knew him and introduced us. He played some smokin' hot dance music with some Latin stuff mixed in that I really liked. It was a hangout for some very attractive Pan Am stewardesses who liked to dance. They were a wild bunch—most of them were German and accustomed to playing around in the nightclubs of Berlin. There were four or five guys, I think they might have been stewards, dancing together—doing poppers. I spotted a small plate of Quaaludes and another plate of coke on top of the bar. Leroy was already into my playlist for the late-night crowd and when he dropped the needle on The Gap Band's "Party Train," the girls went into overdrive. High heels, thigh-high boots, and one or two whips caught my eye. One of the busboys informed me that the girls had arranged it all in advance with Shay Knuth in Catering, ordering twenty bottles of Dom Perignon and several bottles of tequila with sides. The girls had arrived at 2:00 a.m. and requested the bartender not hang around but return every so often to check on the chilled champagne. It was a birthday party and the birthday girl was a big fan of Helmut Newton—which explained everything.

Two of the hottest redheads wearing some sort of matching military garb were pleasuring each other on one of the banquettes. Sitting across from them was the only girl in the room wearing a long dress and on the floor in front of her, under a lot of black velvet, was a guy bobbing his head rhythmically between her legs. I had to laugh because some people never found their way up here—it was perceived as being too far from the dance floor and the main bar, where people thought all the action to be. But as regulars to Studio 54 knew, anything could happen in the Rubber Room—and it usually did. As Grace Jones described it in her recently published book *I'll Never Write My Memoirs*, "It had walls that could be easily wiped down after all the powdery activity that went on. It was a place of secrets and secretions, the in-crowd and inhalations, sucking and snorting."

A few girls were snapping cat o' nine tails, grinding and teasing on each other. One girl wearing nothing more than a tutu, heels, and suspenders danced over to us and grabbed Luciana behind the head and kissed her on the mouth—deeply. Luciana grabbed the girl under her tutu and moved her against the wall. The girl began to writhe under Luciana's touch. I moved over and away. I could tell that they were all really high on Quaaludes, coke, and poppers. The redheads on the banquette were now up and dancing and in their place was a girl licking and sucking the nipples of another while pleasuring herself, and a third girl was spooning coke up their noses. Two girls were standing at the bar pouring champagne on their breasts inviting the others to lick it off. One very big girl was attempting to pleasure herself with the neck of a champagne bottle…and then I saw *him*…there in the middle of it all was the one and only Dudley Moore…laughing his ass off and grooving to the beat. He was feeling no pain, loving every minute of the attention he was getting from the girls surrounding him.

I'd been introduced to Dudley earlier in the evening at the main bar. He was fascinated by Studio 54 and all the sexual possibilities it presented. I didn't know how he ended up in the Rubber Room in the middle of this wild scene but I was happy for him. I was out of coke and didn't want to disappoint so I decided to leave and head back downstairs to my office. Years later in 2002, I was in my car when I heard that Dudley Moore had passed away. Whenever I think of him or see one of his films, in which he was always so brilliant, I remember that night at Studio 54 and I smile. It was so Dudley. In 1983 he did an interview with *Playboy* in which he said, "I think sex is the most important part of anybody's life. What else is there to live for? Chinese food and women. There is nothing else."

Jack Hofsiss and Patti LuPone hosted a benefit for the Laura Dean Dancers and Musicians. That night was another memorable one for me because I was fortunate enough to meet and talk with some of the most creative forces in the music industry, all of whom showed up that evening to support the outstanding talents and contributions to the world of dance by Laura Dean. Laura is a dancer/choreographer having choreographed many ballets, eight of which were for The Joffrey Ballet. She often says that she wears two hats in the world of dance. The dance moves that she created for ballet were derived from her classical ballet training with such greats as Peter Martins of The New York City Ballet. Her creations for The Laura Dean Dancers and Musicians, the foot stomping and twirling arm movement, were derived from her childhood and early dance experience in San Francisco. She composed much of the music for her dance company.

Peter Gabriel, founding member of the group Genesis, a pioneer in sound technology, and the genius behind the cymbal-less drum kit—the sound used by Phil Collins on the brilliant and beautiful "In The Air Tonight"—was in attendance to the delight of the Studio crowd. Peter had a monster-size radio and MTV hit at the time, "Shock The Monkey," his first Top 40 hit in America after leaving Genesis. Laura worked with David Bowie as well, creating the movement for his *Scary Monsters* video in 1981, and with Peter Gabriel on staging and movement for his 1983 tour. John Travolta, David Bowie, Andy Warhol, Richard Gere, Mary McFadden, Melissa Gilbert, and *Interview Magazine's* Bob Colacello were all in attendance, making donations and showing support for Laura. Richard Gere partied hard that night, hanging in the office till the end, along with Keith Richards and Phil Collins. Phil loved the energy of the club that night and we talked about a video shoot at Studio 54 for his next single, "I Don't Care Anymore" on Atlantic Records, but it never came to be.

Hosting a party for the cast of characters on *Saturday Night Live* was always a lot of fun. We never knew what to expect. One great party was in celebration of the film *48 Hrs.* which had been released a few days before, starring Nick Nolte and Eddie Murphy. The musical guest for the *SNL* show that evening was Lionel Richie and the host was Nick Nolte. I heard that Nick showed up for rehearsals on Saturday afternoon and threw up all over Eddie. Nick was too sick to go on after partying with me the night before at Studio, so it was decided that Eddie Murphy would step in and host, the first time ever an active member of the *SNL* cast had been given the honor of hosting the show. The show was a huge success from the opening monologue when Eddie said "and LIVE from New York it's the Eddie Murphy Show." Supposedly that pissed some people off. The *SNL* parties were always very private, with invitations going to cast members and their personally invited guests only. They liked to unwind after a grueling week of preparation for the show, which has always been performed in front of a live audience. We reserved the Rubber Room for them, which they appreciated, and we agreed once again to let them use the fire escape on Fifty-Third Street to enter the club. They requested that it be specified on the invitation. It was insane—watching them climb the five stories up to the Rubber Room on an outdoor fire escape, but they loved it. They were all such children—they loved doing the unexpected and naughty. Joe Piscopo, Julia Louis-Dreyfus, Brad Hall, Clint Smith, Eddie Murphy, Lionel Richie, the *SNL* crew, and all their invited friends did their thing that night after the show in the Rubber Room. Nick Nolte has had his ups and downs since Studio but has always managed to land on his feet and do really good work as an actor. In 2017, Nick earned a Golden Globe (Best Actor) nomination, for his work on the 2016 TV series *Graves*.

JUST WHEN YOU THOUGHT IT WAS SAFE TO GO OUT ON SATURDAY NIGHT, IT'S...

SATURDAY NIGHT LIVE

Nick Nolte, Lionel Ritchie,
&
the cast of Saturday Night Live
request the pleasure
of your company at their

Christmas Party

Saturday, December 11, 1 am

Studio 54
Fire Escape Entrance (229 W. 53rd)

Complimentary admission for two with this invitation.

Nick Nolte got so high partying with me the night before at Studio, he threw up all over Eddie Murphy the following day at the SNL rehearsal. The only way to get into the SNL after-party was the fire escape entrance. Guests had no choice but to climb seventy-five feet up the outside of the building to the Rubber Room. This tickled John Belushi and Gilda Radner.

Chapter Twenty-Three:
It's Raining Men

HALLOWEEN WAS ALWAYS THE biggest night of the year, drawing crowds of over 2,500. People showed up in the most outlandish, creative, and ridiculous costumes. Some women wore nothing more than body paint, which may have inspired Hugh Hefner, years later in the 1990s, to have painted women walking through the crowds at parties in the Playboy Mansion. One year, we spent $50,000 transforming the main entrance hall into a haunted mansion that included live monsters jumping out at our guests as they made their way across rickety bridges through a graveyard, while howling and other very strange loud noises played in the background. Once people made it past that scene, instead of going through the four double doors into the club itself, people were guided left to what was normally a dead-end side room that housed the public telephones. Surprise! We broke through the wall so that revelers found themselves in a strange outdoor courtyard, where bloodied actors screamed as they were being hanged or guillotined on scaffolding. To this day I am convinced, as are other members of my staff, that Michael O. dropped in some live rats that were scurrying around under a bridge they built for that night. I was so freaked out that my first thought that night was, "This is so frightening, will my insurance cover us if someone has a heart attack?" Finally, guests were guided through a large hole we cut in the next wall and voilà—they were back in the main room of the club, where the scene can only be described as something out of a Fellini movie.

The End of Tour Party for Sting and The Police was a blast. Millie Kaiserman, a stunning black beauty from Louisiana, was known for her chili. She was so excited when I told her about the upcoming event for The Police that we came up with the idea to serve her delicious chili for Sting's private gathering of one hundred people behind the scrim. At 8:00 p.m. on the night of the event I received a call from Millie at my penthouse. "Mark, I need some help getting the chili to Studio." I called my office at Studio and caught Denise Chatman just as she was leaving to go home and change clothes for the evenings' event. I told her to stay at Studio and I would send my car and driver to take her to Millie's apartment, to help get the chili to Studio. Denise had just smoked a joint of some really good stuff and was not prepared for a 160-quart stainless steel pot filled to the brim with hot chili, and the only person there to help her was Millie, who was wearing a white pantsuit.

Millie went overboard and prepared enough chili to feed the entire club. As they tried lifting this enormous steaming hot *thing* into the trunk of my limo, some of the chili spilled out and splashed all over Millie, Denise, and Fred, my driver. Millie returned to her apartment to change and Denise went on to the club with the chili. People were already there behind the scrim, waiting for Sting and Millie's chili to arrive. John Griffith and David Miskit helped get the monster-size pot of chili to the serving station, complete with all the necessary accessories. Denise turned around to leave for home and a welcome change of clothes but there they were, a line of people with plates in hand, hungry and eager to taste Millie's chili. Denise said "fuck it" and served chili complete with all the sides—sour cream, etc.—to Sting, The Police, and their invited guests for the next few hours. The club was packed to the gills in anticipation of the curtain being raised on Sting and The Police. I had to keep postponing the raising of the scrim because people wouldn't stop eating the chili. Sting was very appreciative and went out of his way to thank all of us and then returned to his corner, basking in the attention of several young beautiful models. Denise received a beautiful bouquet of flowers the next day from A&M Records. As thrilled as I was to host the party for Sting and The Police, it's Millie's chili that I will never forget.

The "Best Of" Awards party was an annual international black-tie event that recognized elegance in lifestyle, as well as the fields of politics, art, culture, and creativity. One year, it was decided that the décor would be Amazonian in theme, since we were honoring São Schlumberger, the glamorous Brazilian wife of Pierre Schlumberger, the oil industry billionaire. We decorated the club in a jungle motif—banana and rubber trees everywhere—with our "hot" busboys wearing only grass loincloths, much to the joy of all our guests. The guest list included our regulars. Special guests that night were Jeanne Moreau (star of Francois Truffaut's *Jules et Jim*), infamous socialite Claus von Bülow, Brooke Shields, Pierre Cardin, Frank Sinatra, Donald and Ivana Trump, and New York Governor Hugh Carey and his wife. After the dinner we shot cash over the dance floor from the confetti cannons. It was quite a sight to watch this illustrious gathering in formal gowns and tuxedos scrambling all over the floor, diving for tens and twenties. The party generated significant press, including a picture of Claus von Bülow and a few companions on the front page of the *New York Post*. Andy Warhol's sidekick and man-about-town Bob Colacello (a regular contributor to *Vanity Fair* magazine) hosted the party welcoming Richard Gere, Marissa Berenson, Diane von Fürstenburg, Hubert de Givenchy, and Valentino.

Celebrity birthday celebrations were always special, and regardless of whom the honoree was, they would invariably become more involved with their guest list, since it was an event of such a personal nature. Maria Burton, the stunning daughter of Elizabeth Taylor and Richard Burton, was no exception. She invited a cool crowd to her birthday party at Studio. The night was a stand-out with Francesco Scavullo, Susan Sarandon, and Christopher Walken, who made the night for everyone with the moves he threw down on the dance floor. Maria clapped with joy as she and everyone else at Studio stopped to watch Walken do his thing. Looking back on the celebration now, I do so with a tinge of sadness. Throughout the evening, Maria's guests Christie Brinkley and Olivier Chandon were all over each other—it was obvious that they were very much in love. Olivier, also known as Olivier Chandon de Brailles, was a French racecar driver and heir to the Moet & Chandon champagne fortune. They had met at a party we hosted for Christie to promote the 1982 Christie Brinkley Calendar. On March 2, 1983, while traveling at one hundred miles per hour in a practice run in West Palm Beach, Florida, Olivier's car jumped the barrier landing upside down in a canal, trapped in his car at the feet, and he drowned. He had just spoken to Christie on the phone, excited to meet her later that evening in Florida.

The Soap Opera Awards was a favorite event, even though I have never been a fan of soaps. Our guests made it a funny and special night for me. At the party were Neil Simon, Christopher Walken, Eddie Murphy, and the handsome and dashing Douglas Fairbanks Jr. He was the original Zorro and Robin Hood in the 1930s and '40s and the host of the first Academy Awards presentation in 1929. Some twenty-five stars from the local soaps all came out for the party benefitting City Meals-on-Wheels. It was quite an honor to spend some time in the company of Douglas Fairbanks Jr. He was a decorated naval officer, awarded the Silver Cross in World War II. He had appeared in one hundred films—true Hollywood royalty and always included on the International Best Dressed list. He was dapper and had quite a sense of humor. For me, an unforgettable experience.

The bridge over the dance floor in Studio was used for numerous occasions, including musical performances by such groups as Wham! starring the late George Michael, Menudo, The Radio City Music Hall Rockettes, New Edition with Bobby Brown, Culture Club and Boy George, Double Exposure, Madonna, The Village People, Carol Williams, RUN—DMC, Loleatta Holloway, Laura Branigan, Rebbie Jackson, El DeBarge, and the Ritchie Family.

Many of these special performances were choreographed by Karin Bacon, the creative sister of Kevin Bacon. Sometimes we invited everyone from the dance floor up to the bridge. It was a real turn-on and people loved it. It was twenty feet above everybody else below, the same perspective one would have if performing on a concert stage. Frankie Crocker said it reminded him of TV shows *Hullabaloo*, *Shindig!* and *Soul Train*—an inspiration to "get your groove on."

The bridge worked for many artists but definitely NOT for Prince. His high-heeled shoes would have been a disaster on the grated floor surface of the bridge. His people had reached out to Denise Chatman by phone to discuss the layout of Studio 54 for a possible free performance by Prince, but in the middle of the conversation Prince took the phone and continued on with Denise, rendering her almost speechless. Prince wanted to visit Studio…incognito. I agreed not to alert the press. It was a gamble, but I had so much respect for the guy, and I really wanted him at Studio on terms he would be comfortable with. I was hoping for an impromptu jam. I spoke to Richard Walters of the Norby Walters Agency, a nice guy and regular at Studio who was in touch with Prince's people; Richard agreed to do whatever he could to help make it happen. A few days earlier I was in my limo on my way to Studio and Frankie Crocker was on WBLS radio, interviewing Prince in advance of his sold-out Little Red Corvette Tour at Radio City Music Hall.

Frankie asked Prince, "I know you are a gifted musician. How many instruments do you play?" A few seconds of silence and then Prince responded: "I play twenty-four, but only nineteen really well." That blew my mind. So a few nights later Denise monitored the back door and when Prince arrived she alerted me. I never would have recognized him in his hat and bandana with three friends under an assumed name. He thanked me and Denise gave him some drink tickets. Prince asked me if they were good for sodas and juice. I told him yes and they took off toward the upper-level balcony and Rubber Room. A few hours later I spotted them all sitting in a dark area of the Rubber Room watching the crowd below and stuffing their faces with candy and drinking sodas of various colors, which explained the knapsack one of them was carrying when they arrived at the back door. I smiled and left them alone. A Prince jam at Studio never happened due to scheduling, but he did return to Studio several times for Frankie Crocker/Dahved Levy events. Prince never went to the DJ booth; he preferred to hang in the shadows and observe.

When a group was too large to perform on the bridge we'd erect a stage at the back of the dance floor to accommodate a full band. We set it up many times but my favorite groups to perform were Lou Reed; The Temptations; Stevie Wonder; Earth, Wind & Fire; Teddy Pendergrass; The Clash; and The Blues Brothers—Dan Aykroyd and John Belushi. Studio was an intimate setting compared to Madison Square Garden. I know there were more and I wish I could remember them…but I can't.

I sent out this Christmas greeting from the staff of Studio 54.
They were a wild bunch, but devoted and hard working.
Photograph by Doug Van.

During the Christmas season of 1982, we hosted an evening celebrating the fiftieth anniversary of the charity Save The Children with a yuletide party "The Night of 100 Trees." It was a Tuesday night event hosted by Maria Burton, and her husband Steve Carson. Evelyn "Champagne" King graciously accepted a personal invite from Maria to sing her hit song "Love Come Down." Studio 54 was so festive and very beautiful that evening, featuring a dazzling array of Christmas trees artfully decorated by many of the Hollywood elite, including Elizabeth Taylor. The trees were quickly gobbled up at an auction that evening, raising oodles of money for Save The Children, after which everyone danced in celebration amongst and around the trees.

We hosted a dinner and roast for noted gossip columnist Liz Smith, which was an unforgettable evening for all those who attended. Her friends, including opera star Beverly Sills, Kathleen Turner, Helen Gurley Brown, Kaye Ballard, and Broadway actress Elaine Stritch, gathered together to give Liz a good-hearted dose of her own gossip. Liz was the original Gossip Girl; a favorite quote by Liz Smith—"Gossip is just news running ahead of itself in a red satin dress." She was born and bred in Texas, but never looked back once she discovered Manhattan and went to work for *Cosmopolitan* magazine and *Sports Illustrated*. So on this very special night for Liz, all heads were covered with cowboy hats, the floors with sawdust, and we served a down-home dinner of Tex-Mex fare catered by my brother Alan from his Tennessee Mountain restaurant in SoHo. Other guests included Liberace, Diane Sawyer, Marvin Hamlisch, Pia Lindström, and Mariel Hemingway. Highlights of the evening included emcee Gloria Steinem reading telegrams from Carol Channing, Lily Tomlin, and Mike Wallace. It was a night of light-hearted "bitchiness" mixed with a dose of down-home Texas hospitality and much love and affection.

"Welcome Home Peter Beard" was how the invitation read, and it was a glorious night. When Peter entered the main room with beautiful wife Cheryl Tiegs on his arm, as hundreds of friends including numerous major celebrities applauded his return to Manhattan, we knew it would be a fun-filled evening. He had just returned to New York from his beloved home in Africa. Any time spent with Peter was always interesting. He surrounded himself with people one would never find boring. He was an heir to two fortunes, the Great Northern Railway on his mother's side and Lorillard Tobacco on his father's side. Peter travelled with and shot the Rolling Stones American Tour in 1972. Peter Beard was and is one of the nicest guys in the world, beloved in every way by the models he photographed and all the people fortunate enough to know him. Peter enjoyed shooting in my penthouse—it was filled with an abundance of natural light during the day, so whenever he requested to use it I was only too happy to oblige.

Parties for Elite Models and its founder John Casablancas were always chock-full of the hottest models of the day. The girls loved him and showed up for any event he hosted. Johnny loved hanging on the stairs above the backdoor stage entrance that led to my office rather than in a VIP section or on a banquette reserved for him in the main room. Maybe he didn't like loud music but I believe he was drawn to the "behind the scenes" action of the club. It was always a scene on the stairs and people "in the know" like Johnny knew that most celebrities, especially those who loved Sister Cocaine, would make their way to the back of the club and up the stairs to my office at some point in the night. He and Stephanie Seymour, Paulina Porizkova, Iman, Carol Alt, Kim Alexis, Elle Macpherson, and a host of others, whether they were signed to his Elite Models or not, loved him and could be found sitting on the "not-so-fancy" back stairs with bottles of champagne and glasses in hand, having a great time. In order to get to my office on nights that Johnny and his guests were there, my other guests, A-list celebrities from the worlds of fashion, music, sports, film, and theater, had to climb over Johnny and his collection of beauties lining the steps. It made for great fun for everyone.

Brooke Shields hosted a party at Studio 54 to launch the I Love Central Park campaign, created by Fran Moss. I agreed to do the event because, like everyone who has ever lived in Manhattan, I loved Central Park. It was our oasis. But the truth is I was most excited because Allison Steele, the sultry-voiced Disc Jockey known to young boys and men everywhere as "The Nightbird," was on the committee for the event and I was finally going to meet her. Allison Steele ruled in the 1960s and '70s. She would stay with you all night long from midnight to dawn, on WNEW-FM Radio. Boutiques selling a line of gifts and athletic gear, imprinted with the striking green and black I Love Central Park logo, had just been launched at Macy's in Herald Square—attended by Mayor Koch—and the Bloomingdale's at Fifty-Ninth and Third. To the delight of New Yorkers and tourists alike, the merchandise was also available from the ice cream carts with umbrellas throughout Central Park. A percentage of the sales from the I Love Central Park merchandise went to the Central Park Conservancy to help maintain our beautiful park. Michael O.

and his crew strategically placed the same style ice cream carts throughout the club, some filled with ice cream, and others with hundreds of I Love Central Park T-shirts. The walls of Studio were covered with graffiti and big beautiful trees and park benches were everywhere. Being inside of Studio that night felt like being outside in Central Park on a Sunday afternoon. Graffiti artists, break dancers, Grandmaster Flash and The Furious Five, The Sugarhill Gang, Kurtis Blow, Joe Bataan, and Roberto Torres entertained us. It was a happy, outdoor and festive feeling which continued through the night.

The crowd went crazy when all the photographers flashed on Brooke Shields reaching into an ice cream cart—pulling out I Love Central Park T-shirts for everyone. Since the event launched, the I Love Central Park logo, created by Brian Moss, has been declared one of the most innovative designs of the twentieth century. It was a great night for me, since I spent most of it with Allison Steele and Frankie Crocker, drinking champagne and listening to two of the most recognizable voices in broadcasting history. They both had already achieved legendary status in the radio community, having played the records which reflected the musical tastes of the counterculture in the 1960s and '70s on their respective radio shows, blazing a path for the new sound of FM Radio.

We hosted a birthday party for Paul Jabara, who wrote the song "Last Dance" for Donna Summer and "Enough Is Enough," a big hit for Donna and Barbra Streisand. Paul surprised everyone that night with the world premiere of his next big hit, "It's Raining Men." The Weather Girls delighted the crowd, singing what became an iconic song from that era. They performed it that night on the bridge for the first time anywhere, backed up by a cast of characters, including my assistant Shelley Tupper who tore it up as she was known to do, along with all the other dancers. I assure you anyone who was there will never forget seeing The Weather Girls and all the dancers wearing yellow plastic raincoats, singing and dancing on the bridge to "It's Raining Men." Some songs grow on you after hearing them day after day on Top 40 radio and then there's that song that you fall in love with the first time you hear it and you want to hear it over and over, again and again. And that's how we all reacted to hearing "It's Raining Men" for the first time. We all went absolutely crazy, screaming and jumping up and down. Play it again. Play it again. After The Weather Girls left the stage, the DJ played it again and once more later in the evening. It will always remain one of my favorite nights at Studio with my good friend, Paul Jabara. I miss him dearly.

Actor, singer, dancer, choreographer, and Tony Award winner Lee Roy Reams hosted a birthday party for Liliane Montevecchi, the very beautiful and talented film actress, singer, and star of Broadway. This event remains memorable to me and many of my guests that evening because after feeling helpless for so long, we were finally able to do something that would help the fight against AIDS, the horror that was killing so many of our friends and loved ones. A portion of the proceeds from the event that night went to benefit the AIDS Medical Foundation. Liliane Montevecchi had just won the Tony for Best Featured Actress in a musical for her performance in the smash hit on Broadway, *Nine*. Tommy Tune and the entire cast attended. Robin Williams and Christopher Reeve were hanging at the main bar and when Liliane walked over to greet them—they both lost all control and without missing a beat they sandwiched Liliane between them and proceeded to sensually dance and grind around her. Liliane had that effect on men. I will never forget it and neither will anyone else who was lucky enough to be there. She was not only beautiful and possessed great talent but she had a wonderful sense of humor.

Giancarlo Impiglia and nine other painters and sculptors hosted "A Night In Celebration of the Italian Visual Imprint on New York," featuring a musical performance by Laura Branigan singing "Gloria." The evening was to benefit the Order of Sons of Italy in America, New York, which I could relate to, being the grandson of immigrants from Europe. The Order was founded in 1905 to help newly arrived Italian immigrants assimilate into American society. Umberto Tozzi, a handsome Italian singer and composer from Turin, Italy wrote Laura's smash hit "Gloria." It remained on Billboard's Hot 100 for thirty-six weeks and earned Laura a Grammy nomination for Best Pop Female Vocal Performance. The dashing Ahmet Ertegun of Atlantic Records was there, partying behind the mesh curtain with John Travolta, Sylvester Stallone, and the one and only Luciano Pavarotti. Then, Keith Richards and Janice Dickinson, who'd been downstairs working on a song together for Janice in the recording studio Soundworks, appeared to the delight of all. At some point much later that night, Janice lost a magnificent ruby and diamond ring. Shelley Tupper thinks it was a gift from Mick Jagger, Denise Chatman remembers it being from Keith. We did everything we could to help her find it, short of asking DJ Leroy Washington to turn off the music and asking the crowd to join the search. At 5:00 a.m., doors closed, club empty, we continued the search, but it was never found.

STUDIO LOOKED WILD ON the night we hosted a party for model and actress, Margaux Hemingway. She was a six-foot-tall, statuesque beauty and a very sweet and kind person. Margaux was awarded a $1-million contract by Faberge, the first of its kind to a model, to be the spokesperson for the perfume, Babe. She was on the cover of *Time, Vogue, Cosmopolitan, Harper's Bazaar,* and *ELLE* magazines. Michael O. and his crew went all out for Margaux, decorating the club with enormous stuffed animals—I don't mean plush stuffed animals, I mean taxidermy-style stuffed animals. The crowd marveled at the towering nine-foot-tall polar bear, black bear, wolves, deer, and fox that were positioned throughout the club. It was a sight to behold, in homage to Margaux's grandfather Ernest Hemingway, author, wildlife hunter, and big-game fisherman. In 1954, he won the Nobel Prize in Literature for *The Old Man and The Sea.* Margaux Hemingway died in 1996. She is buried in the family plot in Ketchum, Idaho.

We hosted a performance by Bow Wow Wow, which drew a hot crowd. I remember almost nothing about the night except that Rod Stewart, Tina Turner, Cher, Sonny Bono, Valerie Perrine, and Treat Williams were all in attendance, which to me was unforgettable.

I don't remember any of the details about the birthday party for Matt Dillon but I heard everyone had a good time. Denise Chatman remembers nothing except being surrounded by Tom Cruise, Vincent Spano, Patrick Swayze, Ralph Macchio, Rob Lowe, and Matt Dillon as she counted out drink tickets for each of them. Beth Ann Maliner told me the only thing she remembers is Matt coming up to her office to pick up all his presents at the end of the evening and giving her a kiss.

I hosted a party for Debbie Reynolds. She was the star of the 1952 film classic *Singin' In The Rain* and the mother of 1980s film icon Carrie Fisher—*Star Wars'* beloved Princess Leia. Debbie was celebrating her sold-out Broadway run in *Woman of the Year*. Debbie had been divorced from handsome crooner Eddie Fisher for more than twenty years, but she still gave me very explicit instructions barring her ex from entering Studio 54 on the night of her party. In one of the most talked-about divorces in Hollywood history, Eddie Fisher left Debbie Reynolds and married Elizabeth Taylor, Debbie's best friend. (Carrie Fisher died on December 27, 2016, and, to the shock of everyone, Debbie Reynolds died the following day.)

"Welcome to the Twenty-Sixth Birthday Celebration of Maura Moynihan" was a night to remember. I wish I had it on tape. Maura was the daughter of Daniel Patrick Moynihan, the venerable three-term Democratic Senator representing the state of New York. The party was arranged and hosted by Andy Warhol who believed, and I quote, "Maura's going to be a big rock star, she's smart, looks great, and wears thrift shop clothes." So much for that prediction. But it turned out to be a better-than-great evening because Rick James and George Clinton, the Grandmaster of Funk, were hanging out at the main bar throughout the evening. Rick was happy to be at Studio with George Clinton, a man he told me he considered to be "one of the heaviest cats in R&B." But after a few hours of drinking and several trips to my office they got into it, accusing each other of "stealing." This went on for quite some time. Rick was pissed because, as he perceived it, Prince was stealing from him. George countered with "and what about the shit you stole from James Brown and *me* and what about Sly?" Rick thought about that and said, "I took every last motherfuckin' thing I could from Jackie Wilson."

I ordered a round of drinks for tennis star Vitas Gerulaitis, Cheryl Tiegs, Rick Derringer, and Cecilia Peck who were with me at the bar. It was highly entertaining, to say the least and, for me, a history lesson in music. Rick kept grabbing his balls and there was a lot of "Nigga, this" and "Nigga, that" and "Fuck you, motherfucker." If only I had a video of it, it was as funny as any skit you'd see today in reruns of Dave Chappelle's show.

Jackie Wilson's nickname was "Mr. Excitement." He was considered to be a master showman and R&B history will attest to him being one of the most influential and dynamic performers in rock and roll. Everything about him fascinated Rick James. Rick talked about the other artists who had a major influence on his music and songwriting as well when I invited him down to my hotel in the Virgin Islands. He had just finished his Street Songs Tour and was badly in need of some rest and relaxation. We both were. I arranged it so that we spent our days doing nothing but sailing from island to island, dining on great food and good wine, and sleeping under the stars. We sailed from St. Thomas to Tortola to Virgin Gorda. Rick loved the water and learned to swim at a young age. He was a lean and mean competitor in the water as a member of the YMCA Swim and Dive teams in his hometown of Buffalo, New York. When Rick wasn't out on tour he swam in his indoor pool at his home in Buffalo every day. To get to his favorite island drink, "The Painkilla," we had to drop anchor and swim ashore to the Soggy Dollar Bar on the island of Jost Van Dyke. Rick loved the laid-back mindset of island life. We talked a lot about music, his early years, and his first group, The Mynah Birds, with Neil Young and Bruce Palmer. Rick liked to tell me how he was "the luckiest motherfucker alive." If not for a really bad cold, he would have been with Jay Sebring and Sharon Tate in the house on Cielo Drive, on August 9, 1969, the night the Manson Family entered and brutally slaughtered everyone in it.

Looking back, there were so many more parties; some stand out and I remember almost everything, while others are a blur. The Faberge Party attended by Farrah Fawcett, Ryan O'Neal, Joe Namath, and Ricky Schroder was a huge success in the press and yet I remember nothing except that the guests were all A-list celebrities and, as always, our New York crowd cheered at the sight of "Broadway Joe" Namath.

Chapter Twenty-Four:
My Ride Gets Wilder

S TUDIO 54 WAS HOT and my ride was wild, but thanks to my good buddy Rick James life was about to go from Mach 1 to Mach 2. Rick had become a close friend. He was very intelligent and possessed a quick-wit that got us into and out of many a jam. He was at the top of the charts and peak of his career. In 1983, upon realizing that we were both born on February 1, the club threw a small private "Black and White Birthday Party for Mark Fleischman and Rick James."

The photo on the striking invitation showed Rick with his famous dreadlocks alongside a picture of me as a young man in my crisp white Naval Officer's uniform. The main floor at Studio could look like a mosh pit when we were packed to capacity, but on the night of our birthday party we kept the complimentary guest list to seven hundred and up, in the Rubber Room we went for a living room like feeling with flowers and candles everywhere.

The party was graciously hosted by Nick Ashford and Valerie Simpson, and Eddie Murphy presented Rick and me with a birthday cake on the bridge. Nile Rodgers, Lionel Richie, and Chaka Khan then joined us in singing "Happy Birthday." This was an industry crowd, with people from various record labels, radio stations, and several hundred of the most gorgeous models from the top agencies in New York. Rick James held court at the main bar most of the night, surrounded by females of all ages, his entourage and well-wishers. A few feet away stood Frankie Crocker and his good buddy, "Sir" Royce Moore and the legendary, insanely funny DJ, David Rodriguez, along with O. J. Simpson and his stunning blonde girlfriend Nicole Brown. Isaac Hayes was on the dance floor doin' it up with some Alvin Ailey dancers.

At one point, DJ Leroy Washington played an aria from *La Traviata*—requested by Rick—and an aria from *La Bohème* requested by me. The crowd at the bar, not accustomed to hearing opera in a dance club, turned to look at Rick as if to say, "What the fuck—are you down with this?" and there was Rick in all his glory making all the exaggerated moves of a great conductor.

Leroy Washington knew just how to accommodate some unfamiliar new releases requested by various producers and record label heads. Rick took to the live mic he requested and invited everyone to the dance floor for the Etta James classic "At Last" and later in the evening for "To Be Loved" by Jackie Wilson. Lightman Robert DaSilva heard "slow song—drop it down" and the dance floor went romantic and dark. For a party that meant so much to me personally, I am surprised that I remember so little. I do remember the joy I felt in seeing people slow-dancing—a regular happening at Small's in Harlem but not that often at Studio 54. I was in slow-dancing R&B heaven.

Rick always loved his drugs; he enjoyed "the show" of it all and that night was no exception, laying out lines on the main bar and blowing it up with every celebrity. I remember being nervous, worried at first that undercover cops might infiltrate, but after a few drinks and dropping several white pills with 714 stamped on them, I mellowed out and went with the flow. We danced, laughed, drank and enjoyed an endless supply of champagne, cocaine, and Quaaludes, making it a birthday party that I don't remember.

What I do remember is the phone call I took at around 9:00 a.m. the next morning while I was in bed with two hot record company employees. On the phone was John Griffith, night manager at Studio, asking me what to do about the two A-list celebrities who were passed out and handcuffed to the legs of the desk in my office. To this day I don't remember them being at the party. And believe me, they are too famous to forget, and yet I have. Immediately I called Fred, my driver, and within minutes he was at Studio waking them up. Chauffeurs have a way with celebrities. It must be the uniform and the protective bubble of the limousine they represent. Luckily, the keys to the handcuffs were in the pocket of the male celebrity. The female celebrity took one look at Fred in his black uniform and hat, smiled, and sweetly said, "Please take me home, I'm staying at The Sherry Netherland." She then snarled and cursed the male celebrity—reminding him that she intended to leave him over his out-of-control drug abuse, which I supposed was why the male celebrity handcuffed them both to the legs of my desk earlier that morning. Eventually, they broke up. He never recovered from it.

Several times over the years Rick invited me out on tour with him to places like Nashville, Los Angeles, and the Jamaican World Music Festival in Montego Bay, Jamaica. In Jamaica, Gladys Knight, Jimmy Buffett, and The Clash were all on the bill with Rick. The Clash performed their MTV and radio hit "Rock The Casbah." They were a wild bunch. Gladys Knight greeted Rick like her long-lost son and Rick treated her like the royalty she was. Hanging out with Gladys for a bit backstage was a thrill for me. Peter Tosh, Sly and Robbie, and my friend, Jimmy Cliff, were at the show as well, gifting Rick with the best ganja I have ever smoked. It was nonstop spliffs and laughs and insanely good music. I never wanted to leave. But the next day we were off to another venue. I experienced Rick James live and at his best with The Stone City Band and The Mary Jane Girls—his voice and body meeting his every demand. What a talent! This may come as a surprise to many—it certainly did to me—but Rick was a classical music freak. He was a fan of many of the great European composers. In his stash of cassettes for life on the road, he was packing quite a collection of classical and opera.

My time spent on the road with him was unforgettable—not to mention the sexual scenes with groupies who would throw themselves at us at every turn: after parties, getting on and off the tour bus, our limousine, hotel lobbies, and airports. Rick liked staying in the bungalows at The Beverly Hills Hotel but he always had to add extra security when we did. Groupies would always find him. I'm convinced it was hotel staff that tipped them off.

Los Angeles celebrities were screaming for tickets to Rick's Cold Blooded Tour, a one-night-only gig at The Universal Amphitheater. There was a scene that night over "reserved" tickets that I won't ever forget. I was standing backstage, watching Rick do his show, when Prince showed up with a really big bodyguard who appeared to be trying to throw Rod Stewart, his wife Alana, Frank Sinatra's daughter Tina, and her friend out of their front row seats. Alana told us after the show that she told Prince to kiss her ass, she was not moving. Rick admitted to me that the seats were originally promised to Prince but he changed his mind when Rod Stewart and group showed up. Rick loved to fuck with Prince. They would never get along. Rick explained that a few years earlier Rick heard Prince's "I Want To Be Your Lover" and flipped out. They had never met but Rick asked Prince to be the opening act for his upcoming Fire It Up Tour and from the very first moment they met it was a clash of titanic egos. Rick accused Prince of stealing his onstage struts, chants, and microphone moves. Rick was always threatening to throw Prince off the tour as a result.

While Rick was appearing in LA, we stayed at a home owned by Jerry Weintraub, who was promoting Rick's tour. Jerry was a Hollywood legend and very cool guy. He produced tours for Elvis, Sinatra, John Denver, and many others as well as producing the films *Nashville, Diner, The Karate Kid,* and *Oceans 11, 12,* and *13,* appearing briefly in all three *Oceans* films. Jerry Weintraub was a larger than life kind of guy.

It was on Rick's tour in 1983–1984 that I began to understand how wild and crazy the level of unbridled sex is when a rock and roll star goes out on the road. To describe it would be pages and pages of graphic sex scenes, so enough said.

Rick wrote about Studio 54 in his book, *The Confessions of Rick James: Memoirs of a Super Freak* (courtesy of Colossus Books), and he talked about our friendship, saying I had just as much energy as he did ("even for an older guy"). He wrote that I introduced him to Janice Dickinson (who was the world's top model at the time, and who Rick dated for a while). He went on to say he hung out with an interesting crowd during our days together at Studio 54. Rick sang "Happy Birthday" to Kathy Hilton at her Studio 54 birthday party, and then Kathy sent Rick a birthday gift of Baccarat crystal.

In those days, it seemed like Rick lived at Studio 54. Whenever he walked in with his entourage, DJ Leroy Washington would mix "Super Freak" into whatever else he was playing and the predominantly white crowd would go wild, packing the dance floor. As Rick said in his memoir, "The Studio 54 crowd was the most exciting group of people I'd ever met. I was always there, partying and getting high in the office upstairs. But Mark would throw everybody out if I needed a quiet spot to chill." That's true: I did and it wasn't easy. Once groupies got in, they never wanted to leave. Clearing the office was always a delicate task, because nobody ever believed when they heard, "Everyone please take your drinks and personal belongings—we are moving the party downstairs," that we meant *them.* I often overheard, "Don't worry, he means them, not us." Many of my guests had a sense of entitlement. Others just didn't want their moment with any of the celebrities they were hanging with in my office to end. Ever.

Rick had a lot of respect for the talent of Tanya Tucker and they spent many a night hanging out together at Studio 54 and on our many forays downtown exploring New York City's after-hours nightlife. Tanya became a member of our Dawn Patrol and one of the hardest partiers in our crew—though not "the last man standing," as she has claimed. In a 1988 interview with *People,* Tanya said that she was the wildest thing out there and she could stay up longer, drink more, and kick the biggest ass in town. She was definitely on the ragged edge—and we had many an all-nighter to prove it.

In 1981, the same year she got into drugs and alcohol, Tanya's record sales were in decline. Amid the mess that her life was becoming, she ended up on my doorstep delivered by my friend, publicist Joanne Horowitz. Tanya was a major talent and celebrity, and we became good friends, so I put her up at the Executive Hotel and provided her with food, alcohol, and drugs—though it really wasn't that much food. But there was one hell of a party every night to whet her appetite for "the wild." Tanya was troubled. I was told that she got into a fight with her best friend, whom she had invited to stay with her at the hotel, and then knocked her tooth out.

Later that year, Rick struck up a relationship with actress Linda Blair, who had gained fame for her role in *The Exorcist.* As Rick wrote in his memoir, "Linda flew to New York and we hit it off immediately. She is one of the sweetest ladies I've ever known. We went to see Mark Fleischman at a hotel he owned on Madison Avenue in his penthouse, and Mark asked Linda and me to pose for a picture and we both took off our tops. The picture showed up everywhere but we didn't mind." After the impromptu pose, and sensing that the mood was changing, and that I was no longer welcome in the room, I left with the *New York Daily News* photographer Richard Corkery and closed the door behind me. I barely got it shut before we could hear Linda moaning from the other side.

Rick goes on to say, "Linda and I still love each other and have stayed close friends. The only argument we've ever had was on the first night we went out. We were in Mark's office at Studio 54 with Steven Tyler and Ron Wood of the Stones. Linda was busy talking to Steve while I slipped downstairs to get high with Janice Dickinson and her sister Debbie." According to Rick's recently published book *Glow,* he wrote the song "Cold Blooded" about Linda when he found out, after the fact, that she had been pregnant with his child, and had an abortion, giving him no say in the matter.

As I mentioned earlier, we were always looking for angles to get press, but there were a few times when I had something very special but chose not to call them. It was 5:00 a.m. and I was standing at the bar with Jimmy Simpson, older brother to Ray Simpson of the Village People and younger brother to Valerie Simpson of Ashford & Simpson, Michael Johnson of SIR, Ron Tyson of The Temptations, and a bevy of beauties. We were mesmerized, watching Timothy Hutton and Rick James play a game of one-on-one on the dance floor. We were all ripped, roaring, and high as hell. Steve Steckel, from our security team, told me that he paid a friend to build the hoop setup and once a week all the security guys would get a case of beer and play some hoops on the dance floor after closing. Rick spotted it backstage and had his crew pull it out onto the dance floor. What a photo op: "Rick James and Timothy Hutton play hoops at 5:00 a.m. on the dance floor at Studio 54." But I didn't call the press. They were both having so much fun, just like two kids in the street. It was only shortly before that night that I had the pleasure of being introduced to Timothy Hutton. He was a truly humble, nice guy. I will never regret not having called the press that night—but I do wish I had captured the moment in a photo for me personally.

Chapter Twenty-Five:
The Dawn Patrol

AT DAWN IN NEW York City in the early 1980s the possibilities were endless, so I organized a group of night-owl regulars who, like me, never wanted the party to end. Informally, we came to be known as the Dawn Patrol. It was a name conjured up by Nikki Haskell and was meant entirely in jest, but it turned out to be appropriate and it stuck.

The Dawn Patrol was eight or ten regulars—occasionally we welcomed a few adventurous newcomers into the mix—and we would meet several times a week in front of Studio 54 at 4:00 a.m. or 5:00 a.m., climb into limousines, and check out the action at the after-hours clubs. These clubs—which were unlicensed and illegal, usually downtown on the west side—opened at 3:00 a.m. in boarded-up vacant buildings. This was before the meatpacking nightclub district was developed and the neighborhood became chic. In fact, many areas of Manhattan were considered to be dangerous at this point in time. Parties were hosted on multiple floors for thousands of people until as late as noon the next day. Many celebrities were afraid to set foot in places like these by themselves; but I knew the owners, doormen, and staff, so I could guarantee my friends' safety, not to mention a hell of a good time.

In addition to Rick James, Dawn Patrollers included: John Belushi, who was very funny, but had a mean streak when drunk and stoned (I suspected he was freebasing); Liza Minnelli, a sweet and super talented lady who overindulged until she overcame her issues at Betty Ford; Prince Egon von Fürstenberg, the dapper European prince who was always smiling, laughing, and telling jokes in five different languages, loved both boys and girls and could really hold his drugs and alcohol; Lester Persky, actor and producer of films such as *Taxi Driver* and *Shampoo*, who was so much fun but who got so drunk and stoned we often had to carry him to the car; Tanya Tucker; Franco Rossellini, director of the film classic *Caligula,* a very hard partier; Reinaldo Herrera, suave and very much in control, no matter what hour of the night or morning, or what amount of drugs he was doing; Vitas Gerulaitis, a great athlete, who made me sad whenever he would join us—I knew his craving for cocaine was destroying his brilliant tennis career, but I chose to say nothing; Andy Gibb, a sweetheart of a guy who used huge amounts of coke and alcohol to deal with issues he had being the youngest brother of The Bee Gees and reeling from his recent breakup with actress Victoria Principal; Jack Lemmon, the brilliant Oscar-winning actor, witty and charming but seeming extremely sad late at night when speaking about his coke habit; Tony Curtis, legendary actor always chasing women and coke; Tony Danza, a fun-loving guy and TV actor who was always up for a great party; Joe Cocker, rock and roller, always high as a kite; Nick Nolte, actor and absolute wild man; Dodi Fayed, son of Egyptian billionaire Mohamed Al-Fayed, who owned Harrod's of London at the time, always had the most amazing coke. Robin Williams, comedian and Oscar winner, had an enormous appetite for coke and alcohol and appeared to mellow out somewhat when high on coke. Whenever he joined us at Crisco Disco, he'd spend most of the night in the DJ booth, fascinated by the action on the dance floor.

Crisco Disco, named for its DJ booth, which was shaped and painted to look like a giant can of Crisco cooking grease—a popular lubricant for gay men.

The owner was Hank Davis, a tall, lanky, strange man with burning eyes and a raspy voice and always dressed in a tight black leather suit. That, mixed with the near translucent pallor of his skin, made him look like a gay vampire. He lived an illegal life in the shadows, paying off the cops and fire department officials, enabling him to entertain thousands of people after hours every night without proper licensing. Hank always bragged about having the best coke in New York and took particular pleasure in watching us snort a mixture of cocaine and Ketamine, or Special K, a mild hallucinogenic powder that he slipped into the mix unbeknownst to the crowd. Hank liked to make fun of shaving products heir Warrington Gillette and friends, John Flanagan and Michael Van Cleef Ault (Michael now owns Singapore's outrageous club Pangaea) Henri Kessler, now a producer at Paramount; and some of the other young, waspy preppies who sometimes accompanied the Dawn Patrol. Hank took pleasure in referring to them as "the Harvard Boys." He thought of them as young virgins and relished seeing them tripping on his hallucinogenic concoctions. But Hank always treated me and my guests as the ultimate VIPs. Perhaps he believed we legitimized the scene.

We'd pull up to Crisco Disco in the dark of night, just before dawn, on a downtown west-side street surrounded by nothing but deserted buildings. The door opened and BAM! We were always startled to see a thousand people partying in a hot gay music scene. The DJ was Frank Corr and he was brilliant. He played the crowd so well that I hired him to do Thursday nights at Studio 54. We were ushered through the teeming crowd to the innermost VIP areas of the club, which made their home on an upper floor of the venue. First, there was VIP—which was pretty much your standard velvet-roped area that separated the elite from the club's regulars. But beyond VIP was the even smaller, more exclusive, and more intimate MVIP ("most very important person") room for maybe eight of that evening's A-listers. There, at 5:00 a.m. or 6:00 a.m., Hank would dispense booze, drugs (usually cocaine), and whatever other combination of magical powders he could think of to ensure his guests would *feel the party* and remain with him for a few more hours.

With the drinks flowing, and all the free drugs for my guests and me, we'd sit around and share some of our most personal stories. Crazy Hank would be talking, and we'd all be getting messed up on his Special K mix, which created a mini-mescaline trip, kind of like being on Ecstasy, except it didn't last as long. It was actually a reasonably potent hallucinogenic, but luckily no one I knew had any bad trips. One undeniable side effect was that people lost touch with their personal values; inhibitions vanished that might have otherwise served to restrain or protect. These stoned-out conversations went on for hours, and—as you can imagine—being so free of inhibitions, our discussions traveled into really strange, fun, and occasionally very sad places.

Hank, who was rather dramatic and noticeably gay, would enjoy going on about a supposed affair Steve Rubell had with Calvin Klein, spitting while he talked and acting like he was in the know. Steve had been a regular at Crisco. I never believed Hank's story because Calvin's taste in boys was very different from Stevie, and I knew Calvin and Steve to be just best friends. However, I humored Hank and let him tell his tall tales as he was always effusively hospitable to me and my guests.

I was told there was often big drama to contend with, such as the time that Lorna Luft was hanging out in MVIP with a few of her friends when her half-sister Liza Minnelli walked in. Because she and Lorna weren't talking to one another, a common happening between the two sisters, Hank bragged that he walked into MVIP and kicked Lorna out so Liza could have the room. Even though they were both Judy Garland's daughters, Lorna didn't rate as high on Hank's A-List. Liza was a huge star in her own right and, truth is, Hank didn't consider Lorna's dad, talent manager Sid Luft, to be of equal caliber to Liza's dad, Vincente Minnelli, the great director of the films *Gigi, An American in Paris,* and other classics. At Crisco, a hot director trumped a manager.

You never wanted to stay in MVIP for too long, since you'd wind up too disconnected from the party in the VIP Room. Usually, members of our group would spend a little time wandering through the crowd, getting a feel for the scene, then retreat into MVIP for a little while to partake in some party favors and get ready for the next stage of the evening—or morning, as the case may be. Things would get pretty loose up there—particularly when we'd exit MVIP and spend time mixing in VIP. That's where the sex always went down. Where MVIP was small and intimate, VIP was spacious enough to move around in, with big comfortable leather couches to sink into and a well-stocked bar offering free drinks to select people. VIP offered a perfect view of the mayhem one floor below, and you could watch all the goings-on. It was heaven for voyeurs. While some people, possessed by the power of the Frank Corr beat, sweated and danced nonstop, others used the space as a platform to seduce. But the best part about VIP was the darkened corners, perfect for anonymous sexual encounters.

People were always looking for sex in one form or another at Crisco Disco. It wasn't uncommon to see people from MVIP or VIP head down to the lower floors to dance, find someone who captured their fancy, then lead them back upstairs to the hallowed VIP area to get it on. Sometimes you'd go to freshen your drink at the bar, and find yourself dodging people in various states of sexual exploration. Couples making out, guys getting blow jobs, and, in some of the darkened and recessed corners of Crisco Disco, people were fucking. Not the full-on naked kind. People tried to be discreet, working within the confines of clothing, zippers, and buttons, pushing panties aside, allowing for just enough access and the right amount of action to satisfy.

One of the most interesting hallmarks of that pre-AIDS period was the open sexual experimentation happening everywhere in society, and Crisco was no exception. Guys doing it with guys, girl-on-girl—nobody cared and it didn't matter if you identified as homosexual or not. At times you didn't know who you were doing it with—you might know a first name, and sometimes not even that.

I enjoyed this sort of hedonistic play, and while I often found myself at the center of it during my many nights at Crisco Disco, there is one night that stands out far above the rest. I was hanging out in the balcony, checking out the action below, high on Hank's Special K mix. I spotted Robin Williams in the DJ booth with Frank Corr; he had joined us that evening in my limo for the ride down from Studio 54. I smiled to myself, watching him. He was so calm now, standing in the booth moving his hips to the music. We had done a considerable amount of some special mix with Hank in MVIP and that always seemed to calm him down, making him less manic, more mellow and able to relax and just enjoy himself. To quote Frank Corr: "Robin loved the energy of the music and the people. He was an amazing person." I was watching Robin move to the beat and that's when I spotted her—a gorgeous, curvaceous blonde, dancing by herself in her own world as if nobody was watching her. But everyone was. I wanted her. I had to have her, so I made my way down to the dance floor—hoping she'd return to VIP with me.

People were always trying to get in VIP and MVIP, but the only way to get in—if you weren't part of that crowd—was to be invited by one of the A-Listers. The gatekeeper for VIP was a real character, Fred Rothbell-Mista. He wore big black-rimmed glasses and was incredibly cool, with a quick, sarcastic sense of humor. He was well-known in the New York night scene and knew who everyone was. While Hank reigned supreme over MVIP, Fred took care of VIP, and he did so as if he were a secret service agent guarding the Oval Office. He treated it like it was his private domain: nobody got in without his knowing. Even so, he had an appreciation for those who got the invite up, mainly because they always looked so elated to have been chosen, like at the front door at Studio 54.

When I walked out of VIP that night, Fred gave me a knowing look—he had surmised why I was leaving and what I was up to. I gave him a cursory nod and headed for the main floor, intent on finding my goddess and bringing her back upstairs with me. When I found her, she was still gyrating wildly on the dance floor, her long hair whipping around, threatening to lash you if you got in its way. I managed to avoid a whipping and gently took her by the arm to get her attention. She stopped to look at me, curious as to why I'd interrupted her. I smiled and pointed up to the VIP balcony. When she returned the smile, I took that as my cue to lead her upstairs.

Fred unclipped the rope as soon as I approached with my maiden in tow. I didn't look at him or attempt any conversation—I was rock-hard, just thinking about what sex with her would be like. Lucky for me, a couch in one of the more darkened corners of VIP had just vacated. I got her a drink then guided her in the direction of the couch. I slid down onto the soft leather, she smiled and I pulled her on top of me, gently moving my hand up her dress as I kissed her, feeling her tongue entwine with mine while I used my other hand to free one of her sweaty breasts from the confines of her wrap-front top. She moaned, grinding herself into me as I slid my other hand up her dress and around to her ample buttocks.

She ran her hand down my torso and went for the button on my pants, until she felt the chain hanging from my belt loop. She'd found my stash, so I gamely took some out for her and used a little indentation in my thumb to scoop some coke into. I raised it up to her nose, she took it in and immediately asked for more. People would sniff off just about anything in those days, so she knew how to take it as it was given. Once she'd snorted enough coke to satisfy, she went wild. She dropped to her knees and undid my pants. I pulled her mouth off of me and she immediately leapt on top of me, sliding her panties to the side so she could descend on me with her velvety grip. Her hips were bucking so wildly that it was hard for me to hold on to her, so I just let her go and watched her breasts—one free, one still enclosed in her top—as they bounced wildly while she rode me hard. I could feel myself starting to come, so I reached for my little canister of amyl nitrate—like most people, I hung it around my neck when out clubbing. I unscrewed the lid just as my orgasm was starting to crest, and as the amyl nitrate sent a rush of blood to my brain—BOOM—I felt my body shudder to completion. I didn't want her to leave any less satisfied than me, so I gave her a good sniff of amyl nitrate then slid my fingers inside her and worked her g-spot until she came. And when all was done—nothing was said—we kissed and she pulled herself together and slipped out of VIP. I went back to the balcony, where I watched her rejoin the revelers on the dance floor. It was almost as if it had never happened.

The music, lights, and energy, plus the availability of exotic drugs and liquor, topped off by the semiseclusion of the VIP room made for the perfect environment to host anonymous sex. And that's why people went to Crisco

Disco. They didn't care to hang with the same people they'd arrived there with. The idea was to connect, however briefly, with nameless people you'd never see again. Everyone operated under the auspice that you didn't go to Crisco looking for someone to take out to dinner.

By 10:00 a.m., I'd round up what was left of the Dawn Patrol and we'd head outside, blinded by the light of a new day as we headed uptown to breakfast, usually at the Empire Diner on Eighth Avenue. From there, everyone would head home or to whatever hotel they were staying at and crash. This went on for several years.

I'd take Valium to go to sleep, wake up around three in the afternoon, do several lines of coke to get myself going, and repeat the routine of yet another day. Either I didn't realize it or didn't want to admit that my lifestyle—which I loved so much—was doing me in. It was taking me deeper and deeper into a dark place I'd never been to before.

Chapter Twenty-Six:
Return to Paradise

THE EUPHORIA I EXPERIENCED with Angel Dust was mind-blowing, but the bitch came with a hefty price tag.

Self-reflection about moral decay was the last thing on my mind in the spring of 1983. My reality was so twisted and distorted that reason and logic escaped me. The truth is that my pleasure center was in complete control and making all the decisions, which I believed to be absolutely brilliant.

Since willfully consuming myself with Studio 54, I paid no attention to the Virgin Isle Hotel. If you couldn't snort it, dance to it, fuck it, or party with it, I was blind to it. So by 1983, without my focus and personal touch, the hotel property had become increasingly unprofitable. This was all brought to my attention one afternoon while under the grandiose influence of my new friend Angel Dust. I immediately jumped into action organizing a hotel and island promotional event that I believed would single-handedly save the hotel. Convinced that I was brilliant and had it all under control, I abruptly fired the hotel's manager. He was not my appointee, but that of one of my partners, Fred Kasner, co-owner of the travel industry giant Liberty Travel. Fred became the hotel's managing partner around the same time that I opened Studio 54 in New York.

I orchestrated a "Studio 54—Adventure in Paradise" trip to the Virgin Isle Hotel on Memorial Day weekend, 1983. Any rational person would have waited and invited everyone down in November, at the beginning of the next winter season, but no, not me. Angel Dust and I decided that we could convince our crowd and the rest of the traveling public to vacation in the Caribbean during the summer months instead of the Hamptons or other popular summer destinations. I was delusional. People were not going to go to

St. Thomas in the summer. Martha's Vineyard, yes; the Caribbean, no. The trip proved to be very expensive and produced absolutely nothing worthwhile— but it was insane fun.

As part of the entertainment, we booked Two Tons o' Fun, the plus-size singing duo who later became The Weather Girls. The duo had released "It's Raining Men," a huge hit for them on the club scene, after making its debut at Studio 54 in 1982. We put The Girls on an American Airlines flight, but were forced to upgrade them to first class because they were too big to fit in the coach seats. I chartered a plane and flew sixty of Studio 54's regular guests down to the island. I arrived a day early to make the many necessary arrangements for the party weekend. My guests got stoned and drunk on the plane ride down. After a pillow fight broke out, the pilot threatened to land the plane in Atlanta unless everyone returned to their seats immediately. My good friend, Paul Jabara, who wrote "It's Raining Men," flew down for the party, as did Rick James and Vitas Gerulaitis. The next day, I was there at the airport, waiting on the tarmac holding a big basket filled with magic mushrooms.

The Virgin Islands are the sailing capital of the Americas, thanks to the year-round trade winds. Friends and I frequently sailed to the nearby British Virgin Islands, where we would drop anchor off beautiful Tortola, and a local would take us in the late afternoon to a secret spot to search for psilocybin mushrooms found underneath cow patties on one particular side of the mountain above Road Town. Not only did we eat them on the spot, but then we'd return to the sailboat and make magic mushroom soup for dinner, which always helped make our already glorious surroundings even more magical. But, for this special occasion, I sent a bellhop to Tortola to secure the mushrooms so that I could be at the airport to greet my guests personally and pop a fresh mushroom in each person's mouth right on the tarmac as they de-planed. I was nuts to do such a thing to my unsuspecting guests; within an hour everyone was so fucking high. It set the stage for a party that would last for days.

The debauchery that took place over the next ninety-six-hour period was completely off the charts, even for this outrageous crowd, and me, their ever-present host. Aside from the unbridled sex, drugs, and 151-proof rum, my guests enjoyed the beach and playing all the games typical—and some not so typical—of a Caribbean beach vacation, thanks to Shelley Tupper. She arranged snorkeling excursions on Jacque Cousteau's sailboat and endless matches of strip volleyball at the beach. We had a big turnout for the Treasure

Hunt, the treasure being a nice little gift-wrapped bag of cocaine. Tennis great Vitas Gerulaitis played a match against Chris Atkins who had just starred in *Blue Lagoon* with Brooke Shields. My guest, fashion designer Stephen Burrows, advised me on the party décor, enhancing the atmosphere of the various staged events. Almost from the moment the plane landed, I was put in the position of arranging itineraries. Everyone there was my friend—and some were women I'd already had sex with—so many of them came to me with their requests, telling me who liked who, who wanted to sleep with who, and so on. For all I know, in the end, just about everyone wound up making it with everyone else on that trip. At first, I was occupied advising my guests about the various activities on the island and, as a good host, arranging the beach parties and a spectacular torchlit poolside dinner dance with entertainment by The Weather Girls. But finally, once everyone had settled in and were enjoying the arranged activities and their personal routines, I was free to pursue my own adventures.

One afternoon was an all-out sex fest that took place in my secluded poolside suite, the same place I had the tryst with the beauty queen five years earlier. This time, I was in the bedroom with a Ford model who was an undeniably stunning gal with a great body. We were making out on the bed, peeling each other's bathing suits off, when I heard a knock at the door. Had I not been in the position of host for the weekend, I probably would've ignored it. But duty called.

Two women announced themselves through the door—one was a very attractive, slender sales representative for a major cosmetics company and the other her assistant and traveling companion, a large, well-built woman.

"We're looking for coke," said the assistant. "Do you have any?"

"Absolutely," I said, pulling on a pair of shorts. I opened the door and said, "Come on in."

I turned to my new guests, gestured to the bed, and said, "Would you like to join us?"

They looked to the bed, looked at each other, then looked at me and said, "Sure."

And just like that, I was in my first foursome.

The three of us got naked, hopped into bed with the model, and I soon found myself lost in "paradise found." Breasts were rubbing the side of my face, a nipple was in my mouth and I could feel a breast between my legs rubbing against me. I remember thinking, I have to color this moment on my brain, like indelible marker, so I can relive it again and again. I was getting sucked, licked, and swallowed. Hands and tongues were everywhere, making it nearly impossible to tell who was who and what was what. It was heaven. At first I wanted to make sure everyone was happy so I pulled out a vibrating dildo. But then I stopped trying to manage the experience and just had fun. We were all over each other, laughing and giggling, taking our time teasing and taunting one another with fingers and tongues. We snorted coke to keep going. We finally hit our orgasms and collapsed in a pool of sweat—drained—satisfied and smiling. We lay like that for a few minutes utterly exhausted. And then, all I could think about was food. I jumped up, pulled on my bathing suit, the girls put on their bikinis and followed me out the door into the bright sun. We dove into the pool, swam up to the poolside bar, and ordered the most delicious rum drinks and island snacks. We relaxed by the sparkling pool eating and drinking under the most beautiful azure sky, listening to some mellow reggae music. After a while, and to my pleasure, one of the girls suggested we go back to my room for a little more action—and everyone agreed. I was in heaven. If only I could bottle this feeling. This moment. So we slipped back into my room, stripped down, and this time we rubbed coke on each other's genitals. We enjoyed each other all over again, hit our marks, and fell asleep. I understand others on the trip had similar experiences.

Rick James was with a gorgeous very well-known model, at the top of her game in the world of fashion, whose name I am forbidden to mention. They stayed in Rick's room for the entire four days, requesting an endless supply of candles, magnums of champagne, and food from room service, and blasting music from Rick's boom box—dancing, fucking, and playing in the white powder. Rick had his own connection for cocaine on the island, and from what he told me later, he included Chris Atkins in his order for their four days in paradise. It was wild—no one was left out of the action. All my guests were occupied and happy.

Though guests Count Enrico Carimati, business impresario Bo Polk, shaving heir Warrington Gillette, and a number of others paid their own way, many of the girls and celebrities paid half-price, and some were comped by us in full. It turned out to be a very expensive trip, but I hoped that the buzz we generated would catch on and people would return to St. Thomas and the Virgin Isle Hotel. But those hopes were dashed with the onslaught of Hurricane Klaus several months later. The storm ripped through St. Thomas.

It hit the island directly, and the eye of the storm went through the harbor of Charlotte Amalie just below the Virgin Isle Hotel. Every window in the hotel was blown out, and the entire structure was nearly destroyed. Even though we were insured, our coverage was insufficient to rebuild and only provided enough money to pay off the mortgage. Sadly, it was the end of the Virgin Isle Hotel.

I was a train wreck waiting to happen. This was clear to everyone except me. Victoria Leacock was the most down-to-earth of all my assistants. She worked out of the penthouse apartment with me. Upon her arrival, each day at noon, she knocked on my bedroom door to ask how many coffees she should serve, never knowing whether there was one woman in bed with me that day, or two, maybe three. Victoria did her job well and was always calm and levelheaded in a time of crisis. She recently recalled how she entered my bedroom late one afternoon and found me lying on the floor next to the safe where I kept all my drugs. I did not appear to be breathing. Not knowing what to do, she called my best friend, Dr. Bob Millman, who had more clinical knowledge of drugs than practically anyone else alive. She asked Bob if she should call 911.

"Is there any drug paraphernalia around?" he asked.

"Only a vial of coke," said Victoria.

Bob thought about that for a moment, then said, "Don't call nine-one-one. If he really is dead, he's dead. You can always call later. On the other hand, if the police show up and find him alive and in the possession of drugs, he'll be really upset with you."

Bob knew how sensitive the authorities were to any mention of drug use at Studio 54, and he clearly knew me very well. In any event, he made the right call. I woke up a few hours later and didn't remember a thing.

I had developed such an insatiable appetite for drugs and kinky sex, I continued to pick up late-night strays and bring them home. One night, I arrived home with two bimbos who joined me in the Jacuzzi and then in bed where we enjoyed a wild sex scene until I passed out. The next thing I knew, it was morning and my father was in my bedroom waving his arms and yelling at me, "Meshuggena. Look at you. Is this any way for a man to carry on? Your poor Mother, she should never know from this. Mark, I'm talking to you, are you listening?"

The girls had double-locked the front door and taken the phone off the hook. They were having so much fun they decided they didn't want to leave.

My apartment was inviting. Floor-to-ceiling glass sliding doors and terraces that opened up to the Manhattan skyline at night, and everywhere you went was beautiful cream-colored plush carpeting. My kitchen pantry was always chock-full of goodies—ice cream, candies, pastries, imported cheeses, and lots of champagne. The girls had a blast—and passed out. When Victoria Leacock arrived to work that morning she reported to the front desk of the building that she was locked out. Security was called and when they couldn't rouse anyone inside the apartment, they called my father. My father arrived, frantic and thinking the worst. He feared I was dead. He immediately ordered a locksmith to open the door. They barged into my bedroom and found me with two naked girls, one dildo, and two vibrators. I was sound asleep! My father lost it. Now that I was alive, he wanted to kill me.

My world was spiraling out of control, but I was determined to hang on, full steam ahead. After all, I was the host of the party. It was who I was and who I was destined to be. Studio 54 couldn't survive without me. But the truth is, I was going deeper and deeper into a place where the party never ends. I was so happy with my drugs, alcohol, and wild sex—the kind of sex you attract when you stay up all night doing insane amounts of coke and other exotic drugs.

Sycophants were in abundance, always trying to give me new drugs—I never turned them down. On a few different occasions I tried both crack and heroin and got so high, and enjoyed it so much, that I never did either one again. They are both highly addictive and, back in the 1980s, very expensive. I decided to remain true to my friends Angel Dust, cocaine, Quaaludes, vodka, and scotch. They were loyal, dependable, affordable, and I was able to function productively and undetected. I was cool, smooth, and taking care of business. Or so I thought.

One night (early morning) I hooked up with an older, very attractive European princess. She'd been partying all night with friends in the club but at one point left her group to dance and hang out with me. After inviting her to my office for drinks and cocaine gifted to me from some guy in the hope that I would agree to book his son's bar mitzvah, I ended up in her Park Avenue apartment having sex until the drugs ran out. I was accustomed to really good coke but this stuff had been cut with something that made me so jittery that I had to take three or four Valium to calm my nerves. I passed out in her bed.

When I awakened, I realized it was the next day—very late the next day. I called my answering service and listened to several hysterical messages from one of my live-in assistants, wondering where I was. There were also at least five hysterical messages from Carmen D'Alessio. She was screaming into the phone in her thick Peruvian accent, "We have Veeee Eye Peeees coming to deeener in your apartment." I had agreed to host a dinner party for French fashion designer Guy Laroche that evening, which I had completely forgotten about. The guest list included many important people in the fashion industry. I fucked up. With just four hours to go until the guests arrived at my penthouse, I called Studio 54, as they were setting up for the evening, and ordered ice, champagne, a bartender, and a busboy to help me with dinner. I then raced to the market and bought baguettes, an assortment of cheese, shrimp, pasta, salad ingredients, fruit, and petit fours. I transformed it all into a beautiful candlelit buffet just as my guests were arriving at my front door. They loved it. However, it was subpar by my standards. It was then that I realized I was losing it.

It became one of many dinner parties I managed to pull off just in the nick of time, in large part because I had assistants who made a valiant attempt to cover my ass whenever I was out of control. There were moments when I admitted to being out of control and that I was no longer taking care of business as I had been so well-trained to do at Cornell. But they were just "moments," nothing life-changing. I continued to drink and do more and more blow and Angel Dust. I'd spent so much time "being" the owner of Studio 54, building this persona that centered around "him," that I had no idea who I was if I wasn't "him," and I wasn't the least bit curious to find out. I was having so much fun that I didn't want it to stop. Ever.

I continued to submit to the darker side of the Studio 54 effect, living a hedonistic lifestyle of drugs, alcohol, kinky sex, and celebrity. I was in a perpetual state of sensory overload and I was losing my mind. I failed to follow up on details that I knew to be important and then I'd compensate for my lapse in judgment or behavior by turning it around in a positive way. That's how I was getting away with a lot of shit. That's what happened in a story that begins at my penthouse after a very long night at Crisco Disco.

Denise Chatman and Shelley Tupper, who worked out of my office at Studio 54, had arranged a coveted meeting for me with two representatives from the Children's Home Aid Society. These ladies were often referred to as the Mayflower Ladies, suggesting they were so very serious and uptight because they still had the splinters in their asses from the voyage to America on the *Mayflower*. New York High Society—Bluebloods to the core. Anyway, it was 3:30 p.m. and my assistants couldn't wake me. My appointment at Studio was at 4:00 p.m. Denise and Shelley were understandably nervous. I finally woke up when I heard someone screaming, "There are two very straight-laced ladies from the Children's Home Aid Society due to arrive in your office at four, and that's thirty minutes from NOW." I couldn't afford to lose this kind of charity event—it was always a prestigious happening on the Society Calendar and in the newspapers.

At 4:00 p.m., I slid into the back seat of my limousine and headed to Studio. Perfect timing. I had time to do a few hits of coke to wake up and listen to the first twenty minutes of Frankie Crocker's radio show. I was in such a good mood when my limo pulled up to the Studio 54 stage door entrance on Fifty-Third Street. I didn't get out right away; I wanted to hear the end of "I Want Your Love" by Chic. I figured that Frankie must be wooing some chick because the song came out five years ago and he opened his show with it, so he was sending some "honey" a message. I jumped out of the car and bounded up the flight of stairs to my office, but when I walked in I was not prepared for what I saw.

The ladies from the Children's Home Aid Society looked exactly like Dana Carvey's 1980s character Church Lady on *Saturday Night Live*. They were wearing little hats with veils, funny shoes and stockings, their white gloved hands were holding purses, they were sitting up very straight and proper, and they were wearing the most unattractive glasses I had ever seen. I knew if I stopped moving and looked at them for just one more minute I would laugh right in their faces so I excused myself and opened what looked like a door to a closet but was really a door to my very small bathroom, toilet only—no sink—no mirrors—two feet away from where they were sitting, and I disappeared inside. I flushed the toilet so they couldn't hear me snorting the coke. Maybe I should offer them some, I thought they looked like they could use a lift. *How am I going to get through this without laughing?* I thought. Just looking at Denise and Shelley was making me laugh. They're both so serious, but I opened the door, stepped out, and said, "Good afternoon, ladies, it is my pleasure to meet with you today." One lady looked up at me, puckering her lips like Lily Tomlin, and shook her head—and the other one looked like she was about to cry. They were really starting to piss me off. "Ladies, I'm here to help you produce an event for your very worthy cause." Shelley was making faces and pointing to her nose. Is she crazy? I can't give her a hit now. What the fuck? I duck back into my bathroom. This is bullshit. Why am I even here—I should be home sleeping. I'm here because I am the best at this—I'm the closer. I better make this next hit a really big one. WOW! OK, I'm ready! Let's do it. A rush to my head and then to my heart and WHOOSH I'm back in a good mood. YES! When I opened the door both ladies looked at me, gasped, and grabbed their purses. One lady looked at me with wide-eyed terror—shaking her head as if I was crazed and going to attack her or something. And then I saw my reflection in the mirror behind the desk where Shelley was sitting. Oh shit! I did look crazy. I looked fucking ridiculous. White stuff on my nose and all over my black cashmere sweater. I looked like I'd been playing in a box of powdered donuts face-first.

I snapped into "protect my ass mode" and very calmly excused myself. I raced down the stairs and across the dance floor and up the stairs to the second-floor men's room, cleaned my face and sweater, ran back down the stairs across the dance floor and up the back stairs, and returned to the meeting that no one will ever forget. I booked the event and it was a huge success.

By 1984 I was more and more out of touch with my surroundings but very much in touch with my pleasure zone. Believing I was invincible, I somehow deduced that as the owner of Studio 54, I could do whatever I wanted to and get away with it. Gwynne Rivers, my former assistant, recently told me about a dinner that I had with her parents back then. Her father and mother had invited me out to dinner to get better acquainted and assure themselves that they weren't remiss as parents in permitting Gwynne to come to Studio 54 after school and work on the parties she was so good at putting together. I arrived at the restaurant so high on Angel Dust that I nodded out in the middle of our conversation, my face just missing a plate of fettuccine Alfredo. They were flabbergasted. Gwynne, clever as she was, told them I was coming down with a bad cold and taking all sorts of cold medicine. She was able to work it out, continued to do her parties at Studio 54, and saved my reputation with her parents.

Gwynne's parents weren't the only ones concerned about the drug culture at Studio 54. The Ecumenical Coalition to Stamp Out Drugs sponsored an event at the nearby Sacred Heart Church on West Fifty-First Street to bring pressure on the authorities to "Shut down Studio 54." Their flyer went on to say, "Studio 54 is a moral obscenity to every decent resident of New York. More than just a protected haven for drug use by the 'beautiful people,' Studio 54 glamorizes marijuana—and cocaine-use to our youth. There must be no 'double standard'—we need a drug-free America. Shutting down Studio 54 will begin the reversal of the spiritual and moral decay of our city. We call on all religious, civic, and other organizations and every moral individual to join our prayer vigil and peaceful demonstration against Studio 54."

I ignored them and their stupid message of "no more drugs." My body was screaming, "MORE DRUGS NOW MOTHERFUCKER OR I'M SHUTTING THIS PARTY DOWN!" My body turned against me. I had developed a tolerance to it all and what once got me so very high no longer worked. My body was screaming at me, demanding I give it stronger and greater quantities to achieve the same level of happiness. I began experimenting with an even wilder combination of drugs in an effort to reach a new high. And then it happened—the drugs stopped working. I was getting these angry IMMUNE …IMMUNE messages. My body was DEMANDING more. The coke no longer made me feel good—it burned my nose, sometimes causing it to bleed. I had done so much damage to my nasal membranes from years of snorting night and day. I felt trapped in my body, which didn't feel like *my* body anymore. And the worst part of all? My dick turned against me. I was having trouble getting it up. And still I refused to stop. I was determined to find something that would work. I went on a mission to find a new protocol. Two shots of 151-proof alcohol, two Quaaludes, and a big snort of coke felt good. So what if it burned my nose and made it bleed. The goal was to get fucked up, stay there, and never come down.

I had become a lowlife. Bereft of any feeling of humanity. One early morning Rick James dropped by the penthouse with his model friend Tina and said, "I've got a great idea for you, Mark. I'd like Tina to come live with you." I said yes—even though saying yes meant moving Bobbie out. Rick said that Bobbie had been badmouthing me behind my back. True or false, my behavior was inexcusable. It was 5:00 a.m. and I was really stoned—I'd reached a point where I just didn't care anymore, so I agreed to switch Bobbie for Tina in my apartment. Bobbie didn't take it very well—she cried and demanded of Rick, "Why did you say those things about me? They weren't true!" I calmed Bobbie down and assured her she would keep her lucrative VIP-area bartending job at Studio 54. This was out of character for me. Never before had I treated a friend or an employee in this way—but I did.

Tina was tall—maybe six foot one—and gorgeous. Rick wanted to make her a star. He figured that having Tina close to me would pay off for her, plus he wanted me to hook her up with Billy "Tootsie" Tuetsos who could send her out on some go-sees. Billy was a total character—so over the top, you'd think he'd leapt right off the pages of a screenplay. He was short, solid, tough-talking, streetwise, and handsome in a rough-around-the-edges kind of way. He was gay and he knew a lot of people. Billy provided services to famous models—he escorted them places, introduced them to people, and protected them from bad elements. He was a good guy and everybody liked him. One of his biggest clients was Janice Dickinson. He also worked for me, coordinating events in the modeling industry, as he was friends with bookers at all the major agencies, like Monique Pilar at Elite and Joey Hunter at Ford as well as *Interview* magazine editor Daniela Morera.

What I did to Bobbie, moving her out of my apartment to accommodate Rick's protégé, Tina, was so wrong. I would sometimes see Bobbie crying at the club. I was sad about it, but not enough to turn my back on Tina and Sara when they approached me one afternoon asking me if they could take a bath together in my Jacuzzi. I said, "Sure, as long as you invite me."

Into the tub we went, lathering each other up and playing around, getting each other hot and bothered for the action that was set to take place once we'd all toweled off and retired to my bed. I'd like to be able to share with you what it was like to be with curvy Sara and lithe Tina, but the truth is that I can't. It wasn't about the girls anymore, or about giving them pleasure. It was all about me. My wanting and not getting. Why doesn't this feel good? Why is my dick not cooperating? Why am I here—in bed—with these two? Everything that had once been so joyful, playful, and alive for me had now taken on a depressive pallor—and it was about to get worse.

The negative effects of cocaine and Angel Dust were slowly becoming more and more apparent. I was unstable, paranoid, and my judgment had become so impaired that I agreed to host parties that were wrong for the club and, in one case, dangerous. Case in point, the premiere party of the film *Hells Angels Forever*. Chuck Zito was a prominent figure in the Hells Angels motorcycle club and a regular at Studio 54. He attended many of our biggest and most private events, sometimes acting as a bodyguard, providing security to stars like Liza Minnelli. Nikki Haskell, who was paid to book celebrity parties in addition to hosting her cable TV talk show, suggested an after-party for the premiere of the Hells Angels' movie.

I was wary at first, because I remembered the free festival at Altamont Speedway in December 1969. The Hells Angels had agreed to provide security for the Rolling Stones in return for $500 worth of beer. The Angels positioned themselves directly in front of the stage, drinking beer and controlling the crowd with chains and throwing loaded cans of beer at them. When eighteen-year-old Meredith Hunter, Jr., a black American art student from Berkeley, California, approached the stage, he was violently pushed back by the bikers. When he returned to the stage area and took out a gun, he was stabbed to death by Hells Angel Alan Passaro. Everything was caught on camera, becoming a central scene in the documentary film *Gimme Shelter*. Passaro was charged with murder and acquitted on grounds of self-defense. But after Chuck assured me that nothing like that would happen at Studio 54, I was crazy enough to go along with the idea, despite the fact that my King Charles Spaniel, Oliver, given to me by Roy Cohn, seemingly disapproved. While I was meeting with Chuck in the penthouse, Oliver barked at him, then lifted his leg and peed on Chuck's boot. Oliver was a smart dog—I should've listened to him.

Hells Angels Forever premiered at a theater on Fourty-Fourth Street and Broadway. Hundreds of Harley-Davidson motorcycles were impressively parked on Broadway, making quite a statement, blocking traffic and causing great concern. Even though the NYPD were notified in advance of the event, the police appeared totally unprepared. When the movie broke, instead of driving east on Forty-Fourth Street and heading north on Eighth Avenue (a one-way avenue that runs uptown) the motorcycle motorcade drove north on Broadway (a one-way avenue that runs downtown) driving against traffic. They forced cars, buses, and even police cars to side streets. Then the Angels parked their bikes all along Fifty-Fourth Street, completely blocking the street and the front entrance to all traffic, and no one had the nerve to challenge them.

I knew the party was a mistake within minutes of their arrival. It was different from our "usual" atmosphere that night. But what did I expect? I was crazy to book it. Instead of the jovial feeling we were known for creating, my entire staff was intimidated—as they should have been. The Angels and their women drank, danced, and had a good time, but they also muscled anyone who got in their way, including throwing a bartender off the balcony. After that, manager Skip Odeck asked busboy, Oscar Lopez, if he could fill in as bartender for the night. Oscar remembers the evening: "I jumped at the opportunity to tend bar but it was bad… I kept my mouth shut. Bartender George Alvarez and I gave them whatever they wanted once we saw that kid go over the balcony."

They stuffed several patrons headfirst into big trash cans that we had strategically placed around the dance floor, part of the décor, to create a feeling of the street for the party. Finally, Chuck Zito, who appeared in the 2012 season of *Sons of Anarchy,* was able to calm everyone down. I was on edge the entire night until everyone finally left. Miraculously, the bartender wasn't hurt that badly, and the patrons were only bruised. The event was widely covered by the press, and I swore I would never do anything so risky again. The next day when busboy Oscar Lopez showed up for work he was promoted to bartender.

In 1984 I booked another evening that didn't work out the way I anticipated. This time I was on the receiving end of having to deal with someone else's drug and alcohol abuse. It was a one-night performance by the legendary Jerry Lee Lewis. He always drew a big crowd wherever he played and I couldn't wait to hear him rock the house with "Great Balls Of Fire." He stood me up. After a series of calls from "The Killer" saying he was going to be late, but would definitely be there, he never showed. My partner Stanley was ready to kill me. We had to refund our patrons' money and we filed a lawsuit, but it never went anywhere. I learned later that Jerry Lee was far down the path of his own drug and alcohol addiction during that period. He almost died in 1981 as a result of ulcers caused by alcohol, amphetamines, and barbiturates, and in 1986 he checked into the Betty Ford Clinic for an addiction to painkillers.

Chapter Twenty-Seven:
Angel Dust Meets the Whippets

THEN I DID SOMETHING that I couldn't talk my way out of. My judgment was so clouded and my take on reality so distorted that I entered into a business deal that cost me my home. I convinced my partners (including my father and brother) to sell the Executive Hotel to Steve and Ian, and their investor, for cash and forgiveness of my debt from the Studio 54 purchase. While in jail, Steve and Ian had been dreaming about making their next move into the hotel industry. So, in early 1982 they scoured New York looking at various hotel properties but couldn't figure out how to finance a real estate purchase with the stigma of being convicted felons. Then one night, stoned out of my mind at 4:00 a.m., I suggested to Steve, after hearing him vent his frustration, "Maybe you should take a look at my hotel." Steve told Ian and within a few days, Ian brought an architect to look at the building. Together they envisioned the possibilities for converting the Executive Hotel into an elegant boutique hotel. Suddenly Steve and Ian were all over me, like wolves circling their prey, to make the deal. They wanted me to trade my interest in the Executive Hotel for the noncompete debt on Studio 54 that we still owed them.

At that moment in time, I badly wanted to relieve the financial pressure on the operation, which I was feeling personally. Once various entrepreneurs in New York saw how successful Studio 54 was in its first year since reopening, Area, Limelight, Visage, Surf Club, and The Red Parrot were now on the scene, forcing me into the "dancing as fast as I can" syndrome to stay ahead of the competition. I was focused on competing for the best promoters and staging the best events, but because of the money we were paying to Steve and Ian (and for their taxes), we didn't have the cash flow they had back in '77 to stage the numerous extravaganzas they did. Staying one step ahead was kind of like skiing downhill in front of an avalanche. Any second I could be overtaken; I was always looking over my shoulder. I was definitely running for my life and it wasn't just the financial pressure I needed relief from—I needed a rest from the person I'd become.

The Executive Hotel was just breaking even, so I threw out a price of $5 million, although my partners later bumped it to $6 million—25 percent or so of the equity would be my percentage in the trade. Studio 54's debt to Steve and Ian was substantial because we bought the club for no money down to them other than the payment to the state and the IRS over a number of years. Naïvely, I assumed that I would continue to live in the penthouse apartment that I had spent two years building, and knowing Steve and Ian's creative sensibilities, my apartment would wind up on top of a very cool and happening hotel.

However, as we entered into the negotiations, it was quickly apparent that they would insist that my penthouse apartment become part of their new hotel. Although I didn't want to give it up, I wanted relief from the substantial monthly payments, which would stop the moment we signed a preliminary agreement. I naively told myself that the boys weren't going to be able to raise the money, and therefore I had nothing to worry about. My life and happiness were so entwined with being the owner of the most famous club in the world that I would have done almost anything to get relief from the debt, thus enabling me to continue being the owner of Studio 54 forever.

In order to close the deal on the Executive Hotel, which Steve and Ian so desperately needed as part of the plan to restart their careers, they increased the pressure on me for back payments. Had I been on my game, I might have handled the situation differently, including possibly filing a Chapter XI with Studio 54 to stall or compromise their debt rather than trade my interest in the hotel. But I didn't. Unbeknownst to me, they had been in the planning stages of opening Palladium, an enormous nightclub downtown on Fourteenth Street, as consultants to two wealthy investors while still collecting the noncompete payments from me. I thought we were friends. I really didn't think they would scheme against me, but in actuality, they were two tough former nightclub owners, hardened by a prison term and understandably looking out for their own futures. My lapse in judgment and my clouded, delusional mind were a direct result of all the shit I was putting in my body on a daily basis.

I also believed that Studio 54 could live on for at least another fifteen years and that I would make millions. I was paying less than $15,000 per month in rent, which I had negotiated while the boys were serving time. I hadn't figured the cost of what the drugs were doing to me into the equation. And who could have known that one of the deadliest viruses known to mankind would completely change the New York night-scene within a year?

At that point I was too fucked up and discombobulated to deal with legal issues. I didn't look out for *me*. I left everything in the hands of my father, who wanted to cash out his interest in the hotel: his attorney Manny Zimmer, who represented the Executive Hotel partners; and my partner in Studio 54, Stanley Tate, who liked the idea of debt relief and wanted to make the deal fly as well. I assumed they would protect me personally, but they didn't. I didn't have an attorney present at the negotiations, representing my interests specifically, which was an irreversible and costly mistake on my part.

My partners were happy because the Executive Hotel was only breaking even, and yet they managed to sell it to Steve, Ian, and their investor for a million dollars more than it was worth, making a handsome profit, having paid so little for it in 1968. Within a year and toward the end of the hotel renovation, the Executive Hotel, now renamed Morgans, would no longer be my home. I was forced to move out of my beautiful duplex that I loved so much.

In retrospect, it was blatantly obvious that Steve and Ian had enlisted the support of everyone around me, including my partners at the Executive Hotel and my father's chosen attorney. They were continually meeting with my partners to ensure that they could get a deal structured, and the truth is I was always too busy and too stoned to attend. It was not a subtle manipulation, it was easy to spot, but they got away with it because I was no longer "in the game." The warrior spirit that I'd once had was nowhere to be found. Everyone around me was saying, "Oh, don't worry about it, you'll find something else." Our attorney was urging me to finalize the deal. Steve kept schmoozing me, saying the apartment was easily replaceable, telling me, "Don't worry, Bianca just got a great condo for four hundred thousand dollars on Central Park West."

The closing was scheduled in a huge conference room of a major law firm. Everyone was lined up, encouraging me to sign the final documents, but in reality, I didn't have to. The scene was surreal. Not one person in that room was looking out for me, including myself. I was swimming with sharks, experienced in the hunt for fresh blood. Alone, without my warrior spirit,

I didn't stand a chance against this powerful group of Steve and Ian, their investor Phil Pilevsky, their gang of top-flight attorneys, my partners in the hotel, and our lawyer. They sat there looking at me. They all wanted the deal to close. I hesitated, and then I signed. After the closing, I returned to my penthouse and got fucked up with Angel Dust—I got so high, and felt so good, nothing else mattered. Not a fucking thing.

During the renovations of the hotel, Stanley called for a meeting at Steve and Ian's new office to address my erratic behavior and the difficulties Studio 54 was now facing as a result of all the new competition in town. This was meant to be a serious meeting, a sort of "come to Jesus" moment, if you will. I took the elevator down from my penthouse to the office, high as a kite on Angel Dust, in shorts, barefoot and babbling.

When Stanley, Steve, and Ian tried to talk to me about options for reinvigorating the club because it wasn't working as it had during our first two and a half years, I treated them with complete disdain. I remember thinking to myself, "They don't know what they're talking about. If they would just leave me alone and let me do it my way, I can get it back on track." I was delusional and in a steep decline and while Stanley, Steve, Ian, and many others around me could see it—I was in denial. Unbeknownst to me, with Stanley's encouragement, Steve and Ian started looking around for a buyer for Studio 54.

I resented being told what to do by Stanley during our days together at Studio 54. I complained about him, appreciating none of what he tried to tell me. I was convinced that I was right, and I turned a deaf ear. I realize now that Stanley was a good partner. He put up with my drug-induced lunacy for years, but in the end he helped to sell the club and get me out of the deal with some money to show for it.

Reality finally set in about a year later when I had to move out of the penthouse. While I was happy to be relieved of the debt, the price I paid was the loss of my very comfortable and beautiful home. As it turned out, Steve and Ian did far more with the property as Morgans than we would ever have done with it as the Executive Hotel. Ian created an architectural gem out of a not-so-special 150-room, second-rate hotel. It was a task that our original group of partners at the Executive Hotel never would have pulled off—we didn't function as a dynamic, cohesive team. Still, when it came time for me to move, I did not go quietly. My recollection of the events leading up to my moving out was not as clear as that of my assistant, Victoria Leacock, as told to Anthony Haden-Guest in his book *The Last Party:*

> *"They didn't have any trouble getting me out,"* Mark says. *"I had found a new apartment but it wasn't completely ready. They were saying, 'You gotta move!' I said 'Fuck you. I'll move when I can move.'"*

Victoria Leacock remembers it a bit differently. Rubell and Schrager suddenly just appeared. "I was on the telephone taking names for a guest list," she said. "It was about eleven in the morning. Steve and Ian must have got in with their own keys.

"Mark came blasting through the bedroom door with a big gun. It was like Li'l Abner. Steve and Ian ran for the elevator. Then they shouted obscenities from the hallway. But they were talking on the telephone later that day."

Eventually I moved to a nice condo near the club on West Fifty-Sixth Street—but it was depressing compared to my penthouse in the sky. Within six months I rented it out to a Paine Webber executive, and I moved into a bright apartment on Central Park South with an expansive view of the park, which would have made anyone else happy. But by that point, I had completely spiraled into a depression that began six months earlier, when I finally realized that I had to sell Studio 54.

And then AIDS reared its ugly head and took away any joy I still had in life.

Studio 54 became a frightening scene for most of the people who worked and partied there.

Carefree, fun-filled nights were replaced by fear, anticipating the next piece of bad news.

At first, no one understood what was going on, as there was so little information available. People were afraid to go out because we didn't know how the sickness was spreading. We asked, "Is it safe to touch other people, breathe the same air? Does it spread like a cold, or only through body fluids?" No answers. People were scared to sit on any toilet seat other than their own. Michael Johnson, cofounder of SIR, recently told me that he and *Hamptons Magazine* publisher Randy Schindler wore leather gloves for a time—afraid to touch anyone or anything. For the people stricken by AIDS, there were no answers. They were dazed and confused, not knowing what was making them so sick. It was a horrible time and seemed like forever before the medical community jumped in. I was devastated. AIDS had become a full-blown epidemic, and it surrounded me. I was going to more funerals than parties. So many people from my crowd were getting sick, and not getting better. They were dying. For a while the word on the street was that the epidemic in New York had been spread by some of our bartenders, beautiful boys, who desired both men and women. People were afraid to come out and business declined. Quaaludes were banned. The sexual freedom we all enjoyed abruptly ended. The regulars at Studio were now regulars at meetings in basements of local churches reciting the serenity prayer, going to rehab, or gathering at the funerals of friends. It was gut-wrenching to see people who only a year earlier had been strong, healthy, and vibrant now looking like the walking dead. The light and joy went out of everything.

It was my job to make sure we were always on the cutting edge of New York nightlife—but by 1984, I'd lost my focus. Besides making numerous mistakes in handling personnel, promoters, and patrons, I found myself getting into arguments, brought on by my overwhelming sense of paranoia caused by my out-of-control coke habit and alcohol consumption. I foolishly let our super-talented general manager Michael Overington quit over inconsequential issues and a small raise he was asking for. He was scooped up the next day by Steve and Ian, who were clearheaded and knew how to use his talents effectively at Palladium. Luckily we had a real talent waiting in the wings, our assistant manager, David Miskit, who stepped in and filled the void. I became so disconnected from it all that I didn't bother showing up at Studio 54 on some evenings, instead, telling staff and promoters to call me at home and I would deal with any problems over the phone. For the first time, the unthinkable occurred. I lay in bed thinking about life without Studio 54. I wanted out.

My years running Studio 54 were the wildest—a magic carpet ride—a never-ending party and quest for the mother of all highs. But the highs and lows of the ride had taken their toll on me. I was about to call it quits at Studio, and then one day someone introduced me to nitrous oxide and BOOM…the best high ever. I wanted to be back in the game again.

I was ready to return to the party at Studio 54.

Nitrous oxide is a form of laughing gas. It can easily be obtained in head shops all over the country in small whipped cream cartridges, called Whippets, and is commonly used recreationally. The head shops will often provide the user with a canister that breaks the cartridges, thus allowing the gas to be released. Technically, the use of nitrous oxide in this way is illegal, yet it is easily available despite its association with benzodiazepines. Nitrous oxide provided me with a euphoric feeling like nothing I had ever experienced before in my life …and I mean nothing.

This is how you play with Whippets.

You break the cartridge…inhale the gas…SOAR for twenty seconds…and then it's OVER and the minute it's over…you do it AGAIN…

BREAK the cartridge…INHALE…SOAR…it's OVER…

AGAIN…

BREAK…INHALE…SOAR…

AGAIN…

BREAK…INHALE…SOAR…

How fucked up is that?

Once I was introduced to nitrous oxide Whippets, I couldn't stop. But I couldn't go outside either. So I didn't. I was happy to stay home with my new friends the Whippets. The pleasure they gave me paled next to anything or anyone.

The canister and cartridges were cumbersome, noisy, and obvious. I couldn't put them around my neck or hang them from my belt like a vial of coke. No matter how I packed them, the clanging of the cans made so much noise. The only thing that would have worked was to tightly pack them in an attaché case, but I would have looked fucking ridiculous with an attaché case attached to me—taking it everywhere. I became tired of everything—even my nightly adventures with celebrities became a grind. Nothing else made me happy or was worthy of my time but the Whippets. They were so much fun and so pleasurable, but the effect was so short-lived that one quickly becomes a candidate for addiction, creating a psychological dependency like no other. You forget who you are, which contributes to the deterioration of your personality. Nitrous oxide will suck you in, fuck you up, and take you down.

I lost all interest in Studio 54.

Luckily for me, momentum kept Studio 54 going until Stanley Tate and I were able to make a deal with a buyer, at which time it was still the most famous club in the world, and one of the most successful in New York. I was sad when the Studio 54 sale documents were signed. I had truly loved the experience of owning and operating the most famous club in the world and partying every night with the rich and famous. But at the same time I was relieved. I no longer had the pressure of creating an event every night to keep Studio 54 operating at the highest level. I was reminded of something Steve Rubell had said during one of my visits with him in the New York Federal prison: "I hate it here, but I'm happy I don't have the strain of entertaining every night."

We sold Studio 54 to Frank Cashman, a know-it-all type who against my advice started to commercialize the club, destroying the successful business within one year. He advertised on the radio, ruining any chance of attracting celebrities, and refused to offer complimentary drinks to the few remaining VIPs. It was over. More than a year after the sale, Cashman defaulted on the last year or so of payments. I considered stepping back in, but the price of the required insurance for one year was well over $1 million because of numerous pending insurance claims, including one by basketball star David Thompson who was suing Studio 54 for $10 million claiming he was pushed down the stairs there one night. Steve Steckel from security had this to say recently, "One of the tech-crew guys, I don't remember his name but he was short, about five foot three, didn't like it when he saw Dave Thompson grab Penny's ass as she was walking up the stairs." Penny worked in coat check. He confronted the six-foot-four Thompson, a scuffle ensued, and Thompson fell down the stairs. Who pushed who—I don't know.

Between the sale of Studio 54 and several hotels that I owned an interest in, I had enough money and, by rights, I should have been happy. But I wasn't. I missed being the Lord of the Night. The world I'd created in my penthouse by day, and at Studio 54 by night, was gone. All I wanted to do was stay in bed all day, watch TV, feel sorry for myself, and wonder where it all went wrong.

I no longer had an endless array of women available to me. So I called Sara, who had been one of my live-in assistants a year earlier at Studio 54. She was an extremely sexy woman, and she enjoyed participating in the occasional ménage à trois that I put together, so I hired her once again and moved her into my guest room on Central Park South. She'd pick up groceries, prepare meals, and walk Oliver. Sara became my enabler, making sure that my beloved Whippets were always on hand to hang out with. I was living in Oblivion, USA and wanted to keep it that way.

Sara liked to walk around practically naked and we had sex often in one form or another—and while the sex was good, when you're as depressed as I was, nothing penetrates the depression. In other words, there was no satisfaction to be had. But I didn't stop trying, I wouldn't give up. When I got bored of sex with just Sara, she'd invite her friend Susan over, and the three of us would make it together. Susan would give me hour-long blow jobs while I fondled Sara and caressed her large breasts, drinking vodka and sniffing amyl nitrate simultaneously. Sometimes Susan would mount me—when my dick cooperated—and gyrate while Sara sat on my face, fondling Susan's breasts. This was extremely pleasurable, and then it was over. My dick stopped working—turned on me—just like the drugs.

One day, some months later in the spring of 1985, while lying in bed with the blinds drawn to block out the sunshine and the view of Central Park, Laurie Lister, my former girlfriend, showed up at my apartment demanding to know why I had dropped out of sight. She marched into my bedroom and was horrified by what she saw. She immediately started rummaging through my drawers and found all kinds of drug paraphernalia, including boxes of empty Whippets. You'd think that I would have objected to her barging in on me like that—but I didn't. I just lay there. I was totally out of it.

Laurie was irate, waving her arms in the air and yelling, "This has got to stop! You're ruining your life! I'm calling Bob."

Laurie called Bob Millman. Bob came over and together they took control. Bob declared, "You have to go to rehab at the Betty Ford Center."

I was reluctant at first; I just wanted to remain in bed in my semiconscious, self-pitying state. This was years before the days of social celebrity rehab centers that are considered fashionable today. However, I realized that Laurie and Bob were concerned because they both cared so much about me, so I started to think seriously about rehab. I had recently broken my front tooth trying to get high off a nitrous oxide canister and brushing my teeth at the same time. Can you imagine? I wouldn't put the Whippets aside long enough to brush my teeth. I looked ridiculous. Half of my front tooth was missing. When I was forced to leave my apartment to go to the dentist, I discovered I'd gained twenty pounds from the inactivity and I could no longer fit into most of my clothes. In theory, I agreed that I had to do something about my condition before I deteriorated further. I'd heard that Betty Ford had done wonders for many entertainers from the LA scene, and for Liza Minnelli, whose drinking and drugging I knew firsthand to be out of control until she finally went to Betty Ford.

So I got a temporary cap on my front tooth, bought some clothes that were a few sizes larger, and boarded a plane headed to Betty Ford in Palm Springs. I was hoping to save my life.

Chapter Twenty-Eight:
The Betty Ford Effect

THE INSTRUCTION PACKET FOR Betty Ford specifically advises patients not to drink on the plane en route to rehab. But the thought of not getting high or having a drink for the rest of my life—if I made it through the program successfully—made me determined to indulge myself one last time with a pick-me-up before breakfast. So I dropped the two Quaaludes that Laurie hadn't found when she ransacked my apartment, and ordered a Bloody Mary. And then I ordered three more. By the time I landed in sunny Palm Springs in April of 1985, I was smashed.

Staff members met me at the airport and brought me to the check-in area at Administration, where I walked straight to the couch and passed out. A few hours later, I woke up with a hangover, craving some sort of stimulant, but there was nothing to be found. My belongings were searched for drugs, and then I was shown to my room, given some detox medication which made me nauseous, and eventually went back to sleep.

The first three days were disorienting and difficult. I desperately wanted something to jumpstart me. Depriving my body of all the chemical substances that kept me in an altered state for the past four years sent my system into shock. I wanted out, I wanted a drink, I wanted a woman in my bed—and I wanted it *now*!

I had no choice but to deal with waking up and living minute to minute in a sober state deprived of the substances I'd been using for years. At first, time stood still—very still. I had no concept of time—only that I wasn't getting what I wanted. After what seemed like an eternity, I began living hour to hour. Eventually, I made it to day to day and that's when I started to make progress. I didn't appreciate the dormitory-style accomodations. I was sleeping in a twin bed and sharing my space with a twenty-five-year-old male roommate, but I accepted it.

I also accpeted the fact that the routine of individual and group therapy sessions was helping. After attending several group discussions and sharing stories, there was no doubt that my degree of drug intake and all the other insane shit I did topped them all. But I was progressing, learning how to make it through the day without drugs and alcohol. I returned to reading, a lifelong passion, which I had made no time for in the past four years.

I soon befriended an anesthesiologist from Chicago who was serving time in rehab for getting caught with his hands in the hospital's medicine cabinet. Early every morning, before it became too hot, we'd run for an hour on the track, talking about life and how we both ended up at Betty Ford. It was both intellectually and physically therapeutic. Within a month I lost most of the weight I had recently gained, was able to fit into my old clothes, and was generally feeling okay without drugs and alcohol. I was conscious about my diet and growing physically stronger each day. The anesthesiologist graduated from the program and returned to Chicago to resume his practice while I continued to run each morning alone, contemplating what had gone wrong in my life—a life so promising—fifteen years earlier when I was a young man of thirty.

Then one day Andy Gibb checked himself into Betty Ford. When I met Andy at Studio 54 in the early 1980s, he had been consoling himself with liquor and cocaine, heartbroken over his breakup with actress Victoria Principal. While I was happy to see him again, our conversations took me back to the worst parts of my cocaine and alcohol binges. Andy was a sweet, fun, good-looking guy who had been an occasional member of the Dawn Patrol at Studio. He would show up at my office from time to time, and occasionally at my apartment, and we would do coke together. He really loved cocaine, and every now and then he'd ask me to buy some for him, which I would.

Seeing Andy at Betty Ford reminded me of a day back in early 1983 when I received a call from a panicked Zev Buffman, the producer of *Joseph and the Amazing Technicolor Dreamcoat*, the Broadway musical that Andy had secured a starring role in. It was just a few hours before his evening performance and once again, Andy was nowhere to be found. He had missed twelve performances since his opening night a few months earlier. I put out feelers to some of the night people asking where he might be, but no one I knew could find him.

He never made it to the theatre that night. Buffman sacked the twenty-four-year-old heartthrob. It was a decision he did not take lightly. Buffman was a fan of Andy and enjoyed being around him, but the fact is, Andy didn't show up enough and audiences were buying tickets to see him, not his understudy.

Andy was blackballed from Broadway as a result. I imagine this only served to speed up his spiral deeper into depression and more drugs. It was a shame because had he remained in that production he would have earned an enormous amount of good press, which would have led to other projects. I believe the routine and self-esteem earned from such rewarding work would have saved him. "Of the five Josephs we've had so far, Andy was definitely the best actor," conceded Zev Buffman.

Fast-forward to April 1985. Andy showed up at Betty Ford only to walk out of treatment after just three days into the six-week program. The counselor predicted he'd be dead soon—and sadly, within a few years and just five days after his thirtieth birthday, he was.

After four weeks I decided I'd had enough and made plans to leave the Betty Ford Clinic. I wanted to continue to improve but I felt I had learned everything there was to learn from the therapists and counselors during my stay so far. I didn't think I had the same level of psychological problems to tackle as the other patients. To this day I believe that it takes a lot more than drugs to make you a drug addict. It's a mental thing. I acknowledged the benefits, but I didn't find most of the therapists to be inspirational role models. They sat around all day drinking coffee and smoking cigarettes, appearing to have their own issues with unhealthy addictions to nicotine and caffeine. And that didn't work for me. But I had to admit, even though I questioned *their* personal addictions, they forced me to face some important truths about my own.

I was bullshitting myself, and the therapists, when I told them that my drug use was a part of my job at Studio 54 and that it was expected of me. During group therapy sessions, we discussed the timeline of my drug use, and it became clear to me that my drug abuse started years before Studio 54. I started drinking in college at Cornell, and then took it to another level while running the officers' club in the navy. I jumped in, drinking from noon until closing, and became accustomed to a constant buzz. I could have handled it differently, but I didn't. It was more fun to drink with the officers and other guests. It never occurred to me to request that the bartenders water down my drinks. When I first started to smoke marijuana, it inspired creativity and sharpened my perception. It relaxed me and helped me focus. I drank less and told myself—that's good. Smoke more, drink less, avoid hangovers. So, I started each day with a huge joint and continued smoking throughout the day and into the evening. I abused it. I was operating in a haze of pot, and getting away with it.

Tripping on acid can be a powerful learning experience, as documented by many doctors of the 1960s. It can be a path to unlocking the mysteries of the subconscious when taken with guidance and respect for its mind-altering effects. I abused its positive powers and took it way too often. I was a thirty-year-old whiz kid in the late 1960s, on a journey enhanced, I thought, by the wisdom gleaned from my experiences with hallucinogenic drugs. I was young and rising fast; the early success went to my head, leaving me to conclude that I could do no wrong. Being stoned and tripping your brains out is not conducive to success on any level—certainly not when you're at the helm of a multimillion-dollar company and calling all the shots. I took unnecessary risks in business. I told myself that my mind-expanding, mind-altering trips imparted so much knowledge and wisdom to my psyche that they alone would guide me and ensure my success. What a crock. It derailed me.

Then there was cocaine. I did it seven days a week, twelve months a year, for nearly four years at Studio 54. Looking back, I could have kept my drug use under control but I chose not to. I jumped into the party life with reckless abandon. I spent four years of my life doing coke every night and every day, plus Angel Dust, ketamine, Quaaludes, cognac, vodka, scotch, whiskey, and then Valium to go to sleep. That was the routine—day in and day out. People have often asked, "Mark, why did you drink and do so many drugs?" The short answer is, "Because I could."

I blamed everything on Studio 54. I didn't remember, or I chose not to admit, that I was heavily into cocaine long before Studio, particularly in the Virgin Islands. There was a positive and a negative effect to Studio 54 that everyone who worked or hung out there had to deal with. Some people set curfews and imposed limits on their alcohol and drug consumption while others gave not a moment of thought to any of it. It was a dream come true—with celebrities, great music, exotic drugs, dancing all night, beautiful people, and being in the moment, even if the moment is 5:00 a.m. and you're expected in the office at 9:00 a.m. We all had to choose, "Do I stay, or do I go?" I chose to stay.

After four weeks at Betty Ford, I was detoxed and feeling reasonably fit. I was in a better place emotionally and starting to feel a familiar optimism and can-do attitude. Then word reached me about problems at Water's Edge—a restaurant built on a barge on the East River in Manhattan, which I had optioned while looking for a high-profile project to follow my run at Studio 54. I was supposedly actively operating it under a management contract. I had acquired an option at Water's Edge during negotiations at an all-night cocaine marathon in a law office. Many of us participating in the negotiations, including my attorney, had spent much of that night on breaks in the bathroom blowing magic up our noses. I had been so far out there—I was negotiating from another planet and from that perspective it appeared to be a good deal. But the next day I woke up and admitted I wanted nothing to do with it. I hoped the deal wouldn't go through. But it did, and I was stuck with a major responsibility. I thought I could recreate the famous River Café on the Brooklyn waterfront that Buzzy O'Keeffe opened a few years earlier, but I was in no shape to do anything of the sort.

Water's Edge had been opened a year earlier by an inexperienced restaurateur and did well at first because of the great view of Manhattan. That was until the famed *New York Times* food critic Mimi Sheraton gave it a seriously bad review, and people just stopped going. You can see why a deal like this would attract me, as I'd already brought numerous businesses back from the brink of death and normally enjoyed a challenge of this nature. However, at this point in my life, I, like Water's Edge, was too far gone.

My former publicist and friend, Ed Gifford (and his wife and partner, Michael), who had exited my life five years earlier because of my association with Steve and Ian, came back and agreed to represent me at Water's Edge. We hired a chef who had been a sous-chef under acclaimed chef Jean-Jacques Rachou, owner of La Côte Basque. Ed was a real foodie who immediately connected with our chef, but all of this wasn't enough to save Water's Edge. My concentrated involvement was essential to any chance of success, but I started drinking heavily from the moment I signed the deal and assumed management control in January 1985, before I went to Betty Ford.

Each working day began with a drink at 11:30 a.m. when I arrived at Water's Edge. I'd walk directly to the bar and waiting for me would be a gorgeous, perfectly chilled, straight-up vodka martini in a large glass with three olives. And then I'd drink throughout the day. I was so out of it from drinking day and night, and playing with the Whippets as often as possible, that I did something very foolish. I forever ruined my friendship with Christie Brinkley. Just after I took over the restaurant in March 1985, I booked the wedding party of Christie and Billy Joel. Even though I should have known that Christie would not want me talking to the press, I gave Cindy Adams a scoop when she called me for a story to put in her column. I gave her Christie and Billy's menu for the wedding reception. After it appeared in the *New York Post*, Christie, who wanted no prepress and deserved that courtesy, was furious and almost cancelled the event. No apologies I made could have satisfied her, as she trusted me to protect her on her wedding day. It's difficult to say whether the Water's Edge would have succeeded had I been up to the challenge. Despite its glorious view of the Manhattan skyline at its mooring in Long Island City, and the Giffords' best efforts, the simple fact may be that Sheraton's original scathing review had been its death knell and I should never have bought it in the first place.

Even though I'd arranged for my father to look after the restaurant operations for six weeks while I was in treatment at Betty Ford, he called me after only four weeks and announced that he was tired of dealing with my problems, and that I should return home and solve them myself. Wracked with guilt about how I had let him down, behaving in such an inappropriate way with my out-of-control behavior at age forty-five, I told my counselors that I had no choice but to return to New York. They were disappointed and tried convincing me to remain, explaining that because the blood test taken when I first arrived showed such a variety of drugs in my system, I would benefit greatly from the full six weeks. The counselors predicted that if I left early, I would slip just like Andy Gibb did. As it happened, they were right, but I didn't die.

Betty Ford was not my cure-all, but it did educate me about the damaging effects of drug and alcohol abuse. I admitted to how clearheaded I felt after abstaining for more than a month. And though most rehab clinics back then missed the boat by not including a serious physical fitness program, I learned the benefits of that on my own by jogging every day. Nonetheless, the real objective of any rehabilitation program is to get patients to feel good about themselves without drugs.

The counselors at Betty Ford advised me to sever ties with anyone associated with my alcohol and drug use. Once I returned to New York, that's exactly what I did. As much as it pained me, this meant ending my relationship with my assistant, sex kitten, and enabler, Sara. She had phoned me several times while I was in rehab, but as dictated by my counselors at Betty Ford, I did not return her calls. Later on, l learned that Sara had swallowed every pill in my medicine cabinet in an attempt to kill herself, which freaked me out. She was a good person and undeserving of anything but kindness in her life. I am grateful that she recovered. The Twelve-Step Program requires that you make amends with anyone you may have hurt. I made a feeble attempt at best. Other than my mother, my father, and Sara, I honestly felt I hadn't hurt anyone except myself. But there were others, and over time I admitted to that and attempted to make amends. I attended AA meetings occasionally, but somehow I could not wholeheartedly embrace the Twelve-Step Program.

Back in New York, I returned to work on Water's Edge Restaurant, which was losing money. I couldn't think of anything brilliant that would turn it around—and honestly, at that particular time in my life, the last thing I needed was to have a bar as part of my day-to-day life. So I decided to sell the option I had on the property. To do that, I hired a marine architect to create a set of plans that transformed the barge into a two-level catering establishment with spectacular views of the East River and the Manhattan skyline. Then, I presented the plans to a well-known Long Island catering company owned by Marika and Stuart Somerstein that specialized in kosher weddings and bar mitzvahs. I knew Stuart from working together as assistant stewards in the kitchen at Brown's Hotel in the Catskills Mountains in a summer program required by the Cornell Hotel School. We shook hands on a fair purchase price of $500,000 and agreed to meet at my lawyer Irwin Underweiser's office. I felt good—this deal meant I'd recoup the money I'd spent on the down payment and cover my operational losses. I was pleased with myself.

I was dismayed, however, when I learned upon arrival at my lawyer's office that the Somersteins and their attorney had reneged on the deal. I was so furious that I walked out, headed around the corner to the Friars Club, and ordered a shot of 101-proof Wild Turkey with a beer chaser. It was my first drink since Betty Ford, and it wouldn't be my last.

The alcohol calmed me down, and I returned to the law office. Irwin told me that while I had been at the Friars Club, he'd had a calm conversation with the buyers and their attorney and he had persuaded them to agree to a reduced purchase price. He said that if I was amenable to shaving $200,000 off the purchase price and extending payments, he could still structure a deal. I ended up losing money, but I didn't care. I was rid of a situation that would bring only trouble at this juncture of my life.

I slipped, started drinking again, and just about abandoned my physical fitness regimen altogether. I also stopped going to AA meetings. But there was a positive aspect to this relapse. It was nothing like my binges in the Studio 54 days. I was more aware now. My past behavior had deeply disturbed me, and I cared that I was losing control of my recovery. At first, I craved alcohol even while I was abstaining from it. Before long I was depressed again and started drinking at home during the day. Most of the willpower I had gained from the Betty Ford experience had dissipated.

For the first time in my adult life, I had nothing to do and way too much time on my hands. Without even one project to occupy my time, I found myself sitting in my apartment all day, looking out at Central Park and wondering what went wrong. I knew that I had to find myself. To my credit, though, I was not in bed, the blinds were not drawn, and I was fully dressed. That was progress compared to my condition before Betty Ford.

Then, one day in late 1985, I received a visit from my songwriter buddy, Paul Jabara. He could not believe my condition and how unhappy I appeared to be. He begged me to go to Rancho La Puerta, an organic fitness center located on a three-thousand-acre nature preserve in the mountains of Baja California, to rehabilitate myself.

Chapter Twenty-Nine:
My Place in the Sun

A CCORDING TO THE BROCHURE they sent me, Rancho La Puerta was founded by Edmond Szekely and his wife, Deborah, in 1940 in Tecate, Mexico, an hour southeast of San Diego. The Ranch, as it's known among its devotees, sits at the base of Mount Kuchumaa, a sacred mountain that means "Exalted High Place" in the ancient Yuman and Kumeyaay native language.

Szekely was a philosopher, theologian, biochemist, nutritionist, and historian. He was a true Renaissance-man, and an environmentalist long before it became fashionable. The Romanian-born Szekely founded Rancho La Puerta to integrate ancient ideas about health and wisdom into a modern-day lifestyle. His personal philosophy, known as the "School of Life," sought to appreciate and protect nature and transform people's understanding about the care and feeding of their bodies. This is a process through which we can become the "owners" of our whole being in every sense of the word. Thirty years before the Human Potential Movement, Szekely embodied ideas that espoused good health, long life, and the interdependence of mind, body, and spirit—not to mention the importance of respecting the health of the air, water, and soil on which we depend for life itself. Szekely also believed that it was never too late to reinvent oneself. That spoke to me.

Aldous Huxley, whose books I devoured during my acid trip days in the late 1960s, traveled there often from his home in Death Valley, California. Burt Lancaster, who starred in two of my favorite movies, *Sweet Smell of Success* and *Elmer Gantry*, was another frequent visitor. Although it wasn't an official rehab clinic, The Ranch sounded like such a magical setting that I could not get there fast enough. I immediately booked a week's stay and flew to San Diego with the intention of turning my life around once and for all.

Edmond and Deborah Szekely chose the location for Rancho La Puerta not only for its proximity to Mount Kuchumaa but because the weather in northern Baja was conducive to their ideas of well-being. While there on a scientific commission sponsored by the French government to study various regions and their relation to human health, Edmond Szekely discovered that the climate in the San Diego County area, just over the border, is one of the healthiest in the world—a perfect balance of desert temperatures, low-humidity, and the cool breeze of the ocean at 1,600 feet in elevation. Couple that with the fact that Tecate, Mexico, as Szekely discovered, has the same northern latitude as Galilee where Jesus of Nazareth was reared, and you have an environment that can "open the door," so to speak. Rancho La Puerta means "The Ranch of the Door," named so for the arch, created by two oak trees, welcoming you to The Ranch and new beginnings, physically and spiritually. I yearned for a new beginning. I wanted to make it right this time.

The Ranch was so much more beautiful than I had imagined. Winding brick pathways threaded through groves of oak, birch, and eucalyptus trees. Clusters of beautiful flowering bushes and cacti surrounded the quaint Mexican-Colonial-inspired stone-and-clay-tiled casitas, gyms, and yoga studios. There was a quarter-mile running track with a vineyard at its center. A slab of slate was set into rocks that had a new enlightened saying chalked onto it each day, such as "Your actions today are tomorrow's memories." They also had a sprawling organic garden with every kind of fruit and vegetable imaginable, used in the preparation of the delicious meals served in a lovely indoor/outdoor dining area, and free-roaming, happy chickens provided fresh eggs every morning. All this was nestled in a green valley beside an arroyo at the base of the towering Mount Kuchumaa. It was serene but at the same time encouraged one to go further, deeper, seek out more, learn, get healthy, and be strong. Besides the organic food and physical exercise programs, The Ranch featured guest lecturers each week, who provided stimulating information about the path to enlightenment.

The Kumeyaay's ancestors originally settled this land thousands of years ago after migrating from Asia across the Bering land bridge and down the coast of North America. They ended up in the mountains of Baja, California after reaching what is now San Diego and heading east, following what is known today as the Tijuana River. They settled in the valley at the base of Mount Kuchumaa, the highest mountain in Southern California. This "Exalted

High Place" embodies the spirit, energy, and rhythm that pervades throughout Rancho La Puerta.

Once I'd settled in, I resolved to get in shape. I began each day with an early-morning, three-and-a-half-mile hike on the lower plateaus of the mountain, which was carpeted with yellow California buttercups and accented by blue sage, giving a feeling of the Land of Oz. I hiked up the steep trail in a trance-like state as the sun rose, and I felt stirrings deep within. After breakfast, I followed the suggested fitness program with strength training, stretching, yoga, lunch, then aerobic dance, tai chi, and swimming. Alone at the end of each day I would make my way back to the mountain to experience the magnificence of the sun setting in the west. I didn't know it at the time, but this was the beginning of my spiritual awakening. After five days of significant physical activity and organic fruits and vegetables, I could feel my inner spirit coming alive.

I was starting to feel healthy, strong, confident, and happy.

I was so intrigued by it all that I arranged to meet with the owner, whom I discovered to be a remarkable woman. Deborah Szekely had developed the rustic facility into a full-scale fitness center after her husband died. She was a vibrant woman, the mother of the modern spa-movement, and she was credited with being the first to recognize the benefits of aerobic dancing. Though The Ranch was full, she somehow found a vacant casita and I was able to stay another week. On Saturday, the day most guests leave and new guests arrive, I joined a small group of fitness instructors led by Phyllis Pilgrim, The Ranch's fitness director, an Englishwoman. This was not a part of the program, but we embarked on a day-long, nearly fifteen-mile round trip hike to the top of Mount Kuchumaa. As we climbed, Phyllis told me of the harrowing years she spent in a Japanese World War II POW camp as a young girl after living in Indonesia, where her father had been a diplomat. Climbing nearly three thousand feet through brush on unused trails was a grueling challenge since I was not in great shape. But the beauty of the mountain and the thrill of reaching the top at such a fast pace gave me an unusual feeling of pride and accomplishment. This was a welcome emotion to experience after the emptiness of the last several years.

I was running out of gas, but finally we broke for the lunch we'd packed and rested at the summit. I gazed upon the Pacific Ocean to the west, the sprawling farms of the Imperial Valley and the Sonoran Desert to the east, the green hills and valleys of California to the north, and the city of Tecate below to the south. I was overwhelmed. I had an epiphany. I'd hiked mountains similar in size before, but this was a hike of a different nature. To say it took my breath away is an understatement. I was grateful to be here and by the grace of God to be alive. I had experienced a similar sensation years earlier, a "close to God" moment, at the ancient Sun and Moon pyramids in Teotihuacan outside of Mexico City after swallowing some acid. This time I was on a natural high and at that moment I prayed, "Please God let this feeling never leave me."

The hike down the mountain was hard on my knees and by the time I got back to The Ranch, I was so tired I passed out before dinner. On Sunday morning, however, I awoke at 6:00 a.m., still exhilarated by Saturday's experience, and I went on an early-morning five-mile mountain hike, which now seemed like a snap.

After breakfast, I visited the small library hoping to learn more about the mountain. In a book called *Cuchama and Sacred Mountains* by W. Y. Evans-Wentz featuring Mount Kuchumaa, Mount Sinai, and other mystical mountains, I read about the long history of shamans who chose young boys from nearby Native American tribes to come to Mount Kuchumaa. There, these young boys would go through a mystical rite of passage and be initiated into the ways of their tribe. The spiritual setting of Mount Kuchumaa gave the young boys the solitude they needed to receive guidance and wisdom.

I was so drawn to the mountain that I went back every day. As the second week progressed, I went on five-mile hikes by myself on the lower ridges of the mountain early each morning. I began noticing all the different perspectives, particularly when the sun rose over the eastern valley, illuminating the hundreds of granite boulders nestled into the chaparral that made up the lower two-thirds of the peak. When I returned each evening, I found myself captivated by the profound white glow of the mountain against the full moon. It was a surreal landscape.

I would often sit next to a boulder that, after thousands of years of being weathered by the rain and sun, now resembled a huge skull. As I gazed intently upon the vast beauty before me, I felt a calm and clarity that brought me back to those nights in the early 1970s, when I wandered through the dark woods near my farmhouse in Vermont. Barefoot, alone, and with no fear whatsoever, as if I were an Indian warrior, the master of all I surveyed. This was different, but the magic of those experiences nearly two decades before induced by hallucinogens was not lost on me.

At Rancho La Puerta, I discovered how much better life was when you approached each day by eating right and exercising. It was beginning to sink in, that I had to think before I put something in my mouth. "If you take care of your body, your body will take care of you" became my new motto. After nearly destroying myself, this concept was crucial for me to comprehend and fully adopt as I tried to embrace sobriety. With my newfound energy and the awakened spirituality that I took from the magical mountain, I was beginning to feel high on life—an old expression, but a new concept for me. When I look back to the nights wandering around the Vermont woods in the black of night with only the moon to guide me, I can relate to how it laid the groundwork for the spiritual turnaround I was now experiencing nearly two decades later. I was on a path to enlightenment back then but I chose to take a detour at one of those crossroads life presents you with. But now, high in the mountains of Baja California, I came to embrace once again the "way of the warrior," as Carlos Castaneda put it in the *Don Juan Trilogy*. I wanted to take control of myself, my life, and my career.

As I sat atop the plateau, I took a long, hard look at some aspects of my life, past and present—particularly the choices I had made. I was looking inward, not with self-pity, but rather with an excitement to learn, a desire for understanding, awareness, perspective, and truth. A considerable amount of my depression came from guilt. There was so much time wasted, money squandered, opportunities lost. Time gone, but not lost if I could put the lessons learned from those bad choices into action. Then they would not be mistakes at all; they would be learning blocks, not stumbling blocks. With that goal in mind, I felt armed, wiser; knowledge is power. Fueled by a stirring of my Samurai-warrior spirit, I wanted to channel everything I'd learned, turn my life around, and realize my potential and destiny.

Chapter Thirty:
Laurie and Hilary

WHILE MY LIFE AND career were floundering in 1985 and 1986, Laurie Lister was rapidly becoming a top-player in the publishing industry after leaving *Penthouse*. She went from being an associate editor at William Morrow to a senior editor/vice president at Simon & Schuster, commanding a significant salary in the publishing industry at the age of thirty-two. She edited a number of high-profile books, including Joe Klein's biography of designer Oleg Cassini who, in addition to creating the look for First Lady Jacqueline Kennedy, was married to legendary Hollywood beauty Gene Tierney. Laurie also edited Wolf Blitzer's autobiography and *Mafia Princess*, written by Mafia kingpin Sam Giancana's daughter, among others. During the year after Studio 54 but before Betty Ford, I called Laurie a number of times, wanting to have dinner and maybe rekindle our relationship. I wanted to pick up where we left off before Studio 54, but she wanted nothing to do with me—with her sharp, perceptive eyes and ears, she could always tell when I was doing drugs.

However, she decided to give me another chance. After all, it was Laurie who arranged the intervention and it was Laurie who visited me at Betty Ford. She believed in me to her core and we began seeing each other again. The positive energy and lessons gleaned from my experience at Rancho La Puerta in 1986 and the changes I made to integrate them into a new and healthy lifestyle gave Laurie the confidence she needed to believe that I truly had changed. When she told me some months later that she was pregnant, I knew in a heartbeat that I was ready to start a family with her.

Aileen Mehle (aka Suzy Knickerbocker) got it right in the last line of our wedding announcement in her social column in the *New York Post* on July 11, 1986 when she said:

Mark Fleischman, once the big man at Studio 54, is getting
married on August 10 at his home in Garrison, New York. The
bride-to-be is lovely Laurie Lister, a Vice President and Senior
Editor at Simon & Schuster. Mark gave up the flashy disco-life
a couple of years ago, sold Studio 54, and settled into the hotel
and restaurant business. And not a moment too soon.

We had a beautiful outdoor wedding. Steve and Ian gifted us with a
magnificent, elaborate flower installation created by Robert Isabell, a highly in-
demand floral designer. Robert created, with Ian's input, a magical atmosphere,
and well-known Westchester caterer Abigail Kirsch prepared the food. The
event was a huge success. Our one hundred or so guests included my mother
and father, Uncle Hy, cousins, Laurie's family, and our close friends, including
Bob and Eva Shaye and their beautiful daughters Katja and Juno. My brother
Alan was my best man, as I had been in his wedding a year earlier.

Me and my parents with three-month-old Hilary.

Then, two events occurred over the course of two years that forever
changed my life. The first was the birth of our daughter, Hilary, on February
18, 1987. I was in the delivery room for close to twenty-four hours while
Laurie was in labor. Finally, she delivered, and when the nurse put the baby
in my arms, I declared, "She's a redhead!" I was consumed with love. I'd heard
that taking part in the birth of your child is the most gratifying experience of
all—it's true—it was a natural high. The moment Hilary was born, I knew that
I would love this child dearly for the rest of my life. I was beside myself with
happiness. Because I worked from home and Laurie worked from 7:00 a.m. to
7:00 p.m. at Simon & Schuster, I was able to spend serious quality time with

my little girl. Hilary was cute, happy, and smart right from the beginning. I remember how proud I felt when I bumped into Antonia de Portago one day at a local supermarket with my beautiful Hilary slung on my back. Antonia could hardly believe it: the Lord of the Night was now a doting father with this fabulous child. And now, thirty years later, Hilary continues to light up my life. She made me so proud as a graduate of Mount Holyoke and, now, as a director with an international private investigation firm. Recently, Hilary married a fabulous guy in an old-fashioned wedding ceremony in New Orleans, and I could not be happier for the couple.

The second event occurred about a year later, in March 1988. My father died of a heart attack. He suffered for a week in the hospital, and I suffered along with him. I was beside myself with sorrow. He blamed me for permitting him to have an operation a few years earlier to relieve blockage in one leg when he could have had a less invasive procedure. He suggested I was responsible for his condition, believing that as his eldest son I should have somehow prevented this from happening even though I wasn't there at the time. The doctor explained to me that my father was irrational and not in his right mind, but that did little to console me. I was devastated, and when it was my mother's time years later, I more than made up for it when she passed away at age ninety-six with me by her side at my home in Malibu.

My father's death had a profound impact on me. He and I had gone into business a number of times together, and he taught me so many valuable lessons that still apply to this day. I found myself deep in circumspection, fueled by loss and regret. My father meant the world to me. At times I tried to tell myself that I'd surpassed him in business. He ran small second-class hotels while I chose more well-known, high-profile enterprises. I was the guy who could take a failed business and turn it into gold—or so the press had said over the years. I had read so many glowing articles written about my exploits that I thought I could do no wrong. I believed I was destined to be greater and more successful than anyone before me in my family—what nonsense. My father and my grandfather were great businessmen and my uncle, Hy Zausner, had been the largest importer of Danish cheese in the US. He was also the visionary who founded the Port Washington Tennis Academy, nurturing such unknowns as John McEnroe and Vitas Gerulaitis. These men always made money, while I frittered away opportunities and millions of dollars, getting high and leading a hedonistic lifestyle.

But it wasn't until after my father died that I appreciated the point of view expressed by him and my mother, having lived through The Depression, World War II, and, in my father's case, World War I, while he was still in Romania. You might say I was no different than some of my fellow baby boomers who didn't grow up until they reached their forties. I didn't make it to mature adulthood until I was nearly fifty. Before losing my father, I hadn't allowed myself to admit how much I depended on him, psychologically and emotionally. And then he was gone—and I longed to tell him. For the first time in my life, I knew that the only one I could rely on was me.

So, in March 1988, I gave the eulogy at my father's memorial service, which was officiated by the fiery Rabbi Hecht. On that day I made a pact with myself. I thought about my responsibility to Hilary and Laurie. I thought about my father—the pride he took in his granddaughter, the joy she brought him, and the pleasure he would never know watching her grow up. Right then and there I knew I had to make something happen—hit a home run in my chosen field of endeavor—for me, for Hilary, and for my father. I sensed he was still watching me.

A return to Rancho La Puerta was imperative to any future personal growth. I was convinced that any hope I had of finding the spiritual strength and guidance necessary to meet my goals was to be found there. The challenge ahead: to succeed in an evermore competitive world in which I was no longer one of the leaders of the pack.

Laurie was not thrilled. Who could blame her? Hilary was just over a year old and I didn't want to leave her—even for a week. Laurie could not fathom my running off to "Mount Cuchi-Cuchi," as she referred to Mount Kuchumaa. I explained to her that this wasn't a time for vacation but a time to prepare myself for what I hoped was to be a new beginning for me. There was more to be had from The Ranch and the spiritual mountain. I had to pick up where I left off and finish what I had started two years earlier. I was eager to apply the sensibilities gained during my first trip to The Ranch along with the wisdom and good sense that my father would have espoused. I was also ready to apply the lessons I'd learned over the years from my numerous business misadventures. I had given up drugs and hard liquor, but I was still drinking too much wine, which slowed me down. In a word, this was about getting my mojo back. To be successful in that quest I had to be in peak condition—physically, spiritually, and mentally. No excuses. It was a fight to the bitter end to reinvent myself in business.

In the spring of 1988, I returned to my place in the sun, hoping The Ranch was as special as I remembered. It was. This time I dove into the hiking and exercise program and by the end of the week I was closer to top condition. The organic vegetables (which at the time were not yet available in New York) together with an extreme exercise program made me feel healthy and strong. I was on a natural high. It was on this trip that I finally gave up the one-pack-a-day smoking habit that I had picked up at Betty Ford. I was also magically drawn back each day to the sacred Mount Kuchumaa, where I hiked alone for five miles every morning and watched the sun come up over the horizon, casting the early-morning glow from the rays of the sun on the granite boulders that clung to the mountain. It was majestic. I appreciated the warmth of the sun on my back as I hiked in that cold desert air and I felt very much at peace. I loved The Ranch and what it did for me. How it took me to my innermost place within, to my core.

Chapter Thirty-One:
Tatou

WHEN I RETURNED TO New York I felt like a new human being. I swore that I would not have a sip of wine or puff of a joint until I hit "it" out of the park—whatever "it" happened to be. I still didn't know what my next project was going to be, so I scoured New York City trying to figure out what was missing. What was there a need for, an absence of—what was Manhattan lacking at night? If I could figure that out, I could then fill that void and make a real score. I went to all the happening restaurants, frequently bumping into people I knew from Studio 54 days. The one take I heard, repeatedly, was how tired people were of the current loud club scene and how even though nothing had been as much fun as Studio 54, they longed for a place to party at night that wasn't as loud, was more intimate, played good music, and served fine cuisine, but still was good for dancing.

Before I knew it, the idea percolated in my head for a new kind of restaurant/nightclub in midtown Manhattan, a place that would combine the sophistication of the old-time supper clubs of the 1930s and '40s like the famed Stork Club and El Morocco in Manhattan and the Cocoanut Grove in Hollywood, with the magic of Studio 54—taken down a notch, of course. I envisioned an elegantly dressed host that would greet patrons at the door and maintain a dress code. Every night would have the atmosphere of New Year's Eve but with fine dining, cocktails, and dancing, all under one roof. VIP raised dining platforms with plush booths would be designed and placed to overlook the main floor, which would begin each night as a formal dining room with white tablecloths, candles with elegant shades, and gold brocade upholstered chairs, while a live band played blues or blues-oriented jazz on the main stage from 7:00 p.m. to 11:00 p.m. As the evening progressed, the computerized lights would gradually begin to dim as the live music ever so subtly became louder while evolving into a sensuous dance beat. Some of our guests would then call it an evening and retire to their homes and others would stay and join in as a younger, upscale crowd arrived for dancing, drinks, or late supper. By 11:00 p.m., all tables in the center would be cleared. The blues band would call it a night, and guests would dance to music by current DJs, accented by soft pulsating lights hidden in the soffits, while late-night diners watched from platforms on both sides. The entire concept of the modern-day supper club came to me at once as if in a dream.

I had the perfect name for the place: Tatou, an homage to my days as a Naval officer in the early 1960s, when I ran the officers' club at Naval Air Engineering Station Lakehurst. "Tattoo" was the name given to the musical military parade at sunset in the British military and the name of the US military bugle call at the end of the day (call to the bar), and I loved the sound of the word. However, I was worried Tattoo might be misconstrued and a turnoff to fine diners, mistaken for an ink parlor, so I gave it a French spelling, Tatou. My plan was to usher in the dawn of a new experience for New Yorkers with a twist on a bygone era: the 1940s club scene. A sophisticated night out on the town. It was exactly what my formal training at the Cornell Hotel School, together with my experiences at Studio 54, had taught me how to do very well. I had pulled off components of this scene many times before. This time, with a clear head, I could actually visualize it a year before I would make it happen.

I searched Manhattan for the right location and a few months later I found it. The perfect building with a shuttered restaurant in midtown on East Fiftieth Street between Lexington and Third Avenues. Talk about history and aura— this place had it. In the 1940s it was known as Club Versailles where Edith Piaf and Judy Garland performed, and Desi Arnaz conducted the house band. In 1958 Morris Levy took it over and it became a jazz/comedy club known as the Round Table. Singer Pearl Williams opened but was shut down by the police after only a few weeks for her foul-mouthed routine, but not before Sinatra and the Rat Pack had their chance to howl with laughter at her shtick. It became a favorite late-night hang out. The joint had character and charisma. The space boasted high ceilings and a private upstairs space; it was exactly what I had in mind for the type of innovative nightspot I wanted to create, and it appeared to be waiting for the right concept, and me.

I raised the $1.5 million that I needed from my personal funds, family, and investors, including model Oren Stevens who I worked with on the McGovern campaign in '72, and I convinced Deszo "Desi" Szonntagh, the chef from the popular restaurant Provence in Greenwich Village, to join me as chef/partner to create an innovative menu. Couri Hay, my buddy from the Studio 54 days, became a partner and managed our press. Once again, my brother Alan became my key business partner. I went to Chicago and spent a few days visiting the numerous blues clubs in the Rush Street–area, in order to personally experience "the blues" in a restaurant setting. I was particularly impressed by Buddy Guy's place, where he held court playing music that sounded like it just came up the Mississippi from Baton Rouge. Chicago was full of great blues performers, but I came to realize that New York was more jazz-oriented, and so I began a new search for music that would complement my vision of the club.

One evening, I headed up to a club in Harlem to hear an eighty-three-year-old pianist and singer named Sammy Price, who was known as the King of Boogie Woogie. He was playing at a funky club in Harlem, and, unlike in my teenage days, this time I had a car and driver wait out front for me. Sammy Price blew me away. He looked and sang like Louis Armstrong, and his old-time boogie-woogie piano playing made my toes curl. Afterward, I went up to him and tried to start a conversation.

Sammy was surrounded by people, and I knew I had to talk fast—and be covert about it, as the club's owner was standing nearby. Almost any entertainer would want to go from a small club in Harlem to a major venue in midtown. Chances are the money would be better and an artist would get more exposure and recognition. I gave it to him straight: "Sammy, I'm opening a large, elegant, old-time thirties supper club in midtown on the east side, and we're going to feature blues music with classical three-star cuisine."

He lit up and said in his raspy Louis Armstrong-like voice: "You're gonna open what?"

I asked, "Would you be interested in joining us?"

"Would I be interested?" he exclaimed while grabbing my hand with a big smile.

He was a brilliant talent and very excited as he searched his bag to give me a cassette of his music before I left. I listened to it in the car on my way back downtown and was convinced I'd found the piano man to complete my vision for Tatou.

I put together all my ideas and plans and met with David Rockwell, who at the time was still in the early stages of what would become a brilliant career as a restaurant and hotel designer. When I told David my idea, he acted as if I'd lost my mind. "Mark, you're asking me to create the impossible," he said. "No restaurant has ever been successful as a discotheque. It's a marriage that is doomed to fail."

"Not if we do it this way," I explained. I then took pen and paper and drew a rough version of the basic layout I had in mind, showing him exactly how, with hidden state-of-the-art sound and lighting systems, we could transform the atmosphere of the main floor from that of a posh restaurant into a fashionable dance club, with platforms on the sides becoming a late-night dining area for sophisticated guests. David still looked at me askance, but I could tell I'd made some progress and he wanted to do the project. "Mark, I admire your passion and creativity," he said. "Let me see what I can do."

David Rockwell took my concept and brought it to life, creating an elegant mahogany dining room draped with rich fabrics that called to mind the "jewel box" theatres of nineteenth-century New Orleans. Our stage had a hand-painted 1920s roll-down curtain and a thirty-five-foot-high painted dome ceiling with three-tiered chandeliers. Gilded plaster Mephistophelian heads sprouted from the lamps that lit up the dance floor, while a red velvet Arabian Nights–boudoir feeling emanated from the VIP club upstairs. It had intimate booths and was decadent, classic, yet modern—just as I had envisioned. David went on to design the first Planet Hollywood (after showing Tatou to the principals), then the W Hotels, the Kodak Theatre (now Dolby Theatre) in Hollywood, the Nobu restaurants, and the redesign of the Hotel Bel-Air, just to name a few.

Tatou opened in mid-1990 during one of New York City's periodic financial meltdowns. It took a few weeks for patrons to comprehend what Tatou was all about. When we cleared the tables on the dance floor at 10:30 p.m., people didn't immediately understand that was the cue to dance. Those first few nights, I'd grab a lady or two and start the dancing. Before the song was over, I'd look around and the dance floor was full. I marveled at how well it all went over. I was able to bring back Frank Corr from Crisco and Studio 54 to play on occasion and DJ Kevin Doyle settled in as my resident DJ playing whatever kept the crowd happy. Diversity in sound has always been a hallmark of my clubs.

Profitable almost from the very outset, Tatou became the most popular watering hole in New York for many years. It took two weeks to get a dinner reservation and there were lines to get into the nightclub. As if that weren't exciting enough, legendary food critic Gael Greene reviewed Tatou soon after opening. You must understand that when it came to restaurant reviews, at that time in New York City, Gael Greene was *the* voice you listened to. She was a passionate, early foodie who wrote with such vibrancy that she gave New Yorkers a new way to think about eating out—as theatre, as seduction, as art. When Gael Greene wrote a positive review, your restaurant could become an overnight sensation, making it impossible for anyone to get a reservation that wasn't weeks out. What follows is an excerpt from Gael Greene's column in *New York* magazine (quoted with her permission) on October 1, 1990, titled "Tatou Parlor," which I believe captured the essence of Tatou:

> *Is it optimism or innocence, transcendent savvy or uniformed leap into a nighttime void? What has possessed a seasoned man-about-town like Mark Fleischman to choose this moment for a supper club with the feel of 1850 New Orleans? With a disco. And a private club. And lunch. And the eighty-two-year-old King of Boogie Woogie tinkling the blues.*

> *What can possibly come next except Santa Claus and the Tooth Fairy? Welcome **Tatou**. Yes, that's French for "tattoo," but Fleischman fell in love with the sound of the word, and he doesn't want to invoke images of tattoo parlors. Think of tattoo as the call of the bugle, a summons to quarters before taps. That's why Tatou's painted cherubs and the logo's angel all brandish a bugle.*

> *Fleischman couldn't resist…he's built a hybrid dream, a disco for grown-ups, like **Au Bar**. A real restaurant with good food, a private club in the mirrored Moroccan Victoriana upstairs. And don't forget the blues. A crazy quilt of make-believe, something for everyone. He hopes. Heaven knows this town could use a hit of innocent fantasy.*

> *It does feel odd, escaping the 1990-reality of East Fiftieth Street to lunch in the charming, old-fashioned stage set David Rockwell has created, with colorful swags of fabric and chairs shrouded in brocade, the mullioned windows ever so slightly*

over-antiqued with faux mildew, the cast-plaster satyrs gilded and aged with lamps on their heads, the bugle-toting cherubs on the stage drop. A live woman, six foot two, got molded in plaster to create the bronzelike Amazons hoisting fringed lamps that flank the stage. If you're not too jaded, you can easily just go with it.

...Chef-partner Deszo Szonntagh (Hungarian-born, Philadelphia-bred) cooked with a French accent for Michel Jean at Provence... Everything gets filtered through his imagination anyways, so nothing is what you'd expect. But most of it is good, even very good. And the desserts by his wife, Phyllis, are dangerously delicious.

The boogie-and-blues king, Sammy Price, and his trio swing. The serving crew, mostly good-looking young people in Art Deco cravats earning their way to somewhere else, serve efficiently without attitude. And the pâtissière (who longs to open her own light-dessert shop someday) proves she is master of all the classic American indulgences...

I can't begin to guess who will love it, who will laugh at it or with it.

"Victorian bordello," one guest summed it up.

Who knows what the first brisk chill of fall will bring? Last week's party for Susan Anton could entice the young men in couturier suspenders to return. A benefit the other night (with Princess Stephanie as host) landed pretty people in Lycra Band-Aids and other migratory birds who might roost awhile. Tatou sounds a clarion call. Let's see who answers."

After that review, Tatou became the undisputed hottest restaurant, bar, and club in Manhattan for many years. In addition to the crowds of New Yorkers and tourists, Tatou attracted a diverse group of celebrities such as Ice-T, Mickey Rourke, Grace Jones, Leroy Neiman, Anthony Quinn and his well-known sons, John Kennedy Jr., Michelle Pfeiffer, Prince Albert and his sister Princess Stephanie of Monaco, Bret Easton Ellis, Tama Janowitz and Jay McInerney, Donald Trump and Ivana Trump (separately), Armand Assante,

Pelé, and Liza Minnelli—she held her forty-fifth birthday party in the upstairs VIP club. Joan Rivers often reserved the VIP room to try out her comedy routines. Ian Schrager raved when he stopped in for dinner with Calvin Klein after hearing all the hullaballoo about Tatou.

A caricature drawn by one of the waiters at Tatou New York depicting the crowd at Tatou:
Grace Jones, Tony Bennett, Jackie Mason, Robin Leach, Liza Minnelli, Sophia Loren, and
Mickey Rourke. Tatou had a six-week wait for reservations.

We hosted many major events over the years, including a performance by Mariah Carey, serving as her introduction to Sony Music executives visiting from Japan; Tony Bennett's fortieth anniversary celebration with Columbia Records; the party for Whitney Houston's "I'm Your Baby Tonight" video which was shot at Tatou; Robin Leach's absolutely packed fiftieth birthday party; and many of the key political social parties during the 1992 Democratic National Convention, including Arnold Schwarzenegger and Maria Shriver at the George McGovern Reunion celebration with her father Sargent Shriver who ran for vice president on the McGovern ticket. Other fundraisers included Peggy Kerry and me hosting a fundraiser for John Kerry's Senatorial campaign and I agreed to host a Republican fundraiser for John McCain.

The most spectacular event of all was a fundraiser for then-presidential candidate Bill Clinton, where he played saxophone for a live audience for the first time since high school with a rented sax and his own mouthpiece. It was quite a thrill to watch him practice in my office, then step onto the stage to perform. We had a backup saxophonist but didn't need him because Clinton was so good. Fifty press members lined the edges of the room as an elite crowd enjoyed the performance. The bursting light from the flash bulbs created an almost strobe-light atmosphere to the performance. Couri Hay later dropped a piece in Page Six that said I had recorded the evening on CD and was going to market Bill Clinton Live at Tatou—a misunderstanding, but an amusing story nonetheless.

Tatou was such a hit that one magazine dubbed me "the father of the modern American supper club." It was so successful, I got offers to open clubs in Moscow (which was too scary) and Tokyo.

The dark, decadent "Upstairs at Tatou" became a very popular night spot for late-night dancing, drinks, and our specialty—a grilled chicken sandwich with roasted peppers and pesto mayonnaise on toasted Artisan bread. The upstairs VIP Lounge attracted musical artists after their concert performances, including Mick Jagger, Jerry Hall, Robert De Niro, and Jackie Mason who always cracked everyone up with his one-liners, while making the rounds looking for hot middle-aged women to screw. There were also late-night decadent scenes reminiscent of nights at Studio 54. An image of Robin Leach comes to mind, of him drinking champagne from a woman's high-heeled shoe and having crème brûlée fed to him in some unique ways by an ever-changing assortment of bombshell blondes and brunettes while lounging on a couch behind a low cocktail table in a dark alcove. The girls would bend over and anybody who spotted the tastes of temptation found Robin laughing, wiping the crème off his face.

Tatou was critically acclaimed for its cuisine by *The New York Times, New York* magazine, and almost every other publication in town. The club was featured on NBC, FOX, and the local TV stations as a new kind of late-night phenomenon, almost to the level of Studio 54. CNN did a national piece on how I was able to successfully open Tatou during the recession of the early 1990s (for a ten-year run), just as I had reopened Studio 54 during the recession of the early 1980s. We were also in the columns regularly orchestrated by Couri.

I've told you about Fred Rothbell Mista, guardian of the VIP area at Crisco Disco in the early 1980s. Well, in 1991, to the delight of our crowd, Fred began performing once a week at Tatou on Sammy's night off, impersonating a Frank Sinatra-type character, spoofing a Las Vegas lounge singer and calling himself Rocco Primavera—wearing his hair in a pompadour and draped with gold chains. He was accompanied by a three-girl group of his own creation, the New Jersey Nightingales. It was a hoot and he became quite popular in his new role.

I hired the Harris Sisters (aka The Screaming Violets) from Studio 54 to run the coat check at Tatou. They performed many times at Tatou to the delight of our crowd. When they received an offer to perform in Australia, I agreed to let them go and run the coatroom long distance, which they did brilliantly.

I opened Tatou Aspen during Christmas 1991. One of our opening parties was an event hosted by Don Henley of the Eagles, a dinner dance to raise money for his favorite charity, Saving Walden Pond. It was arranged by Dan Klores who I hired specifically to publicize the event, but Couri Hay sent out a press release about major stars attending the party. All of a sudden, TV crews and magazines descended on Aspen during Christmas week. Henley became upset when the snowy mall turned into a frenzied premiere similar to a Hollywood opening, and stars like Barbra Streisand, Cher, Jack Nicholson, Sylvester Stallone, Don Johnson, and Melanie Griffith had to run the gauntlet through the snow with lights and cameras blazing. To Henley, the last straw was Robin Leach arriving with his *Lifestyles of the Rich and Famous* camera crew. Henley, who despised the highly successful television show, blocked the entrance. I finally made a quick deal with Don to let Robin in alone without his crew, as he was my close friend.

Tatou Aspen's opening was featured on worldwide TV, and had a major three-page pictorial spread in *People* titled "Revels Without Pause." The story featured photographs of Don Johnson and Don Henley with the caption "Two Dons Against Development"; Cher and her half-sister Georganne LaPiere with the caption, "Were tattoos too taboo at Tatou?"; Sly Stallone and then girlfriend, model Jennifer Flavin—dashing but not too fast—past photographers outside Tatou; and ex-Car Ric Ocasek cruising Tatou with model Paulina Porizkova.

Everything about Tatou Aspen was wonderful until I got into a ski accident and tore all of the ligaments in my knee. I was skiing with Couri Hay, racing through gates on a cloudy, icy day at 4:00 p.m. the day before New Year's, and I caught a tip on a gate.

That night, I went to Tatou on crutches, got drunk, and the next morning I went in for surgery. I spent a week at the Aspen Valley Hospital, which was a brand-new facility at the time. After the surgery I was put in a room with a beautiful picture window facing the slopes of Aspen Highlands, so it wasn't as bad as it could have been. I ended up in a cast for three months and in rehab for another three. Unfortunately, it blew my season at Tatou Aspen because I couldn't be there to take care of what was a cash business. The Tatou Aspen staff were mostly happy-go-lucky ski bums who didn't take their jobs seriously and would have been difficult to manage even if I had been in the position to offer more oversight. Management was loose and cash seeped out in a variety of ways. Our chef told me that even the landlord was coming in after hours and taking steaks from our walk-in refrigerator. At the end of the season, I knew it wasn't going to work, even though we hung on for one more year. Tatou Aspen was not a financial success, but it was an experience. It also gave Tatou Los Angeles, which was in the planning stages, a base for press.

Once again, I was living the life of a nightclub owner, but this time it was a markedly different experience. I was meeting the crème-de-la-crème of society, wearing three-piece suits and living drug-free. My conversations were relevant, rather than drug-addled babble. I enjoyed people, music, and dancing more than ever. That old feeling of a natural high whenever I was responsible for successfully entertaining a large crowd returned to me, and that was the coolest part of all. Running the business with a lucid mind also brought with it the opportunity to make more money. Tatou was a more challenging business to run than Studio 54 because of the fine dining component—which is a complicated process. At Studio, it was drinks, music, lights, pizazz, and entertaining celebrities with free cocaine. Fine dining is highly competitive, and you're always concerned about critical reviews of the food and service—I had to be on top of my game for that. Even though we had a maître d', I found myself hosting and schmoozing both the early—and late-night crowds, buying complimentary rounds of drinks, delivering welcome appetizers to important guests, making sure people were properly seated; and, more than ever, I enjoyed getting people up and dancing at 10:30 p.m.

Before Tatou opened, Laurie decided that she wanted to make the move to Connecticut, where she had grown up. It was important to her to raise Hilary outside of New York City. The move happened after our nanny told us an alarming story about how, on several occasions, a vagrant had spotted Hilary and then followed them both down Second Avenue to the United Nations preschool she attended. Hilary was an eye-catching, adorable two-year-old with long, bright red hair. I agreed to the move.

Once Tatou opened, I worked late almost every night, and I could only join my family in Connecticut on Saturdays and Sundays. As time went by, Laurie settled in as a stay-at-home mom with a social life in Connecticut, and once again I was living the life of a nightclub owner. We ultimately separated. I took Hilary with me on weekends. We spent our days together enjoying the Central Park Zoo and the Museum of Natural History, and then in the evening I would drop her off with my mother on East Fifty-Seventh Street on my way to Tatou. My mother was thrilled to have this precious time with Hilary. She absolutely adored her. Somehow we made the situation work. Laurie and I loved Hilary so much we made certain the separation was as painless as possible for her. It gave me great pleasure to buy and renovate a house for Laurie and Hilary in Westport, Connecticut, ensuring a home for them in a community they loved and would feel rooted in. Then, a few years later, Laurie married Judd Burstein, a very successful attorney from a well-known New York family of lawyers and judges. Finally, Hilary had a full-time father figure in her life who would be there for her, and that was comforting to me.

Chapter Thirty-Two:
Tatou in La La Land

THEN, MIMI LEONARD WALKED back into my life. I had had a crush on Mimi when she was dating Jerry Rubin while I was at New Line Cinema in the late 1970s. Jerry was one of the New Line Presentation speakers, and I would see Mimi from time to time at the office. Mimi and Jerry married in 1977. In 1981, Mimi and Jerry worked for me at Studio 54, successfully promoting their Yuppie Networking Night which continued for several years. During those years, I was so out of my mind, I hardly noticed her. Then a few years later, in 1987, the Rubins and I discussed opening a "networking" oriented restaurant, and again I felt the spark. But then Jerry and Mimi moved to Los Angeles and we lost contact until one very busy night at Tatou in 1991 when the doorman/security sent word that, "Mimi Leonard and her sisters are outside at the ropes."

Mimi was born in Georgia but spent most of her life in New York City, graduating summa cum laude from Columbia University. She was, and is, an energetic, intelligent, beautiful, kind, and impressive woman. She is the daughter of the charming Southern Belle, Emma Jean "EJ" Clifton, who comes from a good old Southern family, and author and educator George Burr Leonard, who wrote extensively about education and human potential. He was president emeritus of the Esalen Institute, former editor of *Look* magazine, a former US Army Air Corps pilot in WWII, and holds a fifth-degree black belt in Aikido. He also developed the Leonard Energy Training (LET) practice for centering the mind, body, and spirit, and, coincidentally, was a regular speaker at Rancho La Puerta years earlier. So you could argue that Mimi's strength, intelligence, and drive were genetic.

I went outside and greeted Mimi, who looked ravishing, together with her two beautiful, blonde half-sisters. I led them through the crowd to the upstairs VIP room and got them drinks. I vividly remember that moment; I was really happy to see her, especially when she confided that she and Jerry had separated. She now had an apartment in New York where she lived with her two young children, Juliet and Adam. She was the same ebullient, charming woman I remembered from years back, and now available. Coincidentally, earlier that week, our creative director at Tatou New York, Susan Ainsworth, had informed me she was moving to Miami. When Mimi, whom I knew as a very successful nightclub marketer, asked me for a job, I hired her on the spot.

About nine months after Mimi had been living in New York and working as our creative director at Tatou, we coincidentally each made plans to visit LA on the same weekend. I was going to check out a restaurant space. Mimi had just recently given me three months' notice as creative director and was going to Los Angeles to look for a rental home. As part of their divorce agreement, Jerry had gotten co-custody of the children and wanted Mimi to move to Beverly Hills, where he was living. Since we were both going to be in LA at the same time, I invited her to join me with Bob and Eva Shaye at New Line Cinema's Premiere of the film *The Player* in Hollywood.

It was a star-studded evening with Nick Nolte, Faye Dunaway, Harry and Shari Belafonte, Whoopi Goldberg, and Burt Reynolds; plus the picture's star, Tim Robbins, and many other movie stars. We went to producer Keith Addis' home in the Hollywood Hills for an after-party in honor of the director, Robert Altman, who was presented with a huge marijuana "stalk." Lighted pipes packed with exceptional weed were passed around to the guests. I hadn't smoked marijuana for a number of years, and after a few tokes I became very relaxed, content, and felt that familiar sense of enlightenment envelop me. We were sitting on a plush leather sofa next to a large stone fireplace. When I looked at Mimi, I had a sense that she was my "it" girl, my one true love, and we were destined to be partners in life. I leaned over and kissed her, our eyes met, and we both knew.

Back in New York the following week, my heart was pounding when we went out on what would be our first real date. We went to dinner, then returned to my apartment, and I remember saying something to the effect that we should "take it slow." But we didn't. We made love and I understood the attraction I'd felt for Mimi over the years. I couldn't stop kissing her. I wanted to hold her forever. This was true lovemaking and very different from the hundreds of mindless sexual encounters I'd had over the years. This time it was with a woman I couldn't get enough of. I was falling in love and loving every minute of it.

On our next date, Mimi shared her feeling that a real relationship needs to be monogamous. When I mulled that over, I came to the sober and comforting realization that Mimi could be my everything. My world was a better place when she was in it. Mimi commanded my attention and respect from the very beginning—even back to the Studio 54 and New Line Cinema days, when she was working with Jerry. She had left her impression on me. A strong, self-assured woman can be an aphrodisiac of lasting potency. I was very comfortable that she was only nine years younger than me rather than someone of a different generation; we both had an affinity for and working with celebrities and promotions in the nightclub business, had children of the same age, a mutual respect and fondness for our mothers and fathers, and we had great sex.

She was a smart, literate, very attractive blonde shiksa who liked Jewish guys. We were a winning combination. The pieces fit together perfectly, without struggle. Mimi loved me as much as I loved her, which enabled us to develop the relationship that has lasted for over twenty-five years.

I had to tell Laurie about Mimi, because our daughter Hilary often went on playdates with Mimi's children, Adam and Juliet. Laurie had always liked Mimi, who had a summer home in Westport, Connecticut, not far from where Laurie and Hilary lived. We'd go up and spend the weekend at Mimi's house with the three kids in tow. Sometimes Mimi and I would be "playing" upstairs, while the kids were playing downstairs with Mimi's Mary Poppins-like nanny, Anavi. Hilary, at five, was just six months older than Juliet and two years older than Adam; she was able to keep Mimi's kids thoroughly entertained, as Anavi supervised. The kids had no idea what was going on upstairs, and Mimi and I enjoyed some stolen moments of adult time.

Then, my friend Grace Robbins, the ex-wife of Harold Robbins, author of *The Carpetbaggers*, found the perfect location for Tatou on Beverly Drive, smack dab in the middle of Beverly Hills. It was perfect. It was a large, fully equipped out-of-business restaurant with two well-appointed kitchens, thirty-foot-high ceilings, four marble restrooms, and an upstairs space with twenty-foot-high ceilings. One of my Japanese investors, Shin Konishi, put up half the money for the kitchen equipment and became a partner.

I set about putting a team together that included Mimi, who by then had moved to Los Angeles. I also offered a modest partnership interest to Rudolf Piper, the tall, blond, well-known German nightclub entrepreneur who managed numerous clubs in New York, including Danceteria, The Tunnel, and Palladium. In return, he helped me to develop and operate the upstairs nightclub. Rudolf and Mimi held auditions and put together a fabulous and great-looking staff comprised, as is usually the case in Los Angeles, mostly of out-of-work actors and actresses. Our Tatou New York chef/partner, Desi Szonntagh, moved to LA and staffed the kitchen.

A key ingredient, once again, was David Rockwell, whose design fulfilled my vision of recreating the elegant Los Angeles supper club of the 1930s, the Cocoanut Grove, in the restaurant space. The upstairs space became a hedonistic red plush discotheque accented by a lot of gold leaf. Downstairs, Tatou Beverly Hills was breathtaking, with plush brocade booths, a stage with an elegant red velvet curtain, gilded mirrors, and cream drapes embroidered with gold fleurs-de-lis. Fabricated metal palms with oversized faded green fronds arched overhead, accented by hanging lighted coconuts. Subtly colored LED lights buried in the tree trunks along with a billowy-tented ceiling, that slowly changed color from white to pink to blue, created a magical atmosphere. I had found a grand theatre chandelier at an auction in Connecticut and shipped it to LA to hang as a centerpiece in the main dining room. The design blew everyone away.

We held a successful soft opening during the 1991 holiday season booked with private Christmas parties. The parties included events for New Line Cinema, a party for Michael Douglas's production company, and a number of other high-profile entertainment industry entities. These were well-received with great food and live music alternating with the best DJs playing popular dance music. The A-list invitees at these parties ate it up. On New Year's Eve, Nikki Haskell, my friend from Studio 54 who grew up in Beverly Hills, cohosted our official opening with Charles Evans. Charles was founder of the very successful fashion label Evan-Picone Apparel, and brother of legendary Hollywood producer Robert Evans. Tatou became the talk of the town. The atmosphere, food, sophisticated blues bands, and the striking upstairs late-night dance club were a delight to the Hollywood crowd.

Within a week, word of mouth spread and we were overwhelmed with calls for dinner reservations in the downstairs supper club. People were waiting up to three weeks to get a table—A-List celebrities were accommodated immediately. There were lines to get into the late-night upstairs club four to five nights per week. I decided early on that—just like at the original Cocoanut Grove in LA and Tatou New York—patrons should be properly dressed. However, before opening, many friends and acquaintances were advising me that Los Angeles was not like New York, and a dress code wouldn't work. I considered this for a few weeks but just before opening I placed a brass plaque by the front door that read: "Jackets Required." To handle what could be a delicate issue at the front door with the dress code, I hired two young, beautiful, smart, and savvy women as my door people. One of them was Christa Miller, who went on to star on *The Drew Carey Show* and *Scrubs*. They dressed in stylish, tailored pant suits and Mimi and I carefully instructed them on the dress code and who should and shouldn't get in. It turned off a few people, but most patrons loved it, creating the feeling that every night was a special occasion.

We were definitely thinking outside the box when we transformed some vacant space into an art gallery that doubled as a living room and cocktail lounge. An old friend from my Studio 54 days, Tony Curtis, provided the art and furnishings. Painting was a lifelong passion for him. When I first came to Los Angeles we bumped into each other while hanging out at Alan Finkelstein and Jack Nicholson's restaurant, Monkey Bar, and renewed our friendship. He looked much better now than during his Studio days and was very excited about opening The Tony Curtis Gallery at our new posh restaurant. He was a fine artist. In 2005, "The Red Table" by Tony Curtis was accepted into the permanent collection of the Museum of Modern Art in New York.

Fabio, the actor/model/author best known for his long flowing hair and six-foot-three perfectly-chiseled body, was a regular at Tatou, holding court, enjoying the attention of all the women. I watched them literally trip over themselves and walk directly into the nearest table once they spotted Fabio. He had that effect on women.

The people attracted to Tatou were mainly in the entertainment industry, and they felt entitled to a higher level of service, which was less common amongst VIPs in Manhattan. They were accustomed to private chefs and considered it a badge of honor as well as their right and privilege to order "off the menu." They ordered anything they felt like eating at that moment and told the waiter to bring it. I remember record producer Richard Perry was part of a scenario that was a royal pain in the ass. He ordered pasta puttanesca, which wasn't on the menu, and he ordered it at a really busy time. It went like this: "Hmmmm, you know what I'd really love? Al dente pappardelle puttanesca. Please prepare it with very ripe, young olives and only fresh plum tomatoes," he said.

Everyone knows about Richard Perry's work with The Pointer Sisters, Barbra Streisand, Rod Stewart, Carly Simon, Art Garfunkel, Diana Ross, and Donna Summer, but Richard Perry produced *Rock, Rhythm & Blues,* a brilliant album with Rick James in the lead on a remake of The Drifters hit "This Magic Moment" and I loved it…so I let him bust my balls.

We followed his directions and soon we began to unofficially call it Pasta a la Perry.

On busy nights, the orders off the menu would cause our chef Desi to freak out, and I'd have to calm him down on the phone, sometimes from three thousand miles away if I happened to be at Tatou New York.

The peculiarities of the Hollywood crowd confounded Chef Desi. One night Suzanne Pleshette (costar of *The Bob Newhart Show*), walked directly into the kitchen and personally took Desi aside to complain about a whiff of garlic in her dinner. The kitchen had to start her entire table all over again. She said she was allergic to garlic and could not be within smelling distance of it. Why she chose not to, discreetly, share that information with the waitstaff when placing her order is beyond me. This and other similar special requests slowed the kitchen down so much that, in the beginning, the service was erratic.

That went on for several weeks until my staff and I analyzed the situation and established the rules of the house with our dining guests. Most of our guests abided by our new policy and ordered from the menu because they wanted to be welcomed in the hottest spot in town. However, the kitchen was prepared to quickly make reasonable substitutions, when doable, for Barbra Streisand, Sharon Stone, or others at that level of fame. As we got to know the rules of the Hollywood pecking order, the kitchen got back on track.

It didn't take long to figure out that the Beverly Hills-crowd didn't spend money like New Yorkers, even though they had plenty of it. Big stars expected comps. Lesser stars wanted free desserts or a round of free drinks. And I soon discovered that people in LA didn't drink nearly as much, usually nothing at lunch. So even though the downstairs restaurant was always packed, our check average was much lower than Tatou New York. We weren't making the kind of profit we were accustomed to.

Before opening, I gave much thought to what kind of crowd we wanted to attract. Mimi and I had a number of meetings with industry movers and shakers like producer Keith Addis and record producer Richard Perry and others to help orchestrate the right Hollywood crowd. But in the end we were still a Beverly Hills clubhouse. The main restaurant attracted an older, wealthier, expensively dressed Beverly Hills crowd, including actor Red Buttons (Academy Award winner for the film *Sayonara* with Marlon Brando), Milton Berle (the baby boomers' Uncle Milty), actor Cesar Romero (the baby boomers' first Joker on TV's *Batman*), comedian Sid Caesar, TV super-producer Aaron Spelling, Sid Luft (third husband of Judy Garland and father of Lorna Luft), and other wealthy entertainment industry old-timers. But it also brought a more current clientele, including Barbra Streisand, Cybill Shepherd, Mike Medavoy and Patricia Duff, Kirk Kerkorian, Hugh Hefner, Steve Wynn, James Coburn, Robin Leach, Leeza Gibbons, Vanna White, Suzanne Pleshette, and the dapper California Speaker of the House, Willie Brown.

However, the upstairs club (which Rudolf helped choreograph) attracted a young, hip crowd including Billy Idol, Madonna, Ali McGraw, Heather Locklear, and the bad girl of the original *Beverly Hills, 90210*, Shannen Doherty, who was often very rowdy. Most nights were jammed, with the exception of Tuesday, which was dead all over LA. However, Rudolf found two young promoters, Lee Main and Craig Katz, whom he called the "twits." They ended up packing the place on Tuesdays with a very young, cool Hollywood and Beverly Hills crowd featuring loads of beautiful girls. Years later, Lee and Craig became extremely successful opening the Sushi Roku, Boa, and Katana restaurants.

The high-powered entertainment industry crowd came with a price—never-ending drama. It was always a challenge. For instance, one night Marvin Davis, the billionaire owner of 20th Century Fox, held an engagement party for his daughter, Nancy. Gloria Allred, the civil rights attorney, spied District Attorney Gil Garcetti and darted over to him and started quite a scene. Gil was the Los Angeles County district attorney and lead prosecutor in the O. J. Simpson trial, which many thought was being mishandled. Everyone in the room was stunned and speechless and then suddenly, they all looked at me—while pointing to Gil who was trying to fend Gloria off. Luckily, Gloria was petite and light, so I was able to disentangle them. Gil fled, and Gloria, who represented the Brown family, calmed down and the other guests carried on as if nothing had happened.

There was a steep learning curve on catering the private parties of the well-to-do crowd of Beverly Hills. I had heard that Barbara Davis, Marvin's wife, always considered herself entitled to a 50-percent discount. Marvin Davis was one of the richest men in town and could easily afford the very best—which he still insisted upon receiving, knowing that his wife Barbara also insisted on the 50-percent discount. I vividly remember Barbara making her bejeweled fingers into a fist to describe the size of the "jumbo shrimp" she demanded be served at their party. She justified it by telling me that she was going to get me "tons of press by inviting loads of Hollywood stars." In the end, I printed up a banquet menu and altered the prices for Barbara to select from, so we could cater the event without losing our shirts and still give her the 50-percent discount.

Chapter Thirty-Three:
Rodney Fires Up Tatou

O N A VERY CROWDED evening, one of the funniest men in the world, Rodney Dangerfield, lit up a joint while sitting in a booth during dinner. I wish I had been there, but I wasn't; I was in New York and Mimi was covering for me. The manager was too scared to just walk up to Rodney and ask him to "please put the joint out." So he found Mimi and asked her to do it. But Mimi was clever enough to stay out of it, avoiding the drama and one-liners she would invite, knowing Rodney's shtick. Can you imagine the material he would have hit her with in front of everyone? Some in the crowd were horrified at his audacity, while most got a chuckle out of it and laughed it off. It caused quite a commotion, but nothing compared to later that evening, when the voluptuous Mamie Van Doren flashed her breasts for a gang of paparazzi waiting outside.

Just another night out on the town in La La Land.

Aaron Tonken was another character at Tatou. He had started out in Hollywood by living with Zsa Zsa Gabor and befriending the older set. By the time I met him, he lived in an unfurnished studio apartment, drove an old car, and was looking for a gig. He had an amazing Rolodex, and I hired him part-time and gave him meals. He starting doing charity-oriented parties at Tatou, which were great for press.

Aaron introduced me to actor Charlton Heston (star of *The Ten Commandments* and winner of the Oscar for Best Actor in *Ben-Hur*), referred to as Chuck by his friends. Chuck's wife, Lydia, a talented and very artistic professional photographer, asked me to arrange a showing of her rather extensive body of work in the Tony Curtis Gallery. For the opening night cocktail party, the Hestons invited many of their friends, including former President Ronald Reagan and First Lady Nancy Reagan. Tony Curtis and his new wife, a young attorney whose most obvious attribute was her unusually large breasts, clearly wanted to be in as many of the pictures with the former president as possible. This seemed to disturb Nancy. She pulled "Ronnie" away, though he appeared to be totally amused by Tony's antics—but not before it was all captured in several pictures, which typified the old Hollywood pecking order.

Aaron also introduced me to Olympic champion Bruce (now Caitlyn) Jenner and his new wife Kris, while Kris's former husband Robert Kardashian, who represented O. J. Simpson, was having dinner on the other side of the restaurant.

I was beginning to see that Aaron had a problem with the truth, and he began to run up large tabs entertaining his celebrity friends. I remember one particularly large tab that Aaron signed for when he brought Dodgers Manager Tommy Lasorda to Tatou. In the case of Tommy Lasorda, I didn't mind being stuck with the bill because I had been a devoted Brooklyn Dodger fan since I was a kid, taking the Long Island Railroad and the subway from Great Neck to Ebbet's field in the early 1950s. The Brooklyn Dodgers brought my hero Jackie Robinson into the majors. Unfortunately, all the kids on my block loved the Yankees and I ended up getting punched around more than once for my loyalty to The Dodgers.

Aaron Tonken finally ended up in jail for skimming charity money, using Hillary and Bill Clinton as hooks. Aaron was conning Denise Rich, who convinced President Clinton to pardon her ex-husband Marc Rich as one of his last acts in office. Aaron recounted many of these stories in his book, *King of Cons*, which he wrote in prison, including the story of Fabio and his manager Peter Paul, who wasn't who we thought he was either. Unbeknownst to all of us at the time, Peter Paul was a former lawyer and entrepreneur who had been convicted of conspiracy and drug dealing and later for securities fraud in connection with his business dealings with *Spider-Man* cocreator Stan Lee, a regular Tatou guest. Peter Paul was also involved in the messy fundraising conspiracy with the Clintons in 2000, and is now serving a ten-year sentence in federal prison.

While all this madness was going on, the press raved about the food and ambiance at Tatou Beverly Hills.

On February 12, 1993, *The Hollywood Reporter* wrote an article titled, "Note-able Cuisine" with the quote: "Tatou evokes the past glamour of Ciro's and The Cocoanut Grove. Chef Desi Szonntagh has created an eclectic menu that should please a sophisticated clientele of industry honchos and foreign fashion plates."

The *Los Angeles Times* on March 7, 1993 said in a piece titled, "Such a Swell Party" by Ruth Reichl, who later became the food critic for *The New York Times* and editor of *Gourmet* magazine: "Eat, smoke, and be merry—it's Tatou where the beautiful people never leave. Tatou is a new phenomenon in Los Angeles—and it's already a hit." In the April 1993 edition of *Vanity Fair*, in a piece titled, "The Club! The Club!" Ruth Reichl wrote: "This is an East Coast fantasy of La-La Land. We don't mind. Here among the palm trees, we enjoy a good show."

When Tatou Beverly Hills first opened, we featured great local blues bands, the same formula that made Tatou New York so successful. As time went by, many of the older crowd began complaining that the music was too loud. I figured it probably wasn't their kind of music, and I started experimenting with other entertainment for the supper club. I started Monday Night Live, together with local singer-songwriter Carol Connors aka Annette Kleinbard, a two-time Oscar nominee best known for composing the theme song "Gonna Fly Now" for the film *Rocky.*

Carol was also well-known for having dated Elvis Presley, Robert Culp (*I Spy*), and David Janssen (*The Fugitive*) back in the day, and she sang lead vocals with the Teddy Bears on their 1958 smash hit "To Know Him Is To Love Him," written and produced by Phil Spector who was also in the group. She knew everyone of a certain age in town and loved the attention Monday Night Live brought her way. We featured up-and-coming singers, hosted by a different celebrity guest host each week. We comped them and their friends for the evening in exchange for their hosting and giving short performances at no charge. They included comics Red Buttons, Fred Travalena, and Norm Crosby, and a host of singers including Freda Payne, Marilyn McCoo and Billy Davis Jr. of The Fifth Dimension, and Frank Sinatra Jr., who always received a standing ovation for his performance whenever he appeared. We also featured other personalities who just wanted to be on stage, such as "Worst Dressed" columnist Mr. (Richard) Blackwell and super-agent Jay Bernstein.

Whereas Monday evenings had been slow, now with Monday Night Live they became packed. It was a very successful promotion, but one that took an enormous amount of organization to pull off each week. A few months into it,

I got a call from Alan (A.K.) Kaufman, one of the owners of the China Club in New York and Los Angeles, famous for its once-a-week LA Celebrity Rock Jams. He asked me if they could move the very hot Monday Night promotion at The China Club to Tatou. Monday at the China Club was the hottest scene in Hollywood, so of course I said yes. I figured they would start at 10:00 p.m. and I'd cut back Monday Night Live by half an hour, and Tatou would have two evening seatings.

It turned out that putting two concepts together on the same night was an impossibility. The patrons seated at dinner for the Monday Night Live show didn't want to give up their tables once they saw the huge crowd from The China Club impatiently waiting. They sensed something cool was about to happen and wanted to be a part of it. The first night we tried it the celebrity guest host for the early evening show was actor /comic and brother of Michael Douglas, Eric Douglas. Eric refused to end his act at the agreed upon time and kept telling bad jokes. So A.K., the China Club's engineer, cut Eric's sound, and Eric created a scene, throwing a very public temper-tantrum in which he threatened to sue everyone within earshot. Eric appeared to be high and was totally out of control.

The new late-night rock concept with celebrity artists sitting in and performing was a huge success, and the following week I moved Monday Night Live to Tuesdays. From then on, the Monday China Club was not only the best night of the week but also the hottest night in Los Angeles. The coolest entertainment industry crowd fought for tables and, unbeknownst to me until I recently interviewed her, my reservationist the gorgeous blond bombshell, Gail Evertz, who ran the evening for me, made a fortune in tips doling out the key booths.

Besides the booths and tables, the bar scene was standing room only.

Jeff "Skunk" Baxter, a founding member of Steely Dan, put together a six-piece revolving band composed of some very well-known musicians and artists like Graham Nash, Billy Preston, Dave Mason, Gary Busey, Smokey Robinson, Tom Jones, Billy Idol, Lou Rawls, and many others over the years. In itself a great show, it read like a who's who of the music industry. The club was always packed with major stars like Jack Nicholson, Sly Stallone, and Denzel Washington, agents, managers, and record label executives, including Interscope founders Ted Field and Jimmy Iovine. Anna Nicole Smith was known to leave her young son Daniel in the car with her chauffeur while she partied with Sly and others, which was disturbing to our hostesses. It was a major industry scene and everyone table-hopped until 2:00 a.m. when we had to make last call. The key bartender on Monday was Cher's handsome young boyfriend, Rob Camilletti, and the girls flocked to him. Christa Miller and other future TV stars were often the door people designated to deal with potential troublemakers and to keep the wrong people out. The crowd was phenomenal.

The green room where the artists hung out in preparation for their performance was sometimes a crazy drug scene, with A.K. from the China Club providing coke and Tatou providing plenty of free alcohol. On one occasion, it got out of control when Billy Idol exposed himself, threw up, and passed out, forcing us to call the paramedics.

During the other two weeknights I created a number of Las Vegas-type shows, including a Brazilian Samba Revue called the "Girls from Ipanema" starring Christiane Callil. She was surrounded by five hot half-naked girls and two guys, all dancing and wearing vibrant costumes and feathers. On the weekends we continued to have the best in blues bands attended by a very upscale Los Angeles crowd. Tatou remained the most popular place in town until we moved to larger facility in 1995.

Me (right) with Senator Ted Kennedy and his wife, Vicki, at Tatou Los Angeles.

My life, though interesting and exciting, soon became an exhausting commute with a week in Los Angeles followed by a week in New York at Tatou. However, even when I was in New York, which was more or less running itself with my brother Alan watching the purchasing and the money, I was being harassed by the Beverly Hills patrons. At around 9:00 p.m. or 10:00 p.m.

Eastern time, I would get frantic calls about who should get which booth. Reservationist Gail Evertz, who has gone on to become a vice president at Guggenheim Partners in New York, organized who got what tables during the day. She was smart, tough, and knew how to handle Wendy Stark, Victoria McMahon, Barbara Davis, and others of the like. But they could be unrelenting.

People threw the weight of their clients, famous parents, spouses, or exes around to get their way.

I had left Mimi in charge of these social matters, but she was too easily intimidated to deal with it, so I ended up settling petty disputes on the phone from New York most nights. Mimi would call me in New York, desperately trying to head off the clashes that came with Hollywood egos. Among others, Marvel Comics founder Stan Lee used to push Mimi around, using the Hollywood/Beverly Hills mantra, "Don't you know who I am?" Having the "right" booth at Tatou became a nightly issue of critical importance. This is what I had to hear in the nightly phone calls from LA: "Victoria McMahon has a booth but Barbra Streisand wants it. I could ask John Paul DeJoria to move, but he's bringing Wolfgang Puck. Desi's in the kitchen drinking because Suzanne Pleshette accused him of putting garlic in her food again." I would respond, "I don't care if Desi does have a ten-percent interest in Tatou...he knows not to put garlic in Suzanne Pleshette's food!" It went on and on—night after night.

Finally, I had some of the banquettes torn out and added five booths so we had nine in total, which solved the key problem of where VIPs were seated. This went on for over a year until I finally decided I couldn't be in both places full-time *and* keep my sanity. When it came to New York, I'd been there, done that. In the thirty years that I spent in New York as an adult, I did everything one could do—owned every kind of club, every kind of restaurant, been to every kind of show, opera, museum, ballgame, every kind of everything! LA was a new adventure and it wasn't like moving to a small town. To me, LA felt like a West Coast–version of New York. The buildings weren't as tall and there weren't as many of them, but it called to me as it did to many back in the day when the saying went: "Go west, young man, go west."

Chapter Thirty-Four:
The Next Episode

I MOVED TO Los Angeles. I wanted to be with Mimi full-time, and I was hooked on the outdoor lifestyle. In support of that lifestyle, Mimi and I bought a home in the Santa Monica Mountains in Malibu at the center of a system of hiking trails called "The Backbone." We took in a loveable female wolf-shepherd in hopes of keeping the coyotes at bay. We named her Harper after actress Tess Haprer, who originally found the dog. Unfortunately, predators got our two cats before Harper took over.

A Japanese investment group had become so taken with Tatou in New York and Los Angeles that they flew Mimi and me out for a weeklong stay at the elegant Okura Hotel in Tokyo to discuss arrangements for opening a Tatou in the Roppongi neighborhood. Tatou Tokyo opened in 1994 and was successful for more than twenty years and described as "the hot spot for the young and hip. A restaurant that changes into a bar each night at 10:00 p.m."

On a Sunday evening in September 1994, Mimi and I staged a dazzling Hollywood wedding at Tatou. It was a gala black-tie affair and a fitting finale to my foray in Beverly Hills. Many stars who had become a part of our lives in Beverly Hills attended. I really wanted my buddy, Rick James, to be with us on that day but it just didn't work out.

Despite the heavy celebrity and wealthy, bejeweled Beverly Hills matrons and their husbands present at our wedding, it was, at its heart, a family affair. My mother flew out with Hilary and they stayed with Mimi and me in our home. Mimi's father, George Leonard, attended with his wife Annie. Mimi's half-sisters, Emily and Lillie, and her sister Burr (who founded The Bar Method exercise studios in San Francisco in 2001) were there, along with some old friends, which delighted us to no end. Kevin Doyle, the DJ of Tatou New York, joined us and, as his gift, played the dance music for the party, which was a blast. The children from our previous marriages—my daughter Hilary, and Mimi's children Juliet and Adam—all walked down the aisle in the wedding procession.

In 1995, deciding that it was time to move on, the perfect location in Century City became available. I was ecstatic. It was a thirty-thousand-square-foot, two-level property with a beautiful restaurant showroom that could accommodate one thousand guests, two indoor dance floors, a third dance floor outdoors, and another very large room decorated in an exotic Jungle motif. It was a gorgeous and very elegant property—one of the largest nightclubs in LA. Now I could host some really grand parties and special events and make some real money. My partner was Dan Fitzgerald, a contractor who had made millions renovating and flipping mansions, loved nightclubs and girls, and had a reputation for hosting lingerie parties a la Hugh Hefner in his houses to attract buyers. I named it The Century Club.

Once again I imposed a dress code: no sneakers and no jeans, which only worked for a short time. Opening night was packed to capacity with Hollywood and music industry celebrities and friends. I booked the very talented August Darnell, aka Kid Creole, and The Coconuts for the evening's entertainment. The crowd went crazy. Within a week I was slammed with future bookings: Bruce Willis; Blood, Sweat & Tears; Stevie Wonder; Ludacris; Harry Dean Stanton; The Marshall Tucker Band; Dionne Warwick; Snoop Dogg; Wu Tang Clan; Pitbull; and Jay Z, who especially disturbed the LAPD because they didn't like the crowd he attracted.

As always I embraced urban music and I was surprised the first time I heard Dr. Dre rap about The Century Club in his classic "The Next Episode," and I quote: "It's California love, this California bud got a nigga gang of pub, I'm on one, I might bail up in the Century Club." Being the owner/proprietor of a club mentioned in a hit song blew me away.

Rick James came back into my life and joined me for Urban Sunday nights and at many of our "After Film Premieres" and other special events. Since we were located in Century City across the street from the Cineplex Odeon, The Century Club was the perfect venue for film premiere events. We hosted a star-studded event for *The Wedding Planner*. Jennifer Lopez had her team transform the entire club into a beautiful fantasy of white for her guests, costar Matthew McConaughey and hundreds of invited friends including Mark Wahlberg,

Marlee Matlin, and Jon Voight to name a few. There were so many beautiful people there that night but I just don't remember them all. Jim Carrey stole the show at the afterparty for his film *Ace Ventura: Pet Detective* and Cameron Diaz did the same at the afterparty for *The Mask*. The post-premiere party for the film *Dark City* was a great night at The Century Club attended by the very funny Jon Cryer, Kiefer Sutherland, Minnie Driver, Andrew McCarthy, Mimi Rogers, Queen Latifah, Jada Pinkett Smith, Lara Flynn Boyle, and others.

Me and my Century Club partner Dan Fitzgerald discussed a performance by Bruce Wills and his band at our Monday Night Jam.

We welcomed Jodie Foster and Kristen Stewart to the post-premiere party for *Panic Room* and their guests Brad Pitt, Matthew Perry, and others. The film *The Players Club*, directed by Ice Cube, was one of my favorite post-premiere parties attended by my buddy Bernie Mac and guests Jamie Foxx, Babyface, Ice Cube, Jada Pinkett, Boyz II Men, Terrence Howard, Martin Lawrence, Sean "Puffy" Combs, Charlie Murphy, Michael Clarke Duncan, Rick James, and John Singleton. It was a memorable night for me because Rick James and Charlie Murphy spent the entire night trading barbs that were so funny, it should have been recorded as *Live on stage at The Century Club*.

The party for the film *Scary Movie 2* was a wild and funny night with Carmen Electra, Damon Wayans, James Woods, Bill Paxton, and Wes Craven. Many others attended but those were my standout guests that night. There were hundreds of wonderful parties over the years. Dustin Hoffman hosted a very extravagant and over-the-top party, creating a jungle on the patio with live monkeys and birds in the trees to celebrate his daughter's bat mitzvah.

Within a year of opening it was established that Sunday's Urban Music Night at The Century Club featured a crowd that was considered to be black royalty with a smattering of beautiful white girls. The most famous stars and athletes of the day attended, including Michael Jordan, Jamie Foxx, Tyra Banks, Wesley Snipes, Denzel Washington, all of the Lakers including Magic Johnson, Shaquille O'Neil, a very young Kobe Bryant, Venus and Serena Williams, Prince, and Michael Clarke Duncan, who also doubled as a security guard.

On Sunday nights we went through case after case of Cristal as it was a regular happening for Shaq and Michael Jordan to be holding court on opposite sides of the upper balcony surrounded by beautiful girls of all sizes, shapes, and colors, determined to outdo each other in creating a spectacle. One night I thought I might have some real trouble on my hands. I spotted Shaq and Kobe, looking sharp and cool in their custom-tailored suits, standing toe-to-toe in a Mac stare down. Everyone was watching. This was early on in their time together with The Lakers and it was reported that they were always feuding. Then, all of a sudden, they were both laughing. Everyone around them broke out in smiles and more Cristal was poured. I breathed a sigh of relief.

Friday night was dedicated to salsa and R&B and always featured a group of hot well-dressed local Latinos including Mario Lopez, Oscar De La Hoya, Andy Garcia, Paul Rodriguez, and Antonio Villaraigosa, who later became Mayor of Los Angeles. Prince was another frequent guest at our salsa nights. He would sit in the back of the club alone and watch the bands and dancers do their thing to the Latin beat, just like he did at Studio 54. If he and Rick James showed up on the same night, I had to worry because of their rivalry. Ryan Seacrest broadcast *Live from The Century Club* on Fridays, which went over big with his radio audience. This was before he hit gold on TV with *Keeping Up with The Kardashians* and *Live From The Red Carpet*.

The Century Club became the longest-running large supper club in West LA, featuring hundreds of special events and movie premiers. We had a great run for fourteen years, and then it was demolished by the owner of the land to make way for high-rise condos.

In 2003, Mimi and I went into the business of opening exercise studios— The Bar Method of Los Angeles—which became a celebrity favorite, enabling us to franchise twelve more studios in Southern California, from San Diego to Santa Barbara. The hours are much better for someone who is now in his seventies but I am still surrounded by beautiful women—in this case the vibrant staff of teachers and desk managers at our barre-style studios. Our children are grown and living their own lives. Mimi and I live in a duplex penthouse overlooking the Pacific Ocean, which is more spectacular than the one I was so upset about losing thirty years earlier, and this time I have a wonderful partner to share it with. Now, in the twilight of my years, as president of our Homeowners Association, I find myself deeply involved in the running of our club amenities—pools and tennis courts, restaurant and bar. Like I said in the beginning of this book..."I've always had a thing for clubs."

Mount Kuchumaa, where I got my mojo back, became the first sacred mountain to be listed on the National Register of Historical Places by the US Department of Interior, on October 22, 1992. "It represents a natural earthly temple and source of religious wonderment to the Kumeyaay of Southern California."

Generations of Kumeyaay Native Americans and guests at Rancho La Puerta have felt both the physical and spiritual power of Mount Kuchumaa. It holds as much religious importance for the Kumeyaay people today as it did for those in the past. The "indigenous people believed since recorded time, that the peak was imbued with power from one of the Kumeyaay Creator Gods." From day one I believed that the magical feeling I experienced, whenever close to or on the mountain, was healing me. I found strength in that faith. I held onto it and it was enough to get me through the darkest period of my life until I could find the light and faith within myself.

So what better way for me to share this gift with others than to bring the Bar Method to "my place in the sun," Rancho La Puerta, for eight glorious weeks each year? I am so blessed. It has come full circle...as they say.

Chapter Thirty-Five:
The Studio 54 Effect

Some People Were Empowered By It.

Others Were Destroyed By It.

And Some Died From It.

Here Are Their Stories.

ACK IN THE DAY, forty years ago, before cell phone cameras, Facebook, YouTube, Instagram, and Twitter, the press ruled. Newspapers, magazines, and television were the only means available to get the attention of the American public. The press could make you or break you, and the press loved Studio 54. Publicists jammed our phone lines requesting their celebrity clients be put on our guest list. Their clients had only to show up and make nice for the cameras and their pictures would be in newspapers and magazines everywhere in America and around the world the next morning. It was the beginning of celebrity culture. Studio 54 was glamorous, decadent, and safe because photographers respected boundaries; it was a symbiotic relationship. And most importantly, the press never released an unflattering photo and never told the public *everything* that went on the night before. They said it was wild or great fun. Celebrities loved Studio 54—it was *their* playground.

Some celebrities wanted to dance and have fun but remain under the radar. The press respected their wishes, providing a cloak of cover in the dark of night. To others, Studio was like a moth to a flame. They returned night after night wanting to see their faces in the papers again and again. It was their drug of choice—they lived for it.

Discretion was the key to success at Studio 54.

If you were the very popular mayor from another city who came into Studio 54 one night and happened to drink too much and pass out in the balcony in the arms of a beautiful young man—your constituents never found you out. If you were the world famous designer often seen in the pages of *WWD* who swallowed way too many Quaaludes and passed out on a banquette in the Rubber Room, lipstick and mascara mixing with the drool oozing from the corners of your mouth—that image of you never went viral. If you were the well-known national news anchor spotted dancing and snorting coke with a beautiful young girl all night—we had your back. That photo never made the papers and your wife never found out. If you were the young actress adored by millions of young boys and girls who got caught shooting up in a stall in the men's bathroom—the tabloids were never told. And if you were the high society dame who got caught by surprise in the "secret" basement under the "playground" basement, with your wrists tied to an overhead pipe, writhing with pleasure in your sky high heels, getting fucked against the wall by a Park Avenue plastic surgeon—your kinky little secret has remained a secret.

There was much more to it than just sex and drugs. The heart of Studio 54 was the dance floor and the tribal feeling that made you one with others. You were on the beat with the girl over there and the couple dancing nearby—strangers a few hours ago—and now you were one. A guy dances by then around you and kisses you on the neck, a woman twirls, another guy moves in and grinds on you from behind—you are loved and life is beautiful. You are in the moment at Studio 54. You never want this feeling to end. You return night after night to the music, dance floor, drugs, and alcohol. You crave the attention and all the bizarre stuff that goes down when you're hanging with Sister Cocaine at 5:00 a.m. Anyone who has ever hung out with her will tell you—this bitch has the power to make you do some freaky shit. Some of the people in our crowd got so caught up in the collective energy of Studio 54 and blown away by the absence of rules and boundaries that it destroyed them. They returned night after night to live it again and again. It was about pleasure—accountability was tossed aside and some paid for it dearly.

Others were more fortunate—they were able to roll with it and walk away unscathed.

We all believed ourselves to be free to satisfy our lust or passion and follow the object of our desire to whatever end that might be and survive it. The mindset of the 1960s and '70s paved the way for the nonstop party of indulgence and excessive behavior of the 1980s. We eschewed monogamy for the wild side. Don't worry, we have penicillin and the pill, and if you need a little something to break down inhibitions—well go ahead and take a Quaalude—and if you want to go all night long, put some of that powerful white powder up your nose and on your dick. We had pregnancy, disease, and inhibitions under control. So come on down to 54—where anything goes!

Studio 54 didn't force people to make choices and set priorities. The voice within us did. Do I stay, or do I go? It was as simple as that. Do I leave now? It's 2:00 a.m. and I have an important meeting in the office at 9:00 a.m. or do I stay and do another hit and dance another dance? It wasn't easy. People were reluctant to say goodnight. They didn't want to leave, miss out on something, and then, God forbid, hear or read about in the newspaper the next morning. Studio 54 was at the center of the universe—and like I said before—it had the power to suck you in, chew you up, and spit you out.

No one could possibly take credit for the success of Diane von Fürstenberg and her creation, the iconic wrap dress, but Diane. Appearing on the cover of *Newsweek* magazine in 1976, she was referred to as "the most marketable woman since Coco Chanel." Diane partied hard at Studio 54 almost from day one in 1977 but she managed to maintain a balance in her life that protected her from falling. She was a regular on Page Six of the *New York Post* and her picture appeared often on the pages of *People* and the *New York Daily News*. This provided her with a unique vehicle to become an even more relevant and vital force in fashion to generations of younger women. Diane worked the Studio 54 effect—it was a positive in her life.

Today, there are Carolina Herrera boutiques all over the world, yet she wasn't raised for business. In 1968 she married Reinaldo Herrera, a friend she had known since childhood, and entered a social circle of jet-setters that included Princess Margaret—sister to the Queen of England—Andy Warhol, and Mick Jagger. She dressed and carried herself with a blend of classic formality and Latin theatricality, appearing on the International Best Dressed List for the first time in 1972. Then, in 1977, Carolina had another venue in which to shine–Studio 54. She and Reinaldo were often photographed with Halston, Calvin, Bianca, and Mikhail Baryshnikov.

Carolina had been toying with the idea of designing a fabric line, but then in 1980, her friend, Diana Vreeland, editor of *Vogue*, suggested Carolina create a line of dresses instead. She went for it and since then has gone on to design for Jacqueline Kennedy Onassis, Renée Zellweger, Caroline Kennedy, Shakira, Salma Hayek, and many others. Carolina and Reinaldo partied often at Studio 54 over the years and I believe they would both agree that Studio provided an adventure for them and was a positive effect in their lives.

Halston's designs for women were a huge success in the world of fashion long before Studio 54 ever opened. His designs for high-profile women like Jacqueline Kennedy, who wore his pillbox hat to JFK's inauguration, were famous. He was recognized for having dressed Babe Paley, Anjelica Huston, Gene Tierney, Lauren Bacall, Margaux Hemingway, and Elizabeth Taylor out of his Madison Avenue boutique. In February of 1977, Halston unveiled his uniform design for Braniff International Airways stewardesses to critical acclaim. He then designed the uniforms for the New York Police Department, Girl Scouts of America, Avis Rent a Car, and the 1976 US Olympic Team for the Summer Olympics in Montreal. But when Studio 54 opened in April of 1977, photos of Halston with his slicked-back hair and movie star looks hanging out with Studio 54 regulars Liza, Bianca, Calvin, and Warhol and partying with stars like Jack Nicholson, Cher, and Rod Stewart were seen everywhere. Halston was well-known before 1977, but Studio 54 launched him into the upper stratosphere of "supermarket chic" and "trailer-park cool."

Halston died in 1990 from an AIDS-defined illness. He worked the Studio 54 Effect whenever he chose to.

In the early 1970s Bianca Jagger was well known as Mick Jagger's wife. But it wasn't until her well-documented nights of partying at Studio 54 in the late 1970s that Bianca Jagger was referred to as *Bianca*. It was reported that "nothing got started officially at Studio 54" until the Queen Bee arrived. She was referred to as such long before Beyoncé. That's when her star really began to rise. From then on Bianca was perceived to be her own woman, an international jet-setter hanging out with her close friends Andy Warhol and Halston. Bianca's image was everywhere. She was exotic and photogenic. She was a true fashionista: every designer wanted to dress her. The now iconic photo of Bianca riding into Studio 54 on a white horse in celebration of her thirtieth birthday was seen in publications around the world. She was not only desirable, but intelligent, having earned a scholarship to study political science at The Paris Institute of Political Studies.

Bianca knew she had a higher calling than party girl, and in 1981 she began what has evolved into her thirty-year campaign for human rights, social and economic justice, and environmental protection throughout the world. Bianca is the founder and chair of the Bianca Jagger Rights Foundation. She serves as a council of Europe Goodwill Ambassador, member of the Executive Director's Leadership Council of Amnesty International USA, and a trustee of the Amazon Charitable Trust. But it was Studio 54 that gave her the platform on which to get started. Studio 54 was a positive effect in Bianca's life.

Nile Rodgers, a member of the Black Panthers at age sixteen, had a girlfriend who always got into Studio 54, but he couldn't get in without her. He was leader of the group Chic, and they were becoming known after the release of their big hit "Everybody Dance" but hadn't reached the point of superstardom. Nile was turned away from the door more than once and it pissed him off. On New Year's Eve after being rejected once again, he returned home with Bernard Edwards, a fellow band member and writing partner, and together they wrote a song called "Fuck Off," which was later changed to "Freak Out" and became the huge hit "Le Freak" with the well-known lyric "Just come on down, to fifty-four, find a spot out on the floor." It was number one on the *Billboard* Hot 100 charts and remained at number one on the disco charts for seven weeks. After that, Nile was treated with more respect at Studio 54. He went on to write and produce for Madonna, Sister Sledge, Diana Ross, and David Bowie. In 2014, Nile Rodgers picked up two Grammy Awards, including Record of the Year for Daft Punk's "Get Lucky," which he cowrote with Pharrell Williams. In his memoir, *Le Freak*, Nile wrote: "By not getting what we wanted, we got much more than we ever imagined." Nile harnessed the positive energy of Studio 54 and rode it past the moon to another galaxy.

Then there was Joanne Horowitz. Back in the day, Joanne was responsible for bringing in many celebrities to Studio 54. She was paid on a sliding scale ranging from $30 to $250 depending on the celebrity and their level of importance to the press. She brought in major stars like Cher, Michael Jackson, and Warren Beatty—and for the first time photos of celebrities could be seen on the front pages of the *New York Post* and the *New York Daily News*; rather than "blurbs" about them buried in the gossip pages. Today, Joanne manages the very successful career of Kevin Spacey. Back in the day, she arranged for him to get into Studio before he became a star. The effect Studio 54 provided Joanne with was another positive channel through which to work her skills.

The Studio 54 Effect provided DJs Nicky Siano, Tony Smith, Robbie Leslie, and, my personal favorites, Frank Corr and Leroy Washington (the only two resident DJs at the club during my reign) with another venue in which to work their magic—Sirius XM Radio's Studio 54 station. And let's not forget all the DJs who claim to have played at Studio 54—and never did—and how they have benefited. One very well-known DJ who did play at Studio, on occasion, states on his résumé, "In fact, I've played at Studio 54 more than any DJ ever—probably about five hundred nights over the course of six years!" Bullshit. Leroy Washington, who played brilliantly night after night, played Studio more than any other DJ beginning in 1978. He worked the Studio 54 Effect to the bone. He always came through for us. He is a devoted father, plays Studio 54 events around the world, owns a successful tour company in St. Thomas, Virgin Islands, and can be heard on 107.3 six nights a week 10:00 p.m. to 6:00 a.m. Leroy Washington and Nicky Siano were the DJs chosen to play at the Sirius XM Studio 54 Launch Party in Manhattan in 2011.

Frank Corr knew exactly how to work the Studio 54 Effect to his advantage—then and now. He does podcasts and guest spots with Eagle Radio on Live365.com, plays guest spots at Ft. Lauderdale's hottest gay club, Hunter's in Wilton Manors, and is the owner and host of a group of hot vacation rental properties, also in Wilton Manors, a destination that has enjoyed worldwide popularity in the gay community.

Joey Hunter worked the Studio 54 Effect to a positive max for himself and his models, always taking care to protect the image of the Ford Agency. Years later, after leaving Ford, he became president of Modelwire, the company that developed the software program widely used by the modeling industry today.

Peter Beard became famous for his incredible photos and diaries of Africa, the New York arts scene, the fashion world, Hollywood, and the Kennedy clan. Peter enjoyed his nights partying with us and used the power of the Studio 54 Effect to showcase and share his body of work with the world.

As a result of the Studio 54 Effect, Rudolf Piper became my partner in several nightclub ventures down the road and is now a major nightclub impresario in Brazil.

Couri Hay dabbled with the decadent lifestyle that was an element of the Studio 54 Effect, but was careful and survived to do extraordinarily well with his own successful PR firm.

Rick Ferrari partied hard with the Studio 54 Effect during those days, but was strong enough to overcome his addictions and has created a successful Hollywood career as both a manager and an agent.

Michael Fesco, the promoter who produced so many memorable nights (my favorite was "Black Night") always kept it together making the Studio 54 Effect work for him. Michael has garnered much respect in the gay community over the years. This year, 2017, will mark Michael's twenty-first season as the host of "Sea Tea" America's only gay sailing Tea Dance. The Tea sails on ships from Hornblower Cruises out of New York City's West Side Pier 40—Sundays from June to September. Check it out at seatea.com.

Billy "Tootsie" Tuetsos was loved by everyone and very much in demand by the hottest models of the day. He was in the middle of it all when he was with his girls—and he was always with his girls. He advised them, dressed them, escorted them, and protected them. The agencies trusted Billy and he was paid handsomely for his services. The Dynamic Trio of Studio 54 was Patti Hansen, Billy Tootsie, and Shaun Casey. Some days he commandeered the couch and telephone in my office at Studio and worked the Studio 54 Effect the same way…when it suited him and to his advantage. After Studio 54 closed, Billy moved to Ft. Lauderdale and was tragically struck down and killed while riding his bicycle.

Michael Redwine produced numerous hit parties for me at Studio 54 and today enjoys a very successful and lucrative career in real estate in Atlanta, Georgia. He partied hard at Studio 54, leaving all the negatives of the Studio 54 Effect behind, gleaning only the positive, and looks back on it all with humor and joy.

Dahved Levy and his mentor Frankie Crocker produced and promoted many successful Saturday nights at Studio 54. Dahved has always had a laser-like focus in life and worked the positive angle of his experience at Studio to the max. He continues to produce and promote concerts and special events through his very successful website Caribbean Fever, and he owns the upscale cocktail lounge Dick and Jane near the Barclay Center in Brooklyn. You can hear Dahved every Sunday on New York's WBLS radio, 107.5 the number-one-rated Caribbean show in the world, and in 2016 he signed a major deal with Biggs and Roc Nation. Dahved recently shared this with me—"Studio 54 was my eye-opener to the world of entertainment. I met people and saw things there that I never imagined. It made me think outside my box."

Carmen D'Alessio rode the Studio 54 Effect like a rocket to the moon and never looked back. With contacts and style, she has continued on in her very successful career creating events in New York and around the world for more than thirty years now since Studio 54 closed.

Beth Ann Maliner enjoyed her time at Studio 54, working the effect to her advantage and creating memories she will have forever. When Michael Overington left Studio, Beth Ann joined him at The Palladium. In 1985 she moved to Landenberg, Pennsylvania, married, and raised two children. She oversees and manages research dollars in the College of Education and Human Development at the University of Delaware. I saw Beth Ann with her family in tow at the SiriusXM Radio Studio 54 Launch Party in Manhattan in 2011. She hasn't changed a bit and looked so happy.

The Harris Sisters played hard but worked the Studio 54 Effect to the max. They consider themselves fortunate to have experienced such a unique and exciting place and time in history and were very lucky to have survived it. So many didn't and they wouldn't change it for the world. Their very talented brother, George Harris III aka Hibiscus, succumbed to AIDS in 1982—an early casualty of the dreaded disease. The Harris Sisters enjoy spending time with family, maintaining the lifelong friendships they established at Studio 54, performing as The Screaming Violets and writing books. At present, the Harris Sisters are busy promoting their book *Caravan to Oz,* narrated by Tim Robbins.

John Blair dabbled here and there but remained clean for the most part and today he continues to be one of the most successful promoters in New York's gay community. John worked the Studio 54 Effect to his advantage.

Nikki Haskell didn't do drugs but she did do press and as a result of the Studio 54 Effect she walked away with a much higher profile. In later years she made a lot of money with a weight-loss product and now anticipates hosting another TV show.

Alison Gertz, the lovely sixteen-year-old department store heiress, had everything to live for. She was a frequent guest at Studio 54 and often hung out and partied in my office. She was friends with my various assistants and a delight to have around, experimenting with all the effects Studio had to offer. Ali had a crush on one of Studio's beautiful bartenders, Cort Brown. Ali's whole life lay ahead of her—college, a career, marriage, family. No one could have predicted that an ill-fated night of sex with Cort would end her life. Ali was a virgin when she and Cort became intimate in the summer of '82. Six years later, at age twenty-two, Ali was diagnosed with AIDS. It turned out that

Cort was a carrier of the deadly HIV virus. Cort died in the mid-1980s. Alison died in August of 1992. She was just twenty-six years old.

We all felt the effects of Studio 54. But Studio's shirtless bartenders were in the center of everything all night long, every night. Men and women, old and young, wanted to fuck them, cuddle them, support them, tie them up, take them down, get them high, talk to them, befriend them, convert them to straight, convince them they were gay, admire them from afar or from behind a drink at the bar. And maybe, just maybe, take them home and love them for a night. Their job made each of them vulnerable to the Studio 54 Effect. Some had an easy transition to life without Studio 54 and others found it more difficult to adjust. L. J. Kirby was the star of the show, but by 1988 he had had enough of city life and moved to Arizona for the weather and a place where he could enjoy flying gliders and airplanes and riding motorcycles both on and off road. He is devoted to his two young sons, raising them as a single father. L. J. Kirby, John Bello, Scott Baird, Oscar Lopez, George Alvarez, Bob Farrell, Robert Ziehm, Dennis Lazalle, Cort Brown, John O'Connor, Steve Toal, Ron Baruchian, Greg Gurch, Alex McArthur, Sal DeFalco, and identical twins Steve and Jon Learn all worked the Studio 54 Effect positively, then and now. You can only imagine some of the stunts the twins pulled on the girls at the main bar. George Alvarez went on to TV and acting—*General Hospital* for eight years and *Guiding Light* for nine. Alex McArthur appeared as Madonna's boyfriend in her "Papa Don't Preach" video. Studio's handsome Italian, Sal DeFalco, worked the effect of Studio into a force to be reckoned with back then and since, giving more interviews regarding Studio 54 than any other bartender.

Studio 54's busboys, Danny Lopez, Oscar Lopez, and Joe Puga, were such an important part of our success at Studio. They worked their asses off. They were hot, shirtless, in tight shorts and sneakers, and all the celebrities liked and appreciated them. Oscar Lopez was a college kid. He had never smoked a joint in his life and then one night he brought a drink order to Truman Capote, Calvin Klein, and Mick Jagger who were hanging in the basement. Mick said, "Hello, mate," and passed a joint to Oscar. Oscar was about to decline, determined to make it through college and dental school, but changed his mind, said "fuck it," and joined the party. Eventually, Oscar was doing lines of coke next to the cash register behind the bar, along with the other bartenders, but over time he managed to keep the drugs, glitter, and glam in check. Balance was the key to survive Studio 54. They are all very happy in their chosen careers and family life. Oscar lives in Miami and over the years has enjoyed crossing paths with my partner Stanley Tate while dining out. Oscar pursued his dream of becoming a dentist and has a very successful practice in Miami. They all worked the Studio 54 Effect and had big fun with it.

Our head of security, Chuck Garelick, gleaned all that he could from Studio 54 and worked it to his advantage, becoming vice president of Special Events for a security company working such high-profile events as the Victoria's Secret Fashion Show, *Sports Illustrated*'s Swimsuit Issue runway launch, and New York City's Times Square Ball Drop on New Years Eve. In a recent conversation with Chuck, he said: "Not only did I pick Margaret Trudeau's bra up off the floor of the DJ booth back in the day but DJs Nicky Siano and Roy Thode off the floor as well." They loved their Tuinals and Quaaludes.

In 1977, Michael Overington was hired as a bathroom attendant at Studio 54. He used his talent and ingenuity to forge ahead, becoming vice chairman of Ian Schrager's hotel group. He is happily married to Lisa from Studio's coat check and a proud father of two. Michael worked the Studio 54 Effect big time!

I had a great staff. Some employees returned to work at Studio 54 after I reopened it and others were new hires. Skip Odeck, David Miskit, Norval Johnson, and John Griffith were there to give Michael O. the support he needed as day and night managers—and believe me, working at Studio 54 wasn't always easy or glamorous. It was hard work.

David Miskit was a great guy and a very valuable employee. He stepped in as night manager at a crucial time for Studio. He was eventually scooped up by Ian Schrager—David works at the PUBLIC Chicago.

Skip Odeck was the heart and soul of Studio 54. After many years as night manager, he left New York and moved on to Cameo Nightclub on South Beach in Miami and then to Ian Schrager's Delano Hotel. A trusted and valued employee, he is respected and admired by coworkers wherever he goes. Skip kept it all under control at Studio both professionally and personally. Studio was a positive in his life.

Norval Johnson enjoyed every moment he worked at Studio 54 and then moved on to music videos and television as a production designer, working with Rod Stewart, Whitney Houston, Barbra Streisand, KISS, Run-DMC, and Aerosmith. In a recent interview, Norval mentioned how much he enjoyed designing the set used on *Chappelle's Show* in a skit that takes place at Studio 54 with Rick James and Eddie Murphy. He is presently preparing for a gig with Kevin Hart. Norval enjoys the ocean and the redwoods in Mendocino County, California, where he lives with his wife and daughter and looks forward to the annual Studio 54 Alumni Reunions.

Studio 54's tech crew, headed by Neil and Harold Wilson, was unsurpassed and at the top of its game. They were responsible for the sound, lighting, sets, and fly rails. As Neil said, "Making sure the right plug goes into the right hole. Studio was all about the show and the show was LIVE—night after night. Every night was a major event. We took our work very seriously and I am proud of the fact that with all the insane stuff that went on around us every night we never had one mishap. Operating the bridge and all the many moving objects—no one was ever injured." After Studio closed, Neil joined Grace Jones on her yearlong World Tour as her lighting and technical director. He loves what he does and had this to say: "As a nonunion guy, Studio 54 was a chance for me to run a Broadway House." He worked and lived in Rio de Janeiro for twenty-five years with his wife, a Brazilian ballerina. He returned to New York with his three sons and is raising them as a single father.

Melina Brown left Studio to work for Steve and Ian when they took over the Executive Hotel. In time, she and Snoogy moved on to motherhood, enjoying happy and successful lives. Melina lives in Connecticut on a small working farm and rescues dogs from New York City's high-kill shelters. She is the president of her grandfather's foundation—The Radio Drama Network.

Snoogy and Melina were at Studio from the beginning and will always treasure the memories of a time when it governed their lives both night and day. They each worked the positive effect of the experience.

Marc Benecke and Myra Sheer (Steve Rubell's former assistant) successfully launched *The Marc and Myra Show* on the Sirius XM Radio Studio 54 channel, keeping the memories alive and discussing the effects of Studio 54 on every life that stepped within. They both worked the effect in a most positive way.

My production assistant and friend Denise Chatman, whom I reconnected with in 2011 at the Studio 54 Sirius XM Radio Launch Party in Manhattan, made me laugh when she told me she jumped at the opportunity to work in the kitchen with Ina Garten at Barefoot Contessa in East Hampton, anxious to leave the insanity of the Studio 54 Effect behind. She took her Rolodex with her and considers Studio 54 to be the greatest learning experience of her life and motherhood the most rewarding. Denise enjoys marketing and promotion projects, booking DJs and Studio 54 events around the world, and personally DJs at her fundraisers for the Wounded Warrior Project.

The "Girls of Studio 54" and my valued assistants Shelley Tupper, Hilary Clark, Gwynne Rivers, and Victoria Leacock partied hard, sometimes burning the candle at both ends, making headlines and creating a stir. They were given unlimited access to everything: drink tickets, Quaaludes, cocaine, the basement, my office, and the most coveted of all—the Studio 54 guest list. They each embraced different aspects of the Studio 54 Effect and when it was over they moved on to careers and motherhood using all that they had gleaned to their advantage—holding tight to their cherished memories of the wildest party ever.

They each worked the effect to their advantage.

Shelley Tupper is married and lives in Manhattan. She produces corporate events around the world, appears live as a storyteller on occasions, and is trained as an executive coach/positive psychology practitioner.

Gwynne Rivers lives in Maine with her three young children and boyfriend whom she's known since grade school. She is president of the PTA and has never been happier. She considers herself a survivor of her early reckless and crazy years in New York City's night life and says, "But it was fun and I wouldn't trade it for anything." Gwynne embraced the effect and learned along the way.

Hilary Clark lives in the UK, in a charming town near Norwich, not far from the sea, with her husband and two Chihuahuas. She owns a flower shop in the market square and enjoys painting and writing. Her five children come and go from all their various studies and adventures. Hilary had this to say recently:

"Mark Fleischman and I had a great relationship. We both had such fun with each other. Working at Studio 54 was like acting in a wild play every night. It was brilliant and I loved every bit of it. I was very young but also sensible enough to know not to lose myself. I am forever grateful for the experience."

Victoria Leacock Hoffman lives in Washington, DC with her husband and young son. She is a producer, filmmaker, and writer. She was the cinematographer for Jonathan Demme's award-winning AIDS documentary *One Foot on a Banana Peel, the Other Foot in the Grave.* In 1992, she cofounded Love Heals, The Alison Gertz Foundation for AIDS Education, and lectured on their behalf for the following fifteen years. In a recent interview, Victoria shared the following about Studio:

"Working for Mark in nineteen eighty-three for eight months was one of the most adventurous and extreme experiences of my life! I loved many aspects of it and met many lifelong friends, but also lost many to AIDS in the years that followed. Though I have never tried drugs, I witnessed the harsh effects they had on Mark and some of my coworkers. I did enjoy way too much champagne and have been happily sober since nineteen eighty-eight! I am glad so many people made it out and moved on to healthier lives."

Shay Knuth, director of catering, partied hard but never let the effect interfere with putting in the hard work and long hours necessary to make the catering department as lucrative as it was. She left Studio 54 when it all came crashing to an end in 1985 and moved on. Shay lives outside Marbella in Spain and remains a valuable PR asset to Playboy Enterprises Inc.

Some of our friends and guests passed away either directly or indirectly as a result of drug and alcohol abuse, perhaps encouraged by the safe haven the effect of Studio 54 fostered within all of us. Andy Gibb, Vitas Gerulaitis, and John Belushi would stop by on a regular basis to partake in some of the effects Studio had seduced us all with. They enjoyed us way more than whatever or whomever awaited them at home—if not, we wouldn't have had the pleasure of their company as often as we did. They chased the negative rather than the positive—caught it and never let go.

Truman Capote craved the company of "characters," and we had plenty of those at Studio 54. His sarcasm and wit always took the conversation to another level the few times I remember him hanging in my office into the early-morning hours. He thrilled in the back-and-forth banter with the busboys and reveled in "kink" with Japanese psychiatrist Dr. Masao Miyamoto, assistant professor at Cornell University, who authored the book *Straightjacket Society*. I had granted Masao unlimited access while researching a piece for *Playboy*. Truman spoke of writing a book that took place over one night at Studio 54 but, sadly, never did. He died soon after I last saw him in 1984 of liver cancer and the complications of multiple-drug intoxication.

Tinkerbelle, who had a column in the Studio 54 magazine, was another life and talent cut short. Tinkerbelle spent a brief time in the orbit of Andy Warhol in the 1960s. Blonde, very pretty and intelligent, she became a regular contributor to Andy Warhol's *Interview* magazine in the early 1970s. Having become well-known for her biting wit and scathing criticism of others, she landed her own film critic spot with *Newsweek* called *Tinkerbelle Goes To the*

Movies, a video magazine piece. From the first night that Studio 54 opened in 1977, Tinkerbelle was a regular and became immediately addicted to the scene and the measure of notoriety and celebrity it afforded her. It was often seven or eight in the morning before she went home to bed. As a result, she was fired from her job at *Newsweek* in 1978. Finding herself reduced to accepting secretarial jobs to pay the bills, she became increasingly depressed. She jumped to her death from the window of her friend's apartment in 1986. In the words of actress Sylvia Miles, Tinkerbelle had "run out of gas in the fast lane, and when a person like that gets into the fast lane, there's no satisfaction on the other side of the road." Tinkerbelle allowed the Studio 54 Effect to take over and consume her life.

My buddy Rick James began his lifelong abuse of drugs when he was a teenager, falling in love with Sister Cocaine in the 1960s. I was very happy to reconnect with Rick at The Century Club. Once again we were spending time in an office, in a club that I owned, but this time I was straight. In our moments alone together, Rick was insightful, and sometimes sad, but then he always turned it around with something funny. I remember one night very well when Rick reflected on his drug use—"Mark you know me, I'm a people person. But when I was basing it wasn't about anything else but *me*. I didn't give a shit about any other living thing. I lost all sense of humanity. I surrendered—I fell to my knees and I sucked the devil's glass dick."

Rick's health slowly deteriorated until he had a stroke in the 1990s. Rick was found dead in his Los Angeles home on August 6, 2004. The autopsy found a shitload of drugs in his system, which was no surprise to anyone who knew him, and yet I was numb for days after hearing the news. For the rest of my life I will ponder, "What if my friend had chosen to glean more from the positive effects that Studio had to offer rather than the negative? Why didn't he draw on the strength of all those people whom he met at Studio 54, the ones that embraced the positive effect of Studio 54 and whom he found to be, in his own words, "the most interesting people I had ever met in my life"?

Grace Jones worked the Studio 54 Effect positively then and now. She is a great talent. She partied hard, got a handle on any issues she had with drugs, and kept the creative juices flowing through the years in both music and film. She blew my mind in 2012 at Queen Elizabeth II's Diamond Jubilee Concert in London performing with that hula hoop. I enjoyed reading *I'll Never Write*

My Memoirs, a must-read for her fans. She has great style. There will never be another like her, she's all Grace.

Liza Minnelli partied really hard, weathered a troubled marriage and divorce, and then struggled through several extended stays at Betty Ford to reemerge as the incredible talent and star she always was. At times Liza was controlled by the Studio 54 Effect, and then she fought back and won.

Tony Curtis, whose star from the 1950s and '60s diminished when he got involved with drugs and alcohol in the 1970s, was left with a floundering career until he went to Betty Ford in the 1980s. He successfully returned to acting, having appeared in thirty-three films in his career, completed his memoir *American Prince,* and was able to enjoy painting, his lifelong passion. Tony enjoyed the Studio 54 Effect and was almost destroyed by it, but in the end he conquered it. Tony lived to see his dream come true. *Red Table* by Tony Curtis joined the permanent collection of the film and media wing of the Museum of Modern Art in 2005. Tony passed away on September 29, 2010.

Christopher Atkins went from being a big-time partier to a complete teetotaler, living a clean, healthy life as a writer and producer in Hollywood. In the end the Studio 54 Effect was a positive.

Tanya Tucker, whose hard-partying ways landed her at Betty Ford in the late 1980s, got her life together, and returned to her music career. She wrote and published her memoir, then starred in her own reality show, *Tuckerville.* Tanya Tucker was voted the Country Music Association's Female Vocalist of the Year in 1991. She continues to record today. In the end, Tanya won and conquered every negative effect she partied with at Studio. She's a winner.

In 1984, NBA star of the Seattle Supersonics, David Thompson, got into a fight at Studio 54. Witnesses claimed David was stoned and drunk by the time he got into the fight, sometime after 2:00 a.m., with one of our much smaller busboys over a hat check girl. Thompson fell down a flight of stairs and destroyed his left knee, permanently ending his pro basketball career, which had already begun to deteriorate due to his off-court antics and abuse of alcohol. Of course, the way Thompson tells the story is entirely different. In his version, which he tells in his memoir *Skywalker,* he was innocently seeking out the men's room when Studio 54's menacing busboy came at him for no reason, shoving him down the stairs and injuring his knee to such an extent that his return to the ranks of pro-basketball was all but doomed. Only the busboy and Thompson himself probably know what actually happened, but it should be noted that Thompson was a troubled player with a load of talent and a lot of bad habits. Whenever he joined us at Studio, he was seduced by the negative aspect of the Studio 54 Effect.

Thompson sued Studio 54 for $10 million. I was recently asked what became of the lawsuit, and from what I read in Thompson's memoir, it appeared that he did not follow through with it. Word had it Thompson continued to devolve into a life of drugs and alcohol for a number of years. Then, after serving 180 days in jail in 1986 for violating his probation on domestic abuse charges, Thompson found God and sobriety and changed his life. He has been a community relations director for the Charlotte Hornets and a motivational speaker, and now runs kids' basketball clinics. He is a good example of someone who ultimately overcame the negative aspect of the Studio 54 Effect.

Calvin Klein became addicted to the negative effect of Studio 54's nightly offerings of sex, drugs, alcohol, parties, and the nonstop adoration of beautiful young boys early on. But he never allowed the effect to interfere with his responsibility to the company and its people. Ultimately he cleaned up his act and was wise in seeking the help he needed at the Hazelton Clinic. There are designers and then there's Calvin Klein—an American treasure.

Robin Leach, who produced and appeared in *Lifestyles of the Rich and Famous* and who led a decadent, sometimes out-of-control lifestyle, is now living well and happy to be working in Las Vegas promoting products on TV and appearing in commercials. Robin always chose to embrace both the negative and the positive charms of the effect. I am happy it turned out so well for Robin. I was always very fond of him.

Ian Schrager was part of the drug scene at Studio 54, but he was never out of control—he fell under the spell of the Studio 54 Effect, but wasn't overcome by it. However, Studio 54 affected him in a way that has caused him much grief in his lifetime. He flagrantly defrauded the federal government and was found guilty of tax evasion. It was all very public and reported on in the newspapers. Ian, being a very private person, abhorred this kind of attention. It could have been avoided. Studio 54's glamour and lifestyle went to his head. He participated in and fed off of it. He and Steve ended up as convicted felons, and Ian was disbarred as a lawyer.

Ian was quoted in an interview in the British newspaper *London Evening Standard* admitting that he doesn't like to dwell on the Studio 54 years, saying, "It's difficult because I didn't handle the success well. There was nothing you could do at night in the 1970s you couldn't walk away from in the morning. I admire the accomplishment from a distance—we were a couple of guys from Brooklyn—but we created a Frankenstein's monster that almost destroyed us." He went on to say, "I got intoxicated with success and I paid for it." Ian sums up the Studio 54 Effect with that quote, and as one of the most successful people to escape its clutches, he is well qualified to describe it. The experience set him back for several years in his life. But in 1985, Ian reinvented himself and became the cofounder and driving force behind a group of highly successful boutique hotels, first in New York and then nationally and internationally. He was not only a successful hotelier but has become a major superstar in the hospitality industry copied by hoteliers all over the world. In the end, Ian rode the Studio 54 Effect that he and Stevie created far beyond anyone's dreams.

I was happy to learn that Ian Schrager received a Presidential Pardon from President Obama in 2017.

Steve never really outed himself publically in interviews, or with business associates and especially bankers. Whenever it was that Stevie discovered he was gay, the fact is, he was having fun with it and there was no reason not to. By the time he and Ian were at the helm of Studio 54, Steve was doing five or six Quaaludes each night and purchasing enormous amounts of cocaine, which he consumed and shared with others. By 1:00 a.m. on any given night he'd be staggering around Studio, slurring his speech and spitting all over himself when he spoke to people, but everyone loved him anyway. He was Stevie. So up until the crazy moment when he announced that Studio 54 made more money than the Mafia, Steve stayed out of trouble. He always had Ian watching his back. And then AIDS hit and Ian couldn't protect him from that. Steve died of an AIDS-related illness at age forty-five. He embraced all the effects, both negative and positive—sex, drugs, music, alcohol, and most of all the press. He rode the Studio 54 rocket that he and Ian had created to his end.

Steve was just one of many taken from us much too soon. Zoli, the owner of Zoli Agency, succumbed to the virus in 1982 along with a number of Studio 54 bartenders including Cort Brown, Bob Petty, and Randy Kelly; light man Robert DaSilva; DJ Federico Gonzalez, our very talented early-evening DJ at Studio 54 on Jerry Rubin Networking nights; David Rodriguez, Walter Gibbons, and Larry Levan; my good friend and songwriter Paul Jabara; Roy Cohn, George Paul Roselle, Peter Lester, Guy Burgos, Keith Haring, Halston,

Anthony Perkins, Rudolf Nureyev, and Perry Ellis; jewelry designer Aldo Cipullo; and other friends of Studio 54 all died as a result of AIDS.

As you can see, many went off road along the way
They will remain forever in our hearts and memory.
But if those of us who are lucky enough to still be here remember:
The joy in the music
The thrill of the dance
And the magic that was Studio 54…
Then I did a good thing.

Acknowledgments

Mark:

FIRST, I WOULD LIKE to acknowledge Bev Currier, a Bar Method teacher at Rancho La Puerta, who together with a group of fun people at dinner heard some of my stories and kept saying, "You've got to write a book." Then I attended Les Standiford's Creative Writing class, which inspired me to start outlining this book.

I want to acknowledge my beautiful wife Mimi, who was supportive in every way, including helping me with the structure of the manuscript. I would also like to thank my daughter Hilary for her edits, and my writing assistant Amy Lamare whose help in this process has been invaluable. Then, I bumped into music industry maven Denise Chatman at the Sirius XM Studio 54 launch party in 2011 and she helped jog my memory of what happened back in the day.

Denise:

To Brad Guild…I will never forget you. Thank you for insisting, "Now is the time, Denise…before you forget everything!"

Thanks to my buddies at the various gyms I worked out at over the last five years. You all kept me sane. To my friends Wes Bradley, Tony Gioe, Marsha Haber, Bacho Mangual, and Tom Savarese…bless you for never hanging up on me…research is a bitch. To Richard G. Cushing…there will never be another you. To my son Peter and daughter Clara…thank you for your patience and support. You are my greatest productions.

Mark and I would like to thank Mark Kerrigan, the new managing director of Celebrity Bulletin's New York office, for granting us access to the archives and permission to include several copies of Celebrity Bulletin in the book.

Index